SERIES

A Dentist's Guide to the Law

228 Things Every Dentist Should Know

ADA American Dental Association®
America's leading advocate for oral health

Acknowledgements

In 2004 the American Dental Association Division of Legal Affairs thought that ADA members might find value in a publication that addressed various questions about a wide variety of legal issues that arise in their dental practices. So the lawyers in the Division collaborated on the authorship and publication of *Frequently Asked Legal Questions: A Guide for Dentists and the Dental Team*. They were pleased to find an extremely positive response. Members demonstrated a real interest in having written materials available to provide insight and background information on such legal issues. Because this interest continued, and because the law continues to evolve, the ADA published a second edition of *Frequently Asked Legal Questions* in 2010. We now present an updated version, *A Dentist's Guide to the Law: 228 Things Every Dentist Should Know*. The ADA Division of Legal Affairs is thankful to the many ADA members who have supported this publication and who have contacted the ADA with questions about laws and regulations affecting dentistry. These members have provided the impetus for this book and the ideas for its content.

We are also grateful for the valuable assistance of Patrick Cannady, Manager, Dental Informatics; John Malone, Manager, Scientific and Technical Information; Pamela Porembski, D.D.S., Director, Council on Dental Practice; Carolyn Tatar, Senior Manager, Product Development and Sales; Kathryn Pulkrabek, Manager/Editor, Professional Products; Steve Gruninger, Assistant Director, Safety and Biocompatibility; Mary Griffin, Legal Coordinator; Denise Zanders, Legal Coordinator; and our legal interns over the years, with particular thanks to Misti Napier-Burton and Angelique Salib.

About the Book

This publication is intended to be a first-step resource and source of information about a number of legal issues that affect practicing dentists. It sets forth a lot of information in what we hope is a convenient and practical form, and addresses a wide array of legal issues of relevance to dentists and their dental teams. The book features updated links to numerous additional resources, and the appendices contain sample contracts, checklists, and other helpful supplementary materials. Note that while any reader will be able to access the vast majority of these linked resources, we have included a few links to resources that can only be accessed by ADA members. To the extent that you wish to use and revise these materials for your own purposes, we strongly encourage you to consult with legal counsel.

This publication contains updated information on many legal topics, such as the various regulations relating to HIPAA, the Sunshine Act, certain legal aspects of technology for health records and communications, recent changes in the Americans with Disabilities Act, the Payment Card Industry Data Security Standards (PCI DSS), various legal aspects of social media, and the federal Anti-Kickback Statute and Self-Referral (Stark) Law. If there are additional topics that we have not covered, but should cover in future editions, please let us know. If you have suggestions or additional questions, please contact us at *legalbook@ada.org*.

You should be aware that you always have ADA legal counsel working on your behalf:

- Identifying and addressing legal issues of relevance to the dental profession
- Protecting the interests of the ADA and its members
- Filing litigation and amicus curiae briefs that assert positions that serve dentistry
- Generating informational materials that keep our state associations and individual members advised of timely legal issues
- Working with other divisions to provide input into the scope of government regulations
- Assisting in the development of user-friendly seminars and publications to facilitate your compliance with OSHA, HIPAA, and other laws and regulations that affect dental practice

We hope that you will view this publication as still another way in which we are able to continue to support you and your practice on an ongoing basis.

A Letter From ADA's General Counsel

We in the ADA Division of Legal Affairs recognize that members of the dental profession, including members of ADA, are continually faced with issues of law that affect their practices, their businesses, and their everyday lives. We also recognize that our members are not specifically trained in the law and that the legal challenges that beset them are often virtually overwhelming. The healthcare professions, including dentistry, are often subject to federal regulation, actions by insurance carriers, legalistic contracts, and even claims that may escalate into litigation. We have received numerous inquiries from our members regarding matters of law that have come to their attention.

While our members may not always fully understand the many legal issues that confront them, we at ADA take great pride in our ability to understand and help members understand and address those issues. We have received questions from many of our members, and we have attempted to answer those questions knowledgeably and effectively. As an additional avenue for providing information to our members, however, we are pleased to provide this publication, which has been specifically designed to delineate and describe, in plain language, a substantial number of the more relevant issues that you may end up facing.

We are hopeful that our publication will be of meaningful assistance to all who take the time to consult it and to seek to better understand the legal issues that they confront. We invite you, as well, to give us your comments about the publication and about other subject matter that might be of help. We view our Division as a resource to the entire ADA organization, and we look forward to continuing to work with all of you.

Best regards,

J. Craig Busey
General Counsel
The American Dental Association
ADA Division of Legal Affairs
211 E. Chicago Avenue
Chicago, IL 60611-2678

ada.org
legaldivision@ada.org

Disclaimer

The American Dental Association designed *A Dentist's Guide to the Law: 228 Things Every Dentist Should Know* to assist dental practices in understanding certain legal issues. In making these materials available, the ADA does not, nor does it intend to, provide either legal or professional advice. Nothing here represents ADA's legal or professional advice as to any particular situation you may be facing. To get appropriate legal or professional advice, you need to consult directly with a properly qualified professional or with an attorney admitted to practice in your jurisdiction.

A Dentist's Guide to the Law generally discusses certain federal and state laws, but does not and cannot address every federal and state law that could affect a dental practice. Each dental practice must be aware of and comply with applicable state and federal laws. *A Dentist's Guide to the Law* refers to federal and state statutes and regulations, including regulations adopted by agencies such as the U.S. Department of Health and Human Services (HHS) and the Federal Trade Commission (FTC), among others. However, the materials that follow have not been approved by HHS, the FTC, or any other federal or state agency. Dental practices vary widely, and each should address legal issues and develop and implement various compliance programs appropriate to its circumstances and in compliance with all applicable laws and regulations.

We have made every effort to make these materials useful and informative. As a consumer of the information, however, you must understand that the law varies from jurisdiction to jurisdiction, and it sometimes changes more rapidly than these materials. For that reason, we make no representations or warranties of any kind about the completeness, accuracy, or any other quality of these materials or any updates, and **expressly disclaim all warranties, including without limitation all implied warranties (including any warranty as to merchantability and fitness for a particular use)**.

To the extent we have included links to any websites, we intend no endorsement of their content and imply no affiliation with the organizations that provide their content. Nor do we make any representations or warranties about the information provided on those sites, which we do not control in any way.

We welcome your comments and suggestions for *A Dentist's Guide to the Law: 228 Things Every Dentist Should Know.*

A Dentist's Guide to the Law:
228 Things Every Dentist Should Know

Table of Contents

Introduction

Establishing the Dental Practice

Employment Law

Compliance: OSHA, HIPAA, FACTA, COPPA, and the Physician Payments Sunshine Act (Open Payments)

Business Considerations

Payment, Collection, and Reimbursement

The Patient

Appendices

Index

Introduction

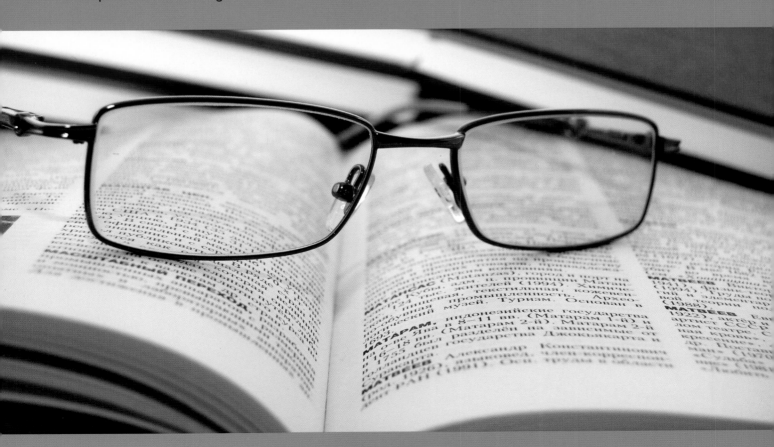

Chapter 1.
How to Use This Book

A wide array of legal issues confronts dentists and their dental teams during the course of their day-to-day practices. Sometimes these issues involve particularly thorny questions about practice management or patient care. This book is here to help. It provides basic legal information on questions that oral health care practitioners have about their practices.

No book could possibly cover every dental legal issue. The topics covered here are those that dentists have frequently asked us over the years.

It's important for you to know both what this book is and what it is not:

- The purpose of the publication is to provide basic answers to frequently asked legal questions. Its focus is on issues confronting dentists and their dental teams in private practice. However, we believe that many of the questions and answers in this book will also be useful for dentists who work in different arenas of the profession, including education and research.

- The answers to the frequently asked questions are informational only, and not a substitute for legal advice. Laws change, and, even more importantly, legal advice requires a careful assessment of the facts of a particular situation, which is then measured against all applicable laws. We don't have all the facts about cases you may be wondering about, and we are not experts in, or able to provide legal advice about, your state law. Indeed, we are not license to practice law outside of Illinois, and we cannot provide personal legal advice with respect to Illinois law, for that matter. We will give you as much information as we reasonably can, but you must consult your lawyer for legal advice.

- Our focus in this book is on federal law. The book references state law in general terms where appropriate, but it is important for you to turn to your state dental society or personal attorney — or perhaps your malpractice carrier — for specific federal, state and local legal information that may apply to you.

- Oftentimes, dentists will ask ADA attorneys questions such as "Should I sign this contract?", "Should I join this plan?", or "Should I fire my HIV-infected hygienist?" This book answers questions from a legal frame. It does not focus on "shoulds" in the sense of ethical, business, or practice considerations. By telling you what the law says, we hope you will have a better context for factoring in ethics and practice perspectives.

Which leads us to the first question:

1. How Should I Use This Book?

This book is a primer that supplies a baseline of legal information that can help you identify, frame, and think through some basic legal issues. While not a substitute for professional advice, think of the book as a way to help you avoid legal problems that might otherwise require you to retain counsel; when retaining a lawyer is appropriate, the book will likely help you and your attorney be more efficient and creative when confronted with dental-legal issues.

Related References and Resources

- Some Laws That Can Affect Dentistry
  ADA.org/DentistGuidetoLaw

- Valuable Federal Government Websites
  ADA.org/DentistGuidetoLaw

2. Will You Give Me a Referral to a Lawyer in My Area?

As a general rule, the ADA does not give lawyer referrals. The ADA does not maintain a listing of lawyers in your area who are (or who claim to be) qualified and sufficiently experienced to handle your legal matter. Lawyer referrals are more properly handled by your state or local dental or bar associations, which are more likely to know local counsel with the expertise you need. On rare occasions, when the issue involved is highly specialized and you are not able to find appropriate counsel, we may be able to identify lawyers reputed to have knowledge in the subject matter area relevant to your situation.

3. What Does a Dentist Need to Know to Select the Right Lawyer?

In a nutshell, you choose an attorney in somewhat the same manner that an attorney would select his or her dentist. The following is designed to help break down and organize the decision-making process.

Why Do You Need an Attorney?

The threshold question is: Why do you need the attorney? Any situation involving your legal rights and obligations is a situation that you should consider consulting with an attorney. Examples of such situations include:

- Purchase/sale of, or starting, a business (such as a dental practice)
- Real estate transactions
- Estate planning (wills, trusts)
- Family matters (divorce, adoption)
- Contractual matters (drafting, review of, disputes over)
- Governmental agencies (investigations, inspections, citations)
- Labor and employment matters
- Litigation (you are being sued or threatened with a lawsuit)
- Criminal matters (you have been arrested or accused of a crime)

Some attorneys practice more as generalists, while some practice in more specialized fields of law. An attorney who might be perfectly qualified to help you defend against an employee's claim of retaliatory discharge may not be the best attorney to help you manage your legal obligations in case of a breach of HIPAA protected health information. Just as you would not go to a gynecologist if you were having migraines, you would not go to an attorney specializing in patents to review an office lease. Thus, to better direct your search, your first step is to understand (even in a broad manner) why it is that you need legal guidance.

Referral Sources

Personal and Professional Referrals. A simple way to start your search is to ask friends, relatives, coworkers, or other members of your community to recommend lawyers with whom they have worked, especially if those people have had legal concerns similar to yours. Professionals with whom you have a business relationship, such as health care professionals and businesspeople, can be helpful, particularly if they work in a field related to the type of law your case concerns. Keep in mind that even if a recommended lawyer does not practice the kind of law you require, she or he might be able to direct you to other reputable lawyers who do. Be careful, however, not to make your decision based solely on another person's recommendation; the lawyer that is right for someone else's case might not be right for yours.

- **Organizations.** Your state or local bar association may have a lawyer referral service. The American Bar Association's directory of lawyer referral services can be found here: *http://apps.americanbar.org/legalservices/lris/directory.*

  If the legal concern relates to your practice, your malpractice carrier might be able to provide you with some guidance in finding a local attorney who has dealt with similar cases.

  Your state dental organization might be able to recommend an attorney. For example, the New York State Dental Association provides has an approved referral list of attorneys and law firms who specialize in dental matters. The list is available at *www.nysdental.org/membership/subpage.cfm?ID=14.*

- **Online.** If you are unsuccessful in obtaining a personal or organizational recommendation for a local attorney who practices in the substantive area you need, you may be able to locate such an attorney through an online search.

Due Diligence

The amount of work you will want to devote to assuring that you have selected the right attorney will likely be proportional to the importance and complexity of the matter. Are you selecting an attorney for your residential real estate closing? The attorney who coaches your daughter's soccer team may do just fine, as might the attorney with an office in the nearby strip mall. Facing a government investigation and substantial fine due to a HIPAA breach? You will likely wish to make sure that your attorney has substantial experience and expertise in HIPAA and regulatory matters.

Interview

For an important legal matter, you will likely want to meet with the attorney for an interview before engaging him or her. Depending on the matter and on your level of comfort, you may wish to interview more than one attorney. Many attorneys will be willing to meet with you at no cost to discuss the possible engagement, but you should make sure that you have agreed upon whether or not you will be charged for this initial meeting.

Considerations as You Prepare to Interview the Attorney

Fees. Advertisements can be misleading. An attorney might advertise a low price that does not include other costs (such as filing fees, copying and fax charges, etc.). Be sure you know whether the attorney will be charging you on a flat-fee basis or by the hour. You will want to have an estimate, in most cases, of how much the attorney's services will cost for your particular matter, and when you will be expected to pay before you hire him or her. You may wish to request a written engagement agreement with the attorney that details the engagement, including fees.

- Be aware that some lawyers charge for an initial interview. As previously noted, you should know ahead of time whether there will be a charge for this initial visit and, if so, how much it will be. The initial meeting by itself does not mean you have committed to hire the attorney.

- There are several types of fee structures:

  o Hourly rates: A fee calculation based on cost per hour for the attorney's services

  o Fixed fee: A flat fee charged for a simple service, such as the review of an agreement, a real estate closing, or an uncontested divorce

  o Contingent fee: A fee consisting of agreed-upon percentage of money the client receives from a settlement, which may include the out-of-pocket costs or expenses incurred in the transaction or lawsuit

  o Miscellaneous fees: Filing fees (physical and e-filing), photocopying, transcription, phone calls, messenger services, serving papers, witness fees, travel expenses, etc. Some lawyers also charge for work done by their paralegals/legal assistants

Practice Record. Though online reviews can be misleading, there are several ways to check an attorney's online reputation. One method is to check your state bar association's website, which may provide information as to whether any complaints, misconduct charges, or malpractice accusations have been filed against the attorney.

Experience. You may wish to ask the prospective attorney to describe the level of his or her experience. Based on the nature of the case, you may not always need the most experienced attorney. A relatively inexperienced attorney might be sufficient for a small matter (such as a residential real estate closing), and hiring such an attorney may save you money. More complex legal matters may call for a more experienced attorney, whose fees are likely to be significantly higher.

Communication. Legal matters require clear, consistent, and reliable communication between client and attorney, especially in a complex or extremely important matter (such as where your dental license may be at risk) which may last for several months or more. You should choose an attorney who commits to respond to calls and emails in a timely manner. You might attempt to test this by sending an email to the law office after an initial visit, detailing a few questions you might have. A delayed response might indicate that the attorney is too busy to give your matter the attention you would want.

Personality. An attorney's personality may be important to you, since you should feel comfortable in his or her presence and working with him or her. You may need to openly share private information so that he/she can effectively represent you to achieve the best outcome. If you withhold information because you do not feel comfortable with your lawyer, that decision could negatively impact your results.

Preparing for the Interview

When you go to the meeting with the attorney, it may be helpful to bring the following:

- A written summary of the issues. For example, for review of an employment agreement, this may consist of a summary of what you believe should be the terms of the agreement (what has been orally promised), concerns that you have with the proposed agreement (e.g., with what is stated, or even omitted, from the proposed agreement), and any other concerns related to the employment.

- In other types of matters, you might bring the names, addresses, and phone numbers of all people or entities involved. The lawyer cannot represent you if he or she has a relationship with anyone who is adverse to your position.

- All documents related to your matter. If you are involved in a lawsuit, bring anything you've received from a court or any person or entity involved in the dispute. Some lawyers might request that you send them the materials ahead of time so they can prepare to meet with you. Provide copies, not the originals. For review of an agreement such as an employment agreement, you should provide a copy of the agreement.

Attorneys often charge by the hour. The more focused and well organized that you are (e.g., all documents supplied to the attorney and well organized), the less work for the attorney and the smaller your legal bill will likely be.

You should also prepare some questions to ask the lawyer. You are essentially conducting a job interview. Depending on the matter, the some or all of the following may be helpful questions:

- Are you experienced in this kind of matter?
- Will you be the lawyer handling this matter, or will an associate be handling this?
- How long do you estimate it will take to complete this matter?
- How much do you estimate your services will cost me?
- What is your fee structure?

Your New Attorney

Once you have hired your lawyer, there are certain expectations for that relationship. You should expect your lawyer to:

- Prepare a written fee agreement, including information about what expenses you will be required to pay and the reasons behind those charges

- Be straightforward and honest in giving you advice

- Tell you the strengths and weaknesses of your case or position

- Keep you informed of the status of the matter and of actions that he or she is taking

- Follow your instructions (as long as they are legal, ethical, and reasonable)

- Protect your interests and consult you when making important decisions regarding your case

- Refrain from representing any other client with interests that conflict with yours during the time that she or he is representing you

- Provide you with copies of all letters and documents related to your matter

- Provide you with an itemized periodic bill of all work done and expenses related to your case

In turn, your lawyer will likely expect the following of you:

- Be present and on time for all appointments and court dates (if applicable)

- Give him or her reliable contact information for you and update him or her whenever your contact information changes

- Be completely honest. Except in very special circumstances, your lawyer must keep information you tell him or her confidential, and it's important that your lawyer have as much information as possible that might help him or her argue your position effectively

If you have problems with your lawyer, such as if you are dissatisfied with the representation, first talk to him or her and see if the problems can be resolved in a mutually satisfactory manner. If you can't resolve the problems, you have a right to fire the lawyer and hire a new one (though, depending on the matter, this may give rise to additional — and sometimes significant — costs).

If you have found an attorney with whom you can work well and whom you trust, you may have found a valuable business advisor on whom you can rely in the future to help with legal problems that may arise. This might include those problems beyond that attorney's expertise — a good attorney will advise you when a matter is beyond his or her (or the firm's) area of expertise, and will likely be able to recommend another attorney with that type of expertise. Thus, spending the time to carefully choose the right attorney to work with you and your practice may pay dividends beyond the current matter.

Related References and Resources

- A Dentist's Guide to Selecting a Lawyer
  ADA.org/en/home-cps/practice/operations/risk-management/a-dentists-guide-to-selecting-a-lawyer

Chapter 2.
Know the Law

Dental practices must comply with a wide array of laws, such as laws that apply to health care providers, employers, and business entities. Understanding these law can help you protect your patients and your practice on a day-to-day basis, and can help you decide when you need help from a lawyer or from another professional, such as an accountant.

4. What Are Some Laws That Apply to Dentistry?

Here are some examples of laws that might apply to a dental practice:

- Dental Practice Acts

- Professional corporation laws

- Tax laws

- Laws that apply to landlords, tenants, and owners of real estate

- Employment laws, such as the Occupational Safety and Health Act (OSHA) and nondiscrimination laws

- Laws on prescribing drugs, such as state prescribing laws and the federal Controlled Substances Act

- Dental records laws

- Patient privacy laws, such as the Health Insurance Portability and Accountability Act of 1996 (HIPAA)

- Laws on insurance, professional liability, and lawsuits

Some laws are federal and others are state or local. Dental practices must understand the requirements of laws on all three levels. For example, the Americans with Disabilities Act (AwDA) is a federal law, but state and local governments may also have disabilities laws, and a dental practice may need to comply with laws on all three levels.

Some laws apply to everyone, and some apply only to certain individuals and entities. Laws such as a state dental practice act are specific to dentistry. Laws such as HIPAA apply to many, but not all, dental practices. Each dental practice should determine which federal, state and local laws apply, and what the dental practice must do to comply. It is important to consider all of the laws that may apply in a given situation.

In this book we often use the word "law" to apply to a number of things, such as:

- Statutes enacted by legislators
- Rules and regulations from government agencies
- Case law from courts

A dental practice must comply with all applicable laws, no matter what the source.

5. What Key Federal Laws Apply in Dentistry?

A number of federal laws may come into play in the dental office, such as antitrust, collections, disability rights, employment, environmental, marketing, malpractice settlement reporting, office safety, patient privacy, taxation, and more. Some are addressed more thoroughly throughout this book.

Federal laws may preempt or override similar state laws. Some federal laws preempt state law but allows more stringent state law requirements to remain in force, as with the AwDA and HIPAA. In such cases, dentists must satisfy both the federal and certain state requirements.

Related References and Resources

- Some Laws That Can Affect Dentistry
  ADA.org/DentistGuidetoLaw

6. What Key State Laws Do I Have to Comply With?

If you are a dentist, your state dental practice act is a key state law with which you must comply. Among other things, the practice act will establish your authority to practice, along with your legal scope of practice. The practice act may address whether and how you may delegate duties to allied dental personnel. It may also specify certain requirements on issues ranging from confidentiality and privacy to insurance requirements and more.

Practice acts are by no means uniform from state to state. For example, recordkeeping requirements may vary. Rules governing allied personnel are sometimes included in the dental practice act, although a state may have a separate act or acts for this purpose (such as a practice act for hygienists). These rules can vary by state as well. For example, certification requirements for dental assistants to do coronal polishing can vary from state to state.

In addition to your state practice act, other state laws will also come into play. State law may be targeted to other (or perhaps all) health care workers in the state (for example, patient privacy rights, or heightened privacy rights for persons infected with HIV). State laws of general applicability statewide must also be followed, such as employment laws that cover all employers in the state. State law may impose requirements not addressed under federal law, or may go beyond the requirements under federal law. Compliance with state law can depend on whether there has been federal preemption, as discussed above.

Chapter 3.
Lawsuits

7. What Are the Penalties for Violating HIPAA?

HIPAA violations can result in civil penalties, and, in some cases, criminal penalties. There are four tiered ranges of civil penalties. The lowest tier is for violations where the dental practice did not know, and by exercising reasonable diligence would not have known, that the dental practice was in violation of HIPAA. Penalties in this tier range from $100 to $50,000. The highest tier involves willful neglect that is not corrected within 30 days. Penalties in this tier can start at $50,000. There is a maximum penalty of $1.5 million for all violations of an identical provision during a calendar year.

In most cases, the maximum penalty amount will not be imposed. Instead, the government will determine the amount of a penalty on a case-by-case basis, depending on the nature and extent of the violation and resulting harm, as well as other aggravating and mitigating factors, which are listed in the HIPAA regulations at 45 CFR 160.408, available online at *www.ecfr.gov/cgi-bin/text-idx?SID=267ddbb0ea4dc25607809aa61c2c7b7b&node=se45.1.160_1408&rgn=div8*.

Examples of the factors include the number of individuals affected, the harm caused to the affected individuals, and the size of the dental practice.

A HIPAA violation can also result in criminal penalties. According to the U.S. Department of Health and Human Services Office for Civil Rights (OCR):

> A person who knowingly obtains or discloses individually identifiable health information in violation of the Privacy Rule may face a criminal penalty of up to $50,000 and up to one-year imprisonment. The criminal penalties increase to $100,000 and up to five years imprisonment if the wrongful conduct involves false pretenses, and to $250,000 and up to 10 years imprisonment if the wrongful conduct involves the intent to sell, transfer, or use identifiable health information for commercial advantage, personal gain or malicious harm. The Department of Justice is responsible for criminal prosecutions under the Privacy Rule.[1]

Related References and Resources

- What are the penalties for violating HIPAA?
  ADA.org/en/member-center/member-benefits/legal-resources

- OCR, HIPAA Enforcement
  www.hhs.gov/ocr/privacy/hipaa/enforcement/index.html

---

[1] Source: OCR, Summary of the HIPAA Privacy Rule, *www.hhs.gov/ocr/privacy/hipaa/understanding/summary* (click on "Enforcement and Penalties for Noncompliance").

8. I've Been Sued. What Do I Do?

We want you to know the law well enough to know when you need to retain counsel. Helping you spot potential legal issues is one of the goals of this publication. The truth is, however, that trying to save money by navigating a legal dispute by yourself can end up costing you far more down the road in terms of money, time, and results than will obtaining sound legal advice when legal issues first emerge.

If you are sued or threatened with suit, contact an attorney. If the dispute has not escalated very far, the attorney may recommend that you try to communicate directly with the other party, and can give you guidance about the best way to do that and about what to say and what not to say. It is best if you do not speak with the attorneys for the other side, and in many states the legal profession ethical code provides that the only thing a lawyer for an adverse or potentially adverse party should tell you is that you should seek legal counsel.

Your lawyer can help you assess your risks and duties in the event a legal action is filed. For example, your attorney can advise you about whether and how to respond to a subpoena for records or about questions you may be asked by representatives for the other party. Parties to a lawsuit are entitled to obtain from each other all information reasonably identified by a properly served request and that may be relevant to the case. This is called "discovery." During a lawsuit, but prior to trial, most courts will err on the side of requiring disclosure, even if the information sought is likely to be ruled irrelevant and inadmissible at trial. If a lawsuit is filed or you have good reason to believe one will be filed, it is important to maintain the status quo with respect to records. For example, once a malpractice claim is made or even threatened, it is a huge mistake to discard or modify patient records. In fact, such conduct may itself create legal liability.

The questions you ask your attorney about legal matters, including legal strategies and tactics, and the legal advice your attorney gives you are protected by what is called the Attorney-Client Privilege. The other side in the legal dispute is not entitled to information about those privileged discussions unless you "waive" the privilege, which is a serious matter your attorney should advise you about. Conversations and other communications with individuals besides your attorney are not privileged and the other party is entitled to learn about them if they are relevant to the case. Discussions you have with ADA staff attorneys are not privileged and information about those discussions is discoverable. ADA attorneys cannot represent members in individual matters. Their client is the ADA and in addition they may not be licensed to practice law in your state.

The legal nature of a document or conversation is what determines whether it is privileged. Labeling or designating information that is not privileged will not make it so. Many people believe that merely designating non-privileged information as "confidential" will protect it from discovery, but that is not true.

You should immediately contact your insurance carrier when a claim is made that may be covered by insurance. Under some circumstances, failure to do so may threaten the availability of insurance coverage.

9. Should I Settle? On What Terms?

Whether to settle depends on your case. This issue invariably arises once the dust clears after you are sued. First-time defendants in malpractice cases sometimes express concern that the attorney provided by the insurance company may be pressuring them to settle the claim. If you are concerned about the advice you are getting from your insurance counsel about settlement, you may wish to consult with your private counsel, who may help you assess the merits of your case and your rights to a full defense as spelled out in your insurance contract. Private counsel can be especially important if a claim is likely to exceed policy limits or the claim is not fully covered.

Dentists often settle claims without admitting liability. Whether to settle can be more of a business issue than a legal one. For example, you may need to consider whether it is worth the time away from the office to have your day in court. If you decide to settle, your counsel will probably try to structure the agreed-upon settlement to avoid any admission of liability. A good settlement will extinguish the patient's rights to sue further on the same facts. The proper ingredients and settlement language may turn on state law. Parties will often agree that the terms of the settlement remain private, and neither the Settlement Agreement itself nor its terms need be placed in the official court record. The Agreement may include penalties in the event a party makes an unauthorized disclosure of the settlement terms.

10. Must a Settlement of a Malpractice Claim Be Reported to the Data Bank?

It depends. If you decide to settle a malpractice claim through your insurance company, the company will need to make a report to the National Practitioner Data Bank (NPDB). Nobody knows for certain what effect being in the Data Bank will have. Some dentists view this as troublesome and will pay out-of-pocket from personal funds to avoid having to report to the Data Bank. Others are not as worried, especially if their Data Bank file is a small one. When assessing your level of discomfort regarding having something entered into your Data Bank file, keep in mind that information about you may already be available through other sources, such as publicly available malpractice "banks" in some states.

11. Will the ADA Represent Me or File a Brief on My Behalf?

The ADA will provide all the information we reasonably can to help you. However, we do not serve as your personal attorneys, and are generally not staffed to function in that capacity, particularly in the case of private business disputes. As for intervening on your behalf, such as by filing a friend of the court brief, the ADA follows Board of Trustee policies. Among other things, the policies focus on whether your case is one of national significance to dentistry; certain financial considerations are also involved.

Related References and Resources

- ADA Criteria for Litigation Assistance
  ADA.org/en/member-center/member-benefits/legal-resources

Chapter 4.
The ADA Legal Division

12. What Do the ADA's Lawyers Do for Me?

The lawyers in the ADA Division of Legal Affairs provide legal guidance to support the ADA's dedication to protecting you, your patients, and the dentist-patient relationship. In addition to supporting this valuable work on behalf of organized dentistry, the Division's lawyers provide useful legal information to members such as explaining provider contract terms through the ADA's Contract Analysis Service, reporting on legal developments, and publishing answers to members' frequently asked legal questions.

In the legal arena, the ADA from time to time files lawsuits to protect the legal rights of dentists and advance the interests of the dental profession generally. For example, the ADA Legal Division spearheaded the filing of three class action suits on behalf of dentists to help stop what we believe to be unlawful practices by insurance companies. The first two suits, against insurance giants Aetna and WellPoint, fought for the rights of non-participating dentists to be fairly treated by the carriers and charge those carriers with breach of contract, unlawful interference with the dentist-patient relationship, and trade libel. The third, against Cigna and other insurers, fought for the rights of participating dentists to fair compensation for services they provide and alleged the carriers violated the federal racketeering statute and other laws. We're proud to report that we obtained an excellent result in the Aetna case. The ADA was extremely pleased with the settlement agreement it reached with Aetna, which brought changes to Aetna's billing practices and reimbursement procedures in a manner unparalleled in the insurance industry. The ADA Legal Division recently filed *an amicus curiae* brief, and solicited filings of *amici curiae* briefs by various state attorneys general, in the *North Carolina Board of Dental Examiners v. Federal Trade Commission* case before the US Supreme Court (the Court's decision in that case is summarized in Appendix 12).

The ADA's Division of Legal Affairs also provides guidance to protect the ADA from lawsuits and defends the ADA if sued. Recent examples include the successful defense of numerous lawsuits against the ADA about its position on dental amalgam, which helps free dentists to continue to offer this treatment option to patients. Our lawyers also advocate on behalf of dentistry by filing "friend of the court" briefs with the U.S. Supreme Court and other appeals courts in appropriate cases involving issues potentially affecting dentists and patients. In addition, the ADA's lawyers often partner with other divisions to work proactively on your behalf. Some great examples include urging the federal government to limit the scope of HIPAA privacy regulations, developing user-friendly seminars and publications to facilitate your understanding of important legal issues and enhance your practice's compliance efforts, and assisting with the ADA's efforts to limit the applicability to dental practices of the federal Red Flags Rule and to promote repeal of the McCarran-Ferguson Act, which exempts insurance companies from certain federal antitrust restrictions.

So in addition to providing you with valuable legal information, protecting the ADA from lawsuits, and defending the ADA when sued, ADA's lawyers are powerful advocates for you and the patients you serve.

Practice Formats: the Business/Legal Structure

Chapter 5.
Practice Formats: the Business/ Legal Structure

When establishing a dental practice, one of the first issues you need to consider is which business structure to use. The choice of practice entity has business, legal, tax, and personal consequences.

As your practice evolves over the years, it may be wise to ask from time to time whether the business organization you chose when you began your practice remains the best format for you now. Your attorney and tax advisor can help you make business and tax planning decisions and can help you file the forms and keep the records that are appropriate to the business arrangement you choose.

Let's look at some of the key considerations in choosing among the various types of legal organizations for conducting a dental practice.

13. What Business Structure Options Do I Have?

Virtually all practices will be conducted in one of the following business formats:

- Sole proprietorship

- General partnership

- Limited partnership or a variation on the partnership format called a limited liability partnership (LLP)

- Corporation, which will be either a "C" corporation or an "S" corporation, and will be a professional corporation or a standard business corporation

- Limited liability company (LLC), which in a few jurisdictions might be a professional LLC

There are positives and negatives connected with each business format, as discussed below. In addition, a given format may simply not be appropriate because of the way you intend to conduct your practice.

14. What Are the Advantages and Disadvantages of a Sole Proprietorship?

A sole proprietorship is the simplest and most common structure chosen to start a business. It is an unincorporated business owned and run by the dentist with no distinction between the business and the owner-dentist. The dentist is entitled to all profits and is responsible for all business's debts, losses and liabilities. This low maintenance business structure costs almost nothing to create and is relatively easy to establish.

Because the dentist and the dentist's business are one and the same, the business itself is not taxed separately — the sole proprietorship income is your income. The dentist reports income or losses and expenses with a Schedule C and the standard Form 1040. Because the dentist is the sole owner of the business, the dentist has complete control over all decisions — he or she isn't required to consult with anyone else when the dentist needs to make decisions or wants to make changes.

Because there is no legal separation between the dentist and the dentist's business, the dentist can be held personally liable for the debts and obligations of the business. This risk extends to any liabilities incurred as a result of employee actions. Note, however, that the dentist will remain liable for professional malpractice individually regardless of business structure.

Furthermore, a prudent dentist will purchase a reasonable amount of professional liability insurance to afford protection (covering legal defense costs as well as any settlement or judgment amounts) from malpractice lawsuits. A sole proprietorship will not afford protection against non-professional liabilities, such as the patient who slips and is injured in the waiting room. A business format such as a corporation will help protect the dentist's personal assets from these non-professional liabilities, but will not protect assets that are part of the practice. To protect practice assets, other types of insurance such as general liability coverage should be considered in these litigious times. However, insurance can be expensive, deductibles and co-pays apply, and potential sources of liability keep expanding. As a dentist starts to accumulate more personal assets outside the practice and the practice itself grows, liability issues become more important and may lead the dentist to conclude that he or she has outgrown the sole proprietorship format. Some other factors that influence the business format decision will be discussed in the subsequent sections.

15. What Are the Pros And Cons of a General Partnership?

A partnership is a business arrangement where two or more dentists own the practice together — for example, if two or more dentists wish to operate a practice together. These dentists should understand the economies of scale achievable by working together and agree upon an arrangement to share costs and profits. The dentists may consider establishing a general partnership, under which the partners share decision-making as well as financial risk. Similar to sole proprietorships, general partnerships retain full, shared liability among the owners. Partners are not only liable for their own actions, but also for the business debts and decisions made by other partners. In addition, the personal assets of all partners can be used to satisfy the partnership's debt.

Another risk is that the vision and enthusiasm that the partners had when they started the practice can sometimes wane. As in a marriage, disagreements or disgruntlement can arise which can cause an unfortunate split of the practice. For that reason, it is very important that a group practice have a formal written agreement setting forth the parties' understanding of the relationship — profits, expenses, decisions, what happens upon termination, and so forth. The agreement should be drafted by an attorney, and should reflect the parties' expectations and understanding of the partnership.

Although the partnership will need to file a separate informational tax return, the partnership does not generally itself pay tax but, rather, income and losses are allocated among the partners based on their agreed percentage, and the partners pay taxes as part of their own personal returns. There is no additional partnership tax (with limited exceptions at the state level in a few jurisdictions).

Next to sole proprietorships, general partnerships are the simplest legal format, requiring less administrative detail and fewer associated costs than the formats to be discussed below. But in a general partnership, liability and decision-making must be shared.

Keep in mind that you must tailor any partnership agreement to meet your needs and to satisfy state law requirements. Your counsel can draft an agreement and help determine what is right for you.

Related References and Resources

- Appendix 1: Checklist of Questions to Ask When Forming a Group Practice

16. Does a Limited Partnership Have Advantages Over a General Partnership?

It depends. A limited partnership differs from a general partnership in that it has two separate classes of membership: a general partner or partners, and limited partners. The general partners hold the management and decision-making authority for the practice. They also are individually charged with liability that might exceed the assets of the practice. The limited partners, on the other hand, do not have decision-making responsibilities, nor are they individually liable for liabilities of the practice (other than their own malpractice) that exceed their own investment in the business. In that sense, limited partners are much like individual stockholders in a public corporation. They have no real say in how the business is operated, but the most they can lose is the money they invested in their limited partnership interest.

At the same time, a limited partnership is similar to a general partnership in many ways. Partners associate together to share profits and expenses, and will have an extensive written agreement setting out the legal and financial elements of operating the practice, dealing with any termination of the business, admitting new partners, and so forth. The limited partnership files an informational tax return but taxes are paid by the individual dentist members, not the partnership itself.

A limited partnership requires more attention to detail and more filings than a general partnership. It can be formed only by making a statutory filing with the Secretary of State or similar governing office in the state of organization. A partnership agreement is essential for that filing and is more elaborate than a general partnership agreement. Annual filings with the state authority also are necessary, as well as federal and state income tax returns.

A limited partnership does have one important advantage over a general partnership, in addition to the fact that limited partners face a finite amount of risk on liabilities of the practice. Although the precise opportunities and limitations are well beyond the scope of this section, generally speaking, a limited partnership can slice and dice profits, losses, tax credits, required investments, and capital gain/loss in any way (proportionate or disproportionate) that the parties choose. To take some simple examples, a limited partner who has more assets to invest in the practice than the others might receive all the profits until that dentist has "recouped" his or her investment, and thereafter profits might be divided according to set percentages. A partner who has substantial other income — such as from a spouse — might negotiate to be allocated more of the anticipated early year losses from the practice. A partner who has substantial net operating loss carryovers from a prior business might want to be allocated more of the taxable income (but not cash flow).

Because of these tax advantages, limited partnerships are attractive formats for specific, one-time investment opportunities. One such example would be a real estate purchase, where certain investors are willing to invest money for profit but have no expertise or interest in managing the property, much less any desire to take on liability risk. The format is much less attractive for an operating business like a dental practice because a dentist who invests money in the practice will usually want to have a vote in how it is run. The new dentist who is associating with an established practice usually has little money to invest and is often taken on as an associate until such time as sufficient mutual trust is developed to allow that dentist to become a "full partner" and participant. At a point in a practice's evolution when employees are being hired, income is increasing, perhaps a lengthy lease is contemplated, and substantial equipment purchases are being made, a corporation or limited liability company as the legal format may become increasingly attractive.

17. What Is There About a Corporation That Would Make Me Want To Incorporate My Practice?

At least theoretically, incorporation is a way to reduce certain legal exposures. A corporation offers the owners of the practice (its shareholders) the ability to separate themselves legally from its operation. These shareholders invest the required start-up capital to get the business running, and the board of directors they elect, who in turn appoint the officers, who in turn are responsible for the day-to-day operations as well as important strategic decisions for this new legal entity, the corporation. As a practical matter, the shareholders, directors, and the officers will be by and large the same persons, at least in all but very large associations. Nonetheless, flexibility is possible with this arrangement. The new dentist who starts as an associate may "buy in" and become a shareholder after some years as a valuable contributor to the practice, but might not be quite ready to assume the same management responsibilities as the founding dentist. So perhaps the associate might become an officer, but not a director.

Because a corporation is a separate legal entity distinct from its shareholder(s), an important advantage of a corporation over the other formats discussed above is that all shareholders have limited liability. In other words, the corporation itself, not the shareholders that own it, is held legally liable for the actions and debts the business incurs, except in the case of fraud or malfeasance. This limited liability

At least theoretically, incorporation is a way to reduce certain legal exposures. A corporation offers the owners of the practice (its shareholders) the ability to separate themselves legally from its operation.

can be comforting to a group of dentists entering a fifteen-year lease, or purchasing $1 million of new equipment. (Note, however, that a bank from which the group may seek financing for that equipment purchase will likely ask for personal guarantees as to any significant loan, defeating the theoretical "limited liability" a corporation structure affords, at least for that transaction.)

A "C" corporation may be less desirable from a tax perspective because there are two layers of tax — the corporation pays tax and after the corporate income tax is paid on the business income, any distributions made to stockholders are taxed again at the stockholders' tax rates as dividends. Income paid to shareholders as wages are also taxed on the shareholder's personal income tax return.

Alternatively, the corporation may be able to make an "S" corporation election. An S corporation is often more attractive to small business owners than a C corporation because an S corporation has some appealing tax benefits and still provides business owners with the liability protection of a corporation. With an S corporation, income and losses are passed through to shareholders and included on their individual tax returns, similar to a partnership, resulting in one level of federal tax to pay. S corporations also have limitations as to who can be a shareholder.

One real tax advantage of forming a corporation is the ability to establish fringe benefit programs in a tax-favored manner. These include medical plans, to a limited extent, retirement plans, and some withholding tax advantages when dealing with employees. The availability of these tax-favored fringe benefits is typically what drives the decision to incorporate. Tax-favored fringe benefits, combined with flexibility in structuring the business relationship among the participants; a greater ability to establish buy-out arrangements among the parties; and a certain legitimacy or successful air that is associated with being organized as a corporation — particularly a professional corporation — all point to why many dental groups ultimately choose to be organized as corporations. It should be noted that many states specifically require an incorporated health care professional to be formally structured as a "professional corporation," or "PC" or "SC." You will need to consult an attorney in your state to determine local requirements.

One real tax advantage of forming a corporation is the ability to establish fringe benefit programs in a tax-favored manner. These include medical plans, to a limited extent, retirement plans, and some withholding tax advantages when dealing with employees.

With these advantages come some negatives that must be considered. A corporation generally involves more maintenance tasks and expense of operation than the other entities mentioned above (although a limited partnership involves many of the same maintenance tasks and expenses as a corporation). A corporation must be registered with the state; annual reports are required; meetings must be held and records of same kept; and a bookkeeper is often necessary to maintain the necessary books and records. Not only must a separate tax return be filed, but corporate-level taxes may have to be paid. For those reasons, the new dentist will frequently defer forming a corporation for a period of time.

18. Will It Help Me to Be a Limited Liability Company?

It depends. A limited liability company is a hybrid type of legal structure that provides the limited liability features of a corporation and the tax efficiencies and operational flexibility of a partnership. The "owners" of an LLC are referred to as "members." Depending on the state, the members can consist of a single individual (one owner), two or more individuals, corporations or other LLCs. Unlike shareholders in a corporation, LLCs are not taxed as a separate business entity. Instead, all profits and losses are "passed through" the business to each member of the LLC. LLC members report profits and losses on their personal federal tax returns, just like the owners of a partnership would. Like a partnership or limited partnership, LLCs have flexibility in determining how profits will be distributed. LLCs are somewhat easier to operate than corporations, as there are no requirements to keep formal minutes or conduct meetings of a board of directors, although some formalities are still required.

Members of an LLC are protected from personal liability for business decisions or actions of the LLC. This means that if the LLC incurs debt or is sued, members' personal assets are usually exempt. This is similar to the liability protections afforded to shareholders of a corporation. Members are not necessarily shielded from wrongful acts, including those of their employees.

You should check with your tax advisor concerning the proper tax election for your particular circumstances (C corporation, S corporation, partnership taxation — the most common election — or sole proprietorship). You should also consult with your lawyer when implementing or becoming a member of an LLC, as there is no "one size fits all" approach when it comes to LLCs.

While all 50 states allow the formation of LLC entities, some states do not allow a health care practice to be conducted as an LLC. Other states require a health care provider choosing the LLC option to be organized as a Professional LLC (PLLC), an entity similar to a professional corporation. Thus, it is important to check the laws of your state and any other state in which you might wish to form your LLC.

19. Should I Create an Operating Agreement If I Choose the LLC or PLLC Format?

Operating Agreements are important, particularly if you plan to have multiple members in the LLC. Using an operating agreement can help to avoid management and ownership misunderstandings that may occur during the business relationship. A carefully drafted operating agreement will establish specific rules and procedures in connection with the operations of the LLC, such as the percentages of ownership, the share and distribution of profits and losses, the rights and responsibilities of each member, how the LLC will be managed, and ownership transitions (such as what happens when a member leaves, dies, retires, becomes disabled, or wishes to sell his or her interest in the LLC, or when the LLC wants to add new members).

Chapter 6.
Dental Office Design

20. What Laws Affect Office Design?

Many federal, state and local laws affect dental office design, including zoning laws, building laws, and disabilities laws such as the Americans with Disabilities Act (AwDA), which imposes minimum requirements regarding accessibility for people with disabilities. Similar state and local disabilities laws may impose more stringent requirements than the AwDA. Zoning laws and building codes may impose a wide array of requirements for purposes such as safety. Zoning laws must typically be addressed in order to commence construction. So, too, may other specific state or local laws, such as those related to environmental hazards.

In addition, federal and state laws on emerging issues such as ergonomics, waste management, privacy, and employee safety may indirectly shape dental office design requirements. For example, a dental practice may wish to include office design elements that could reduce the chance of a data breach by protecting patient information in paper files and on computers.

21. What Does the Americans With Disabilities Act (AwDA) Require for Office Design?

The Americans with Disabilities Act helps guarantee access to "places of public accommodations" for persons with disabilities. Under the Act, and many similar state and local laws, a dental practice is considered a place of public accommodation, so the practice must comply with the Act as well as with applicable state and local accessibility laws. The Act requires that places of public accommodation meet certain accessibility standards. The standards that apply depend on whether the office is an existing facility, being renovated, or new construction.

Related References and Resources

- Americans with Disabilities Act: ADA Guide for Small Businesses
  www.ada.gov/smbusgd.pdf

- Americans with Disabilities Act: Access to Medical Care for Individuals with Mobility Disabilities
  www.ada.gov/medcare_mobility_ta/medcare_ta.htm

- The ADA Practical Guide to Dental Office Design
  adacatalog.org or 1.800.947.4746

22. Isn't There a "Grandfather" Provision That Exempts Me From the AwDA?

No, the AwDA contains no grandfather provision regarding accessibility. Exceptions to the AwDA requirements are extremely limited, such as certain exceptions for buildings that are listed in the National Register of Historic Places or designated as historic under an appropriate state or local law. Private dental offices are viewed as places of public accommodations that must comply with the law. Under the federal law, a lesser standard applies to existing facilities, as opposed to renovated or new ones. In all cases, the federal law sets the minimum requirements and dentists must also comply with any more stringent standards imposed by state or local laws.

23. I Rent My Office Space. Isn't AwDA Compliance the Building Owner's Responsibility?

Landlords and tenants are each responsible for satisfying the accessibility requirements of the AwDA. Typically, they may decide to apportion this responsibility between themselves by contract. For example, the landlord may agree to be responsible for compliance for common areas and the tenant may agree to do the same for his or her office space. While the AwDA allows them to do so, agreeing by contract to apportion who will do what does not vitiate either party's responsibility for the entire portion of the premises that an individual may visit, from curbside to dental chair and back.

Some dentists who lease their office space have anecdotally reported that their landlords would not take needed compliance steps. A lease provision requiring the landlord to do so with respect to common areas, and to indemnify the dentist-tenant for damages should the landlord fail to do so, may be one way to help protect against this risk.

24. What Are the AwDA Requirements for Existing Facilities?

The accessibility requirements for existing facilities are the lowest and easiest-to-meet standard. A dental practice in an existing office that does not require renovation must remove architectural barriers to the extent that doing so is readily achievable, which the Act describes as something that is "easily accomplishable and able to be carried out without much difficulty or expense." The standard of readily achievable barrier removal does not mean the office must be "fully accessible." However, a dentist may wish to undertake an audit of what barriers to access exist, and determine which barriers can be removed without significant difficulty or expense. Keep in mind that other laws, such as state and local accessibility laws, may impose even more stringent requirements that would require additional compliance steps.

Related References and Resources

- Checklist for Existing Facilities
  www.ada.gov/racheck.pdf

25. What Are the AwDA Rules for Renovation and New Construction?

In contrast to the requirements for existing facilities, renovations and new construction must be accessible as defined in the regulations, standards and guidance. These materials are very specific regarding many requirements, such as those pertaining to parking lots, entrances, doors, operatory size, counter heights, restrooms, elevators and more. Let's take a look at a few key points.[2]

Alterations (Renovations)

- Any alteration to a place of public accommodation or a commercial facility after January 26, 1992, shall be made so as to ensure that, to the maximum extent feasible, the altered portions of the facility are readily accessible to and usable by individuals with disabilities, including individuals who use wheelchairs.

- An alteration that affects or could affect the usability of or access to an area of a facility that contains a primary function shall be made so as to ensure that, to the maximum extent feasible, the path of travel to the altered area and the restrooms, telephones, and drinking fountains serving the altered area, are readily accessible to and usable by individuals with disabilities, including individuals who use wheelchairs, unless the cost and scope of such alterations is disproportionate to the cost of the overall alteration.

- Alterations made to provide an accessible path of travel to the altered area will be deemed disproportionate to the overall alteration when the cost exceeds 20 percent of the cost of the alteration to the primary function area.

New Construction

- With limited exceptions, failure to design and construct facilities for first occupancy after January 26, 1993 that are readily accessible to and usable by individuals with disabilities constitutes discrimination in violation of the Act.

- A dental office must have elevators even in situations when other business owners would not. Although elevators are generally not required in facilities under three stories or with fewer than 3,000 square feet per floor, there is an exception for the professional office of a health care provider.

- When a dental practice is located in a private residence, the portion of the residence used exclusively as a residence is not covered by the Act, but that portion used exclusively in the operation of the dental practice or that portion used both for the dental practice and for residential purposes is covered by the new construction and alterations requirements of the Act. The covered portion of the residence extends to those elements used to enter the dental practice, including the homeowner´s front sidewalk, if any, the door or entryway, and hallways; and those portions of the residence, interior or exterior, available to or used by employees or visitors of the dental practice, including restrooms.

---

[2] Source: Americans with Disabilities Act Title III Regulations. Part 36 Nondiscrimination on the Basis of Disability in Public Accommodations and Commercial Facilities (as amended by the final rule published on September 15, 2010), *www.ada.gov/regs2010/titleIII_2010/titleIII_2010_regulations.htm#a402*

26. How Do I Get More Specific Information About the AwDA Accessibility Requirements?

The U. S. Department of Justice has responsibility for enforcing provisions of the Act related to public accommodations. The U.S. Department of Justice Technical Assistance Program provides publications and free information about the AwDA through a toll-free Americans with Disabilities Act Information Line at 1.800.514.0301 and 1.800.514.0383 (TTY). Spanish language service is available.

Related References and Resources

- Americans with Disabilities Act National Network
  https://adata.org and 1.800.949.4232

- Information and Technical Assistance on the Americans with Disabilities Act
  www.ada.gov

27. Do I Still Have to Comply With State And Local Laws?

Yes, in addition to the federal law requirements imposed by the Act, you will also need to comply with any state and local civil rights laws pertaining to disability and access issues that are more stringent than the federal Act.

Many states have human rights laws with accessibility requirements. Local building codes place restrictions in a number of ways that can affect the dental office. For example, plumbing codes may require specific line sizes for drains, based on the number of sinks to be installed. Required setbacks and limits in building height are features that may be determined by local code.

State and local requirements may impose more stringent requirements and even stronger penalties for non-compliance. However, compliance with such state and local requirements alone will not necessarily ensure compliance with the federal Americans with Disabilities Act, since the federal Act may address issues not covered by state or local laws.

28. Does HIPAA Impose Requirements Related to Dental Office Design?

HIPAA does not mandate specific office design features, but the HIPAA rules do require covered entities to have reasonable and appropriate physical safeguards to protect the privacy and security of patient information. Facility security and contingency planning are two areas of the HIPAA Security Rule that may influence dental office design decisions.

For example, HIPAA requires a covered dental practice to adopt reasonable and appropriate policies and procedures to protect patient information and related buildings and equipment from natural and environmental hazards and from unauthorized access. Some of HIPAA's physical security safeguard standards can be adjusted according to factors such as the dental practice's size, complexity, capabilities, and budget.

The HIPAA Privacy Rule requires covered dental practices to reasonably safeguard patient information to limit incidental uses or disclosures made pursuant to an otherwise permitted or required use or disclosure. In some covered dental practices, such reasonable safeguards may involve dental office design decisions. According to the Office for Civil Rights, "[t]he HIPAA Privacy Rule does not require that all risk of incidental use or disclosure be eliminated to satisfy its standards. Rather, the Rule requires only that covered entities implement reasonable safeguards to limit incidental uses or disclosures."[3]

Dentists who are covered by HIPAA probably do not need expensive structural changes such as private, walled-off operatories or overall office soundproofing. However, dentists should evaluate their office designs under applicable federal and state privacy laws to determine which safeguards are required, how to protect patient information in compliance with the law, and which office design choices are reasonable and appropriate to protect the privacy and security of patient information.

Office design features that can help protect privacy and security include:

- Exterior locks on doors and windows

- Locks on nonpublic areas of the dental office

- Workstations that cannot be viewed or accessed by the public

- Secured entrances to areas where patient information is stored

- Consultation areas and operatories where patient information can be discussed without being overheard

- Secure disposal of electronic and paper patient information in accordance with a document retention system that meets applicable federal and state law

- Secure data backup and storage systems

Although HIPAA does not mandate specific dental office design features, HIPAA compliance considerations may influence dental office design trends over time. For example, offices with open operatories may incorporate curtains or sliding doors. Floor plans may help prevent unauthorized access to patient information (for example, floor plans that direct foot traffic flow away from areas where patient information may be accessed, such as the front desk). Products marketed to protect and secure patient information (such as easily locking cabinets) may become more prevalent. While some of these changes may not be specifically required by HIPAA, they may make good compliance sense for both HIPAA and state privacy laws, so they are likely to take root in designers' thinking about dental office design.

---

[3] OCR FAQ, "Is a covered entity required to prevent any incidental use or disclosure of protected health information?" http://www.hhs.gov/ocr/privacy/hipaa/faq/incidential_uses_and_disclosures/206.html

Unauthorized access to patient information can result in reputational and financial harm to the patient; for example, if a Social Security number is stolen, or if patient information is disclosed to an unauthorized individual. Unauthorized use or disclosure of patient information can also cause reputational harm to a dental practice, as well as the financial burden of complying with breach notification laws and the risk of penalties for noncompliance. Keeping privacy and security in mind when designing a dental office can help protect both patients and the dental practice.

Related References and Resources

- Chapter 15: HIPAA, State Law and PCIDSS: Patient Information

- HIPAA 20 Questions
  ADA.org/DentistGuidetoLaw

- OCR Frequently Asked Questions: Is a Covered Entity Required to Prevent Any Incidental Use or Disclosure of Protected Health Information?
  www.hhs.gov/ocr/privacy/hipaa/faq/incidential_uses_and_disclosures/206.html

- The ADA Practical Guide to HIPAA Compliance: Privacy and Security Manual
  adacatalog.org or 1.800.947.4746

29. Will Other Cutting Edge Dental Issues Affect Office Design?

A number of other laws and considerations affecting dental practice have the potential to significantly impact dental office design.

Ergonomics

If and when a federal ergonomics standard is passed, it may dramatically affect dental office design. It may be good risk management to proactively address ergonomics issues in your office design even though there are no current federal legal requirements. Considerations may include adequacy of space, placement of equipment, and four-handed dentistry.

Waste Management

Concerns about waste management may also affect office design. Some waste products that have come under regulatory scrutiny include X-ray fixer and developer; mercury/amalgam in wastewater; solid medical waste (including sharps); and various pharmaceuticals and other chemical substances classified as hazardous or controlled medical wastes. For example, space must be provided for segregating regulated medical waste from other solid waste. Thought should be given to how you will remove mercury/amalgam from the office wastewater. For example, do you have adequate space to install and maintain an amalgam separator. Also, convenient access to plumbing and clean-out points for plumbing can be designed into new construction.

Regulated Drugs

Space design should consider the need to maintain certain classes of drugs in a secure location. Other materials and equipment may also be of value and require a secure storage location. Properly locked cabinets should be included in office design.

Related References and Resources

- Question 70: What if I Suspect an Employee or Co-Worker Is Abusing or Taking Drugs from the Dental Office?

- ADA Statement on Best Management Practices for Amalgam Waste (includes a Practical Guide to Integrating BMPs Into Your Practice)
ADA.org/en/member-center/oral-health-topics/amalgam-waste-best-management

30. Is Video Surveillance Permitted in the Dental Office?

A number of complex federal and state laws regulate workplace surveillance, and a variety of factors may influence the legal risks associated with surveillance activities. For example, before a dental practice implements a surveillance program, it should consider factors such as:

- Where will the camera(s) be installed (e.g., building exterior, reception area, business office, operatory)? Can the camera(s) be installed so as to eliminate the possibility of capturing private areas such as restrooms and changing rooms?

- What is the purpose of the surveillance?

- What information is intended to be captured (and likely to be captured)?

- Will the equipment capture only video, or both audio and video?

- Will the dental practice post a sign alerting the public that surveillance is under way?

- Will the dental practice notify employees of the surveillance program, and have policies and procedures in place concerning the program and the resulting surveillance records?

- Will patient information be recorded, and, if so, how will it be stored (and for how long) and who will have access?

- Will the equipment capture information about patients' dental procedures?

- Will the equipment capture employee information, and might it be used in connection with employment matters such as discipline, promotions, or terminations?

- How might the dental practice act on information obtained through monitoring?

Audio

Surveillance equipment that captures audio may trigger complex federal and state laws, such as laws on wiretapping, eavesdropping, and stored communications. Telephonic monitoring, such as programs to evaluate employees' handling of patient communications, involves additional compliance issues. For example, applicable law may require the dental practice to notify both parties to the call (e.g., the employee and the patient) that the call is being monitored. A qualified attorney can provide information about applicable laws and legal risks, and whether a dental practice might take certain measures to comply with applicable laws and to minimize legal risk.

Monitoring Employees

State law may determine whether, and if so how, an employer is permitted to use video surveillance or other methods to monitor employees. For example, state law may require an employer to have policies in place concerning workplace monitoring, and to provide notice to employees. Even if the laws that apply to an appropriate workplace surveillance program do not require employee notification, providing notice to employees can help an employer defend against potential claim that surveillance was improper.

Security and Safety

A dental practice may wish to use video equipment for security and safety purposes, such as monitoring the building exterior or in public areas such as lobbies and elevators. However, a dental practice that implements a surveillance program for such purposes should also consider how the surveillance records will be reviewed and the steps that the dental practice will take if the records reveal an incident that could compromise safety or security.

Privacy

If patient information such as full face photos or other identifiers is captured by surveillance equipment, the HIPAA Privacy Rule may require appropriate administrative, technical and physical safeguards to protect the privacy of the information. A covered dental practice might meet this obligation through encryption or by otherwise restricting access to the surveillance records. If the surveillance is managed by a vendor, the vendor may meet the HIPPA definition of a "business associate" and may need to sign a compliant business associate agreement with the dental practice. HIPAA and applicable state law should be considered when deciding how to manage retention, access, and disposal of surveillance records.

State employment laws and privacy laws may also govern the surveillance of employees as well as patients and the public. A qualified attorney could help a dental practice determine whether a surveillance program complies with applicable federal and state law.

Clearly, monitoring equipment that captures information or behavior that is deemed private, such as employee break rooms, would pose a much higher legal risks. Monitoring that captures activity in restrooms and similar private areas could result in criminal prosecution as well as lawsuits for damages.

Discoverability

Keep in mind that surveillance records may be discoverable in the event of a lawsuit, such as a malpractice claim or a slip-and-fall. For example, records of an incident that results in an alleged injury to a patient, employee or other individual may need to be retained and turned over to the other side in the event of a lawsuit.

31. Should I Rely on Design Professionals, and What Should Their Contracts Include?

Consulting with design professionals is a good idea if warranted by the scope of your project. As any seasoned dentist knows, the days of dentistry being relatively unregulated have long passed. The importance of keeping up with regulatory developments cannot be understated. These developments will affect not only how you practice, but also the design elements of your practice environment. Relying on experts "in the know" about legal requirements and shaping your contracts with them to protect you and assure compliance is the best way for you to proactively address this important aspect of dental office design.

The interplay of federal, state, and local laws varies from city to city. A prudent dentist will want to consult and rely upon competent professionals for advice. Your lawyer can help you understand what is required, and draft contracts that obligate your architect and contractor to provide services and work product that meets the requirements of all applicable laws. In the best scenario for a dentist, these contracts will contain insurance requirements and indemnification provisions to help protect you if your design team fails to keep you "legal."

32. Do My Exam Chairs Need to Be Accessible to Patients With Disabilities?

As this publication goes to press, the Architectural and Transportation Barriers Compliance Board, a federal agency that develops accessibility guidelines and standards, is developing accessibility standards for medical diagnostic equipment under the Affordable Care Act. Thus, new standards may eventually apply to equipment such as dental exam chairs to help facilitate the provision of care to individuals with disabilities.

Currently, federal statutes such as Title III of the Americans with Disabilities Act, which applies to "public accommodations" such as dental practices, and applicable state and local disabilities laws, provide requirements for accommodating individuals with disabilities and the removal of barriers to access for disabled individuals. State and local disabilities laws may be more stringent than federal laws.

Related References and Resources

- Question 21: What Does the American with Disabilities Act Require for Office Design

- Question 50: Does My Dental Practice Website Need to Be Accessible to People With Disabilities, Such As Someone Who Is Blind or Hard of Hearing?

- Question 164: Can I Claim the Americans With Disabilities Act (AwDA) Tax Credit for Purchases of Intraoral Cameras, Panorex Machines, New Chairs, Etc.?

- Americans with Disabilities Act Access to Medical Care for Individuals with Mobility Disabilities
  www.ada.gov/medcare_mobility_ta/medcare_ta.htm

- The ADA Practical Guide to Dental Office Design
  adacatalog.org or 800.947.4746

33. Should I Have an Automated External Defibrillator (AED) in My Dental Office? If So, Where? What Legal Concerns Are There With Respect to an AED in the Dental Office?

Some dental office locations are required by state law to have automated external defibrillators (AEDs) on site; in some instances, the legal requirement may be contingent on whether the office provides deep sedation.

Regardless of any legal requirement, an on-premises AED may be a prudent investment. We are not aware of any incident where a dentist has been found liable for failure to have an AED on premises. However, if a patient expired from cardiac arrest in a dental office (or, to take another example, an allergic reaction — or even for no discernable reason), it is not farfetched that the decedent's attorney would argue that such an occurrence was reasonably foreseeable, that proper use of the AED would have avoided the death, and that the dentist was negligent (failed to meet the "standard of care") in not having available the AED. The trend towards requiring AEDs is clear — in many jurisdictions, they are required in locations such as health clubs, large office buildings, public transportation centers, schools, etc.

A prudent practice should assure that they are, at absolute minimum, in compliance with applicable law. The practice may wish to check with their insurance carrier regarding legal requirements in their state, coverage with respect to this equipment, and liability-related issues (e.g., the extent to which any risks associated with acquiring the AED may be outweighed by having the AED and trained staff on site, and the availability in your state of "good Samaritan" laws that might provide additional protection for an AED user in the event of a lawsuit). Your state dental society may also be able to provide some guidance in this regard.

The mere purchase of the equipment is not enough. The equipment should be stored in an easily accessible location. Training with respect to the equipment is critical, and in some instances may be legally required (likewise consider which — if not all — of your staff should be trained). Finally, make sure that the equipment is properly maintained. The manufacturer may be able to help you with respect to periodic testing and safety checks.

The trend towards requiring AEDs is clear — in many jurisdictions, they are required in locations such as health clubs, large office buildings, public transportation centers, schools, etc.

Chapter 7.
Practice Marketing

34. What Legal Limits Are There on Advertising My Practice?

Federal, state and sometimes local law laws govern advertising, which can include promotions offered via websites and social media. The central point for dentists is to make sure their promotional efforts are neither false nor misleading in any material respect and that they have a reasonable basis for making any claims announced.

Most state dental practice acts and other state laws prohibit false, misleading or deceptive advertising. Many of these statutes provide that damages (in some cases treble damages plus attorneys' fees) are available to the successful plaintiff. Some state laws regulating professionals also contain specific prohibitions on certain types of advertising claims. It is important to check the advertising regulations and rules in your state before advertising.

If the dental practice is planning to use a trade name, a licensing board permit will likely be required (these are sometimes called "fictitious" or "assumed" name permits). State laws regulating businesses may also require registration of assumed business names in either the state or county offices, depending upon the type of business entity in question.

The Federal Trade Commission (FTC) monitors ads and publicity efforts. The FTC provides helpful resources for businesses interested in federal advertising laws and policies, including unfair or deceptive advertising and federal warranty law.

Unfair or deceptive advertising can include:

- Bait-and-switch tactics
- Deceptive demonstrations or prices
- Defamation of the competition
- Fraudulent contests
- Fraudulent testimonials
- Misleading or unsubstantiated claims
- Misuse of the word "free"

Before you send marketing information to patients (or have another party send it on your behalf), or disclose any patient information for marketing purposes, make sure you do not risk violating applicable federal, state, or local laws, such as consumer protection laws, advertising laws, laws regarding testimonials, privacy laws such as HIPAA, or your state's laws regulating advertising by dentists. You should also understand the impact of any warranties made in an advertising communication.

Your state's dental advertising laws and regulations may restrict the information that may be included in an advertisement, statements about specialties and services, the use of testimonials, claims about quality or results, the use of paid referral services, offers of gifts or inducements to patients or prospective patients, or statements about pain or sedation. These laws may require dentists to retain copies of advertisements for a period of time. For information about your state's laws regulating advertising by dentists, contact a qualified attorney. Your state dental society may also have information about your state's dental advertising laws.

Related References and Resources

- Advertising Basics for Dentists and Dental Associations: A Guide to Federal and State Rules and Standards
  ADA.org/en/member-center/member-benefits/legal-resources

- Advertising and Marketing
  http://business.ftc.gov/advertising-and-marketing

- Frequently Asked Advertising Questions: A Guide for Small Business
  www.business.ftc.gov/documents/bus35-advertising-faqs-guide-small-business

35. What Rules Apply to Dental Specialty Claims?

Many states regulate the conditions under which a dentist who is a specialist may advertise the specialty. Many states also require that a general dentist who offers services in a specialty area clearly state in any advertisement that he or she is a general dentist. There are also ethical considerations.

Related References and Resources

- Advertising Basics for Dentists and Dental Associations: A Guide to Federal and State Rules and Standards
  ADA.org/en/member-center/member-benefits/legal-resources

- ADA Principles of Ethics and Code of Professional Conduct
  ADA.org/en/about-the-ada/principles-of-ethics-code-of-professional-conduct

36. Can I Use ADA Materials or Other Existing Material in Promoting My Practice?

Using material created by and belonging to others may be possible, depending on what you want to use, how you want to use it and whether you obtain permission as required by law.

Let's take a specific example. Say you come across an article on a dental development and you want to place the article on your website — it's good information, and you think it might impress your patients or attract new ones. It is likely that someone, probably the author or publisher, holds the copyright to that article. This is true whether or not the copyright owner has affixed a copyright notice to the article. To reprint the article in full, you will probably need permission from the copyright owner. It is best to secure written permission allowing you to copy the work and use it when, how, and where you want to. Failure to obtain such permission would in most cases be a violation of federal law.

The following works — published or unpublished — are generally covered by U.S. and international copyright laws:

- Text (written works of fiction and non-fiction)
- Musical materials (songs and musical compositions)
- Visual images and materials (illustrations, photographs, and Web page graphics)

Copyright laws make it illegal to use or copy any copyright protected work without obtaining the permission of the copyright owner, unless it falls within one of the narrow legal exceptions. Use of a copyright "notice" (i.e., "© 2014 John D. Smith") is no longer required by law (although it is still a good idea to use such a notice on your own copyrighted material), so materials may be copyright protected even if you cannot find a copyright notice on them.

As noted above, there are some exceptions to the general rule requiring you to obtain copyright permission before using third-party material. One exception is for materials which are in the public domain (this includes some, but not all, materials published by the federal government). Another exception is "fair use," which permits the use of limited portions of a work, including quotes, for purposes such as commentary, criticism, news reporting, and scholarly reports.

There are no "bright line" legal rules stating the specific number of words or percentage of a work allowed by fair use. Whether a particular use qualifies as fair use depends on all the circumstances. Your lawyer can help you determine what constitutes "fair use" of third-party materials, whether materials are in the public domain, and also how to properly use various materials in connection with marketing your practice.

Related References and Resources

- U.S. Copyright Office's Frequently Asked Questions
  www.loc.gov/copyright

37. Can I Use the ADA Logo to Market My Practice? How Can I Use the ADA Logo on My Website? What Rules Apply to the ADA Membership Logo?

You may use the ADA logo in certain approved ways, such as displaying the annual window decal the ADA provides to current members and using items available from the ADA Catalog, such as membership plaques and patient educational materials. However, the use of the ADA logo for practice marketing, such as in advertisements, on your website, or on your practice stationery, is not allowed. You certainly can inform the public and the profession, without using the ADA logo, that you are an ADA member. The ADA logo is a registered trademark of the American Dental Association. It is used to indicate source or sponsorship from or by the ADA itself. For this reason, members cannot identify or market themselves or their practice using it. Of course, it is impermissible to state or imply, whether using the ADA logo or not, that ADA membership represents a special level of certification or qualification.

Although use of the ADA logo is not allowed, the ADA has created two logos that members may use. One is the "Visit ADA.org" button, which member dentists may use to link their website to the ADA's website. The other is the ADA Member logo that identifies you as an ADA member. It must be used only in association with individuals who are members and cannot be used to identify an entire practice, which could give the false impression that a dental practice (as opposed to an individual dentist) can be an ADA member.

"Framing" the ADA website is not allowed. Framing is when a Web page from one website appears inside a "frame" on another website, so that the page appears to be on the second website.

Related References and Resources

- ADA Logos
  ADA.org/en/member-center/member-benefits/logos-multimedia-promotional-toolkits/ada-logos

38. Is My Website Exempt From These Traditional Practice Marketing Rules?

No. The rules that apply to traditional marketing vehicles also apply to marketing on the Internet. Your practice website and social media communications are by no means exempt.

39. Can I Send Information About Products Or Services To Patients, Or Provide Patient Lists To a Company That Wants To Send Them Information?

HIPAA imposes restrictions on covered dental practices that wish to send marketing communications to their patients (or allow others to send marketing communications to their patients). In many cases, the dental practice must have a valid, written patient authorization to use or disclose patient information for marketing communications, and the authorization must contain specific information. Under new rules that took effect on September 23, 2013, if a dental practice (or its business associate) receives "financial remuneration" (dollars) for making a marketing communication from a third party whose product or service is being marketed, or by someone else on the third party's behalf, the dental practice is required to have a patient sign an authorization form if the dental practice will use patient information in order to make the marketing communication (e.g., patient names and addresses, or information about a patient's dental condition). The authorization form must state that the dental practice received payment for making the communication. The new rule does not apply if the dentist receives nonfinancial or in-kind remuneration for making the communication if the communication is for a permissible purpose under HIPAA. There are several exceptions to the authorization requirement. For example, patient authorization is not required for face-to-face communications or for promotional gifts of nominal value.

The September 23, 2013 HIPAA rules also contain restrictions on providing patient lists to others. Under the new rules, even if a disclosure is permitted by HIPAA, a dental practice cannot exchange patient information for remuneration from or on behalf of the recipient of the information without a signed authorization from the patient that states that the dental practice will be remunerated for the disclosure. The new rule applies whether the remuneration is direct or indirect, and it applies whether or not the remuneration is financial (that is, the new rule also applies if the remuneration is nonfinancial or in-kind). There are limited exceptions to the new rule, such as the sale of a dental practice to another HIPAA covered entity (or to a buyer that will become a covered entity after the sale), and for related due diligence.

Related Resources and References

- Chapter 8: Practice Websites (addresses legal issues involved in online marketing)

- Chapter 15: HIPAA, State Law and PCI DSS: Patient Information

- HIPAA 20 Questions
  ADA.org/DentistGuidetoLaw

- HIPAA Privacy and Security
  ADA.org/HIPAA

- ADA Center for Professional Success
  success.ada.org

- OCR Office for Civil Rights (OCR)
  www.hhs.gov/ocr/privacy

- The ADA Practical Guide to HIPAA Compliance: Privacy and Security Manual
  adacatalog.org or 1.800.947.4746

40. What Can I Do If a Negative Rating, Review, or Comment About My Practice Is Posted on a Blog or Website?

Internet ratings sites (Yelp, Healthgrades, DoctorOogle, Bestdentists, Angie's List, RateaDentist, RateMDs, etc.) are almost all inherently unfair. The people posting the ratings are generally anonymous (save for the poster's screen name) so they take no real ownership for the content. Discovering the poster's identity is often impossible (and, where it is possible, will often require expenditure of substantial legal fees). Further, even in the unusual situation where you are able to learn the poster's identity, his or her comments have wide protection as his or her "opinion," as opposed to a factual allegation. The websites on which they post their comments are nearly untouchable from a legal perspective. Even if you are able to discover the identity of the poster and prove (overcoming obstacles to proof such as HIPAA and state privacy laws) that the comment is defamatory (as opposed to opinion), proving damages in such cases is extremely difficult.

Given that these ratings sites likely will be with us for the foreseeable future, and that consumers afford them credibility, it is important to understand how to best navigate them. One 2013 study found that 79 percent of consumers trust online reviews as much as personal recommendations.[4] But first a brief discussion on how we got here, with a real life example:

A parent of a patient of a California dentist wrote the following on Yelp:

> *"1 Star Rating! Let me first say I wish there is a '0' star in Yelp rating. Avoid her like a disease! She treated two cavities...but my son was light headed for several hours after the filling. The filling the dentist used is metallic silver color. The metallic filling...has a small trace of mercury in it. I regret ever going to her."*

---

[4] Anderson, Myles. "2013 Study: 79 percent of Consumers Trust Online Reviews as Much as Personal Recommendations. "Search Engine Land. June 26, 2013. *www.searchengineland.com/2013-study-79-of-consumers-trust-online-reviews-as-much-as-personal-recommendations-164565*. Last accessed on May 28, 2014.

The dentist requested that Yelp remove the review. Yelp did not remove the review. The dentist then filed suit claiming libel, slander, and intentional and negligent infliction of emotional distress against the parents who wrote the review and Yelp, the host of the Internet forum. (This was an unusual case in that the reviewer was known to the dentist.)

The court held that Yelp was entitled to dismissal under California's anti-SLAPP statute. A SLAPP (Strategic Lawsuit Against Public Participation) lawsuit is a suit filed to stifle those who take an adverse position on an issue of public interest. Anti-SLAPP statutes allow courts to dismiss lawsuits which stifle discussion on matters of public importance and for which there is not a reasonable likelihood the plaintiff will prevail. More than half the states currently have such statutes.

The court held that, in this case, dental fillings were a matter of public interest. Because California's anti-SLAPP statute permits the prevailing party to recover attorney's fees, the dentist was ordered to pay over $80,000 of other parties' (Yelp's and the parents') legal fees. This was in addition to any fees the dentist paid to her own attorney, and the cost to the dentist in time and angst.

But wait — there's more! The dentist received considerable publicity over the lawsuit, including newspaper, radio and Internet reporting. The dentist had inadvertently turned one small Web posting into a Web avalanche.

The "Streisand Effect" — the term for what sometimes occurs where an attempt to remove, censor, have deleted or otherwise hide information on the Internet — has the unintended consequence of publicizing the information even more broadly. The term has its genesis in a lawsuit filed by Barbara Streisand seeking to have aerial photographs of her coastal California home removed from the Internet plus $50 million in damages. Before Ms. Streisand filed, the image had been downloaded only six times, two of them by her own attorneys. As a result of her filing the case, the next month more than 420,000 people visited the site. There are a number of examples in the dental realm where a dentist responding to a negative post inadvertently ended up only bringing greater attention to the posting. For example:

- A Yelp reviewer's attorney responds to a dentist's letter:
  www.popehat.com/wp-content/uploads/2013/06/thisissparta.pdf

- Anti-SLAPP dismissal of a suit:
  www.katu.com/news/local/Dentist-loses-defamation-suit-after-former-patient-criticizes-him-online-171622011.html

- Dentists loses on anti-SLAPP and is assessed fees of $43,000 for the first action and $23,000 for the second:
  www.courts.ca.gov/opinions/nonpub/A136463.PDF

- A listing of doctor lawsuits over patient reviews:
  www.digitalcommons.law.scu.edu/cgi/viewcontent.cgi?article=1289&context=historical

A dentist bringing suit to have a negative review removed starts with a few disadvantages:

- The Web host is protected from liability under the Communications Decency Act of 1996 (47 U.S.C. Sec. 230); the host is not a "publisher" of the comment

- It is often difficult and expensive to obtain the identity of the content creator

- Reviews and comments have wide protection as "opinions"[5]

- Medical professionals may be constrained from responding by HIPAA and state privacy laws

- Proving monetary damages is difficult to do

- Where anti-SLAPP laws are applicable, the dentist may be liable for the defendant's legal bills, as well as the dentist's own legal bills

- The lawsuit itself may result in bringing even greater attention (the "Streisand effect") to the negative review

As you look at a posted negative review, take a deep breath and consider:

- How many people will really see the negative review?

- Will this review actually affect the practice/business?

- Is the host of the Internet forum immune under the Communications Decency Act?

- Will you be able to identify the content creator?

- Would it be worth the considerable time, effort, expense and adverse publicity to file and pursue a lawsuit?

- Is there a chance that your response (lawsuit or otherwise) might actually increase the number of people who will read the negative review?[6]

- Is there a means that can be used to remove (or minimize the effect of) the review or to positively position the practice to make up for the negative review?

If litigation is not generally the answer to a negative review, then what is? Well, unfortunately there are no silver bullets.

---

[5] Note that where the allegations in a comment or review are demonstrably false allegations of a material fact (e.g., "this dentist has been found liable for malpractice on more than four occasions", where the dentist had never been held liable for malpractice), such an allegation would likely not be protected as "opinion", and in many cases would likely violate the Web host's own terms of use, and (upon proper demand and proof of the falsity of the statement) might be voluntarily removed by the Web host.

[6] The more a website is "clicked", the more prominently (higher) it may appear in search results. With respect to a negative comment or rating, your "clicking" it (or suggesting that others do so) may actually help move the site to a higher level in a search for your practice!

One thing you might try is to request that the Web host voluntarily remove the offending Web post. On this front, your chances for success are not high, particularly if the Web posting falls into the category of the poster's opinion. You will likely maximize your chance of success in this appeal if you are able to demonstrate that the post violates the Web host's own "Terms of Use." Frequently the Web host's "Terms of Use" prohibit users from posting material that "…infringe[s] a third party's rights, including without limitation any privacy, publicity or intellectual property rights, or that are unlawful, untrue, harassing, libelous, defamatory, abusive, potentially tortious, threatening, harmful …or that is otherwise objectionable."[7] To the extent that your request for removal is able to make the case that the post falls into one of these prohibited categories, you are likely to increase your chances of success in persuading the Web host to voluntarily remove the comment.

You may decide ignoring the negative review is your best response, and often it will be. However, you should evaluate responding on a case-by-case basis. If the person leaving the comment has a large following, appears to be making a measured and justified complaint to anyone who might come across it, or is turning to the Internet as a last resort after already contacting your office, you may want to respond to the review (without violating HIPAA or state privacy law). In those instances where you chose to respond, it is imperative that you remember that your audience is not the individual posting the content; it is the dozens of people who will see your response and judge you (and your practice) on the basis of your response. You do not want to engage in an online debate over the incident that provoked the review. You do not want to appear defensive, confrontational or accusative. You do want to come off as caring, concerned and compassionate. A productive response along these lines might be:

> *"We are sorry that you feel that way. We treat hundreds of patients who are extremely satisfied with our practice, and we want to make sure that you are one of them. Please call our office so that we can see what we can do to make things right."*

Another way to deal with a negative review is by receiving multiple positive reviews, effectively "burying" the negative review amidst a sea of the positive. If a single bad review is all that appears on a Web search, it may stand out. If the negative review is one of many and all the other reviews are positive, the one negative review is more likely to appear as an aberration. One way that a negative comment can be "buried" amidst a quantity of positive comment is for patients who have had positive experiences with your practice to post positive comments and ratings.

However, you need to be cautious in this regard — there are regulations that limit your ability to solicit positive reviews by either compensating (whether by cash or by "in-kind" payment, such as discounts) reviewers or requesting persons associated with your practice (such as your staff) from posting positive comments; reviewers who post such endorsements must disclose that they have been compensated for their review or disclose their relationship to the practice. Making it appear that solicited (e.g., paid for) content originated spontaneously rather than as part of a campaign is sometimes referred to as "astro-turfing." (It takes place at a "grassroots" level, hence the term.)

....

Another way to deal with a negative review is by receiving multiple positive reviews, effectively "burying" the negative review amidst a sea of the positive.

....

---

[7] *Doctoroogle.com*, "Terms of Use", section 1. The terms of use for other rating sites contain similar prohibitions.

....

Likewise, you can seek to have other positive content on your practice posted on the Internet so that a search by a potential patient will yield overwhelmingly positive content. Just make sure that what you say is true. Some means of generating such positive content posted include:

- Get media attention for performing charitable endeavors (these will show up when potential patients search your name on the Web)

- Contribute dental-related content to other websites

- Start a practice-related blog

The majority of people do not go to the second page of a Web search. If you are able to provide sufficient positive content such that the negative comment is pushed off the first page of a search, you will have successfully minimized the chances that someone searching your name will ever see the comment.

To summarize, responding appropriately to a negative review is a difficult and emotion-laden task, but it can be important to do so. Take a few deep breaths before you decide how and if to respond. If you elect to retain an attorney, be aware that on some occasions this course of action has backfired in a number of ways (e.g., bringing even greater publicity to the negative comment, resulting in a dentist forced to pay not only their own legal fees, but those of the defendant). If you elect to seek to have the Web host voluntarily remove the post, review the Web host's own terms of use to see if the post violates those terms. Finally, if you elect to respond to the post online, remember two things:

- Avoid violating HIPAA and state privacy law

- That your "audience" is not the individual comment creator, but the dozens of others who will see your response and will likely judge you and your practice more on your response than on the negative comment itself.

Related References and Resources

- Dentist Pays Sizable Penalty for Not Knowing 47 USC 230 — Wong v. Jing
  www.blog.ericgoldman.org/archives/2011/05/dentist_pays_fi.htm

- Maintaining a Positive Online Reputation
  success.ada.org/en/learn/online-educational-opportunities/online-reputation-management-webinar/maintaining-a-positive-reputation?WT.mc_id=email_huddle

41. Can My Dental Practice Advertise That We Accept Medicaid?

In addition to the rules that apply to advertising generally, a dental practice should review proposed advertising and other published materials that refer to federal health care programs such as Medicare, Medicaid and CHIP to make sure they are in compliance with any additional requirements set by those programs.

For example, a dental practice should avoid using symbols and logos of government agencies in their promotional and other published materials. Government seals and logos, such as the seal of the U.S. Department of Health and Human Services (HHS), may not be used by the private sector on their materials, which could imply that HHS favors or endorses the practice, its services, or its personnel. State agencies likely have similar restrictions on the use of their logos and symbols.

Although not limited to advertising, federal fraud and abuse laws, such as the federal Anti-Kickback Statute (AKS) and beneficiary inducement prohibition, should also be kept in mind when developing advertising and other materials. The AKS is a federal law designed to prohibit the exchange of any remuneration to induce the referral of business covered by a federal health care program. The AKS even applies if remuneration is merely offered or solicited, but not exchanged. The AKS imposes both criminal and civil sanctions.

Under the beneficiary inducement prohibition, a person who offers or gives a Medicare or Medicaid beneficiary any remuneration that the person knows or should know is likely to influence the beneficiary's selection of a particular provider, practitioner, or supplier of items or services covered by Medicare or Medicaid may be liable for civil money penalties. There are certain exceptions to the prohibition.

Advertising the routine waiver of Medicare or Medicaid copays could implicate federal fraud and abuse laws. Your state Medicaid agency may have additional requirements or guidance regarding advertising.

42. Does Our Dental Practice Need to Be Aware of What Federal Laws Apply to Commercial Messages Sent Via Telephone, Email, Fax and Text?

Even if a dental practice does not think of itself as a "telemarketer," laws such as the Telephone Consumer Protection Act may impact the practice's activities, and a dental practice should understand when these federal laws may come into play and where to find out more about them. Even an inadvertent violation could result in penalties.

Telephone Sales Rule and the National Do-Not-Call Registry

The Federal Trade Commission established the National Do-Not-Call Registry (DNC Registry) under the federal Telephone Sales Rule (TSR). Consumers may add their phone numbers to the DNC Registry to limit the telemarketing calls they receive. Indeed, dentists and members of the dental team may have added their telephone numbers to the DNC Registry to limit telemarketing calls.

It appears unlikely that a dental practice's routine appointment reminder calls to patients who have existing appointments would be deemed in violation of the TSR. However, it is conceivable that TSR issues could come up if a dental practice implemented a telephone campaign that could be construed as being for the purpose of selling goods or services, or soliciting consumers, particularly if the campaign included individuals who do not have an "existing business relationship" (as defined in the TSR) with the dental practice.

There are two kinds of "established business relationships" under the TSR:

One is based on the consumer's purchase, rental, or lease of the seller's goods or services, or a financial transaction between the consumer and seller, within 18 months preceding a telemarketing call. The 18-month period runs from the date of the last payment, transaction, or shipment between the consumer and the seller. The other is based on a consumer's inquiry or application regarding a seller's goods or services, and exists for three months starting from the date the consumer makes the inquiry or application. For more information, please see Exemptions to the National Do Not Call Registry Provisions section of Complying with the Telemarketing Sales Rule.[8]

Note that this definition of an "established business relationship" may exclude certain individuals who may be a dental practice's "patients of record."

If the TSR applies, the dental practice must take a number of steps before a telephone call is made. For example, the dental practice must check to make sure that the number is not on the DNC Registry. The dental practice must also maintain its own do-not-call list and add any consumer who has asked not to receive any more calls from or on behalf of the dental practice. Calling a consumer who has asked not to be called potentially exposes a dental practice to a civil penalty. Even if a call is to a telephone number that is not on the DNC Registry or the dental practice's own do-not-call list, additional requirements apply. For example, the caller must provide certain material information to the consumer.

TSR violations can result in civil penalties of up to $16,000 per violation, and violators may also be required to pay redress to injured consumers.

Moreover, whether or not a call is permissible under the TSR, it must comply with other applicable laws, such as the Federal Communication Commission's regulations under the Telephone Consumer Protection Act and the Privacy Rule of the Health Insurance Portability and Accountability Act of 1996 (HIPAA).

A qualified attorney can provide information about how these laws apply to a proposed telephone campaign.

Telephone Consumer Protection Act

The Telephone Consumer Protection Act (TCPA) regulates certain telemarketing "robocalls," text messages, and fax advertisements. Robocalls are communications made using automatic telephone dialing systems. Just make a covered call using equipment that is capable of automatic dialing may violate the act, even if the equipment's automatic dialing feature was not used to make the call. There are exceptions for communications made with the recipient's written "prior express consent" and recipients who have an "established business relationship" with the caller, as these terms are defined under the Act. There is also an exception for certain healthcare messages.

It appears unlikely that the TCPA would apply to dental practice's routine appointment reminder telephone calls and text messages, but these are limitations to the healthcare message exception.

A TCPA violation can result in damages of actual monetary loss or $500, plus $1500 if the violation is deemed "willful" or "knowing." TCPA compliance is complex and the penalties are severe. A qualified attorney can evaluate a dental practice's proposed use of telephone, text or fax communications to determine whether the TCPA may come into play.

---

[8] Q&A for Telemarketers & Sellers About DNC Provisions in TSR *http://business.ftc.gov/documents/alt129-qa-telemarketers-sellers-about-dnc-provisions-tsr*

CAN-SPAM

The CAN-SPAM Act is a federal law that applies to commercial messages sent via email. The FTC, which enforces the CAN-SPAM Act, defines an emailed commercial message as "any electronic mail message the primary purpose of which is the commercial advertisement or promotion of a commercial product or service,' including email that promotes content on commercial websites." The FTC notes that there is no exception under CAN-SPAM for business-to-business email.

CAN-SPAM establishes requirements for commercial messages, such as the requirement that each email give the recipient the right to opt out of future emails. Opt out requests must be honored within the timeframe established by the Act. Other requirements also apply, such as the requirement that the email include the sender's valid physical postal address.

The penalties for a CAN-SPAM violation can be severe. Each separate email in violation of the CAN-SPAM Act is subject to penalties of up to $16,000.

A Canadian anti-spam law that took effect on July 1, 2014 imposes severe penalties on individuals and businesses that send commercial electronic messages without consent.

HIPAA

The HIPAA Privacy Rule requires covered dental practices to permit patients to request to receive communications by alternative means or at alternative locations, and covered dental practices must accommodate reasonable requests. Thus, phoning, emailing or texting a patient who has reasonably requested to be contacted only by another means could violate HIPAA, whether or not the telephone call or text implicates the TSR, TCPA, CAN-SPAM Act, or other federal or state law. In addition, HIPAA restricts certain marketing communications, whether the covered entity makes the communication, or a third party makes the communication either on behalf of the covered entity or using information supplied by the covered entity, such as patients' names and contact information.

Related References and Resources

- Question 121: What Effect Did the 2013 Omnibus Final Rule Have On HIPAA Compliance? (Scroll down to "Subsidized Marketing Communications" and "Sale of Patient Information")

- Q&A for Telemarketers & Sellers About DNC Provisions in TSR
  http://business.ftc.gov/documents/alt129-qa-telemarketers-sellers-about-dnc-provisions-tsr

- CAN-SPAM Act: A Compliance Guide for Business
  www.business.ftc.gov/documents/bus61-can-spam-act-compliance-guide-business

- CRTC, Canada's Anti-SPAM Legislation
  www.crtc.gc.ca/eng/casl-lcap.htm

- Section 164.522(b) of the HIPAA Privacy Rule
  www.ecfr.gov/cgi-bin/retrieveECFR?gp=&SID=69b3abd350f5647b3b0b902ad1ef897d&r=SECTION&n=se45.1.164_1522

Chapter 8.
Practice Websites

Let's revisit and expand upon some marketing considerations for an increasingly important marketing vehicle: your practice website.

43. What Are Some of the Liability Issues With Practice Websites?

Dental practice websites can enhance the doctor-patient relationship, promote patient care and health, and be a useful marketing tool.

However, it's very easy for a dentist with a practice website to unwittingly take on legal exposure. Among the liability issues are: malpractice (for example, if you are viewed as giving professional advice online); false or misleading advertising; trademark and copyright violations; and breaching patient privacy. This risk will vary depending on the nature of your site, the extent of interactivity, etc.

These issues often come into play when you use electronic media other than your website. For example, when you send emails or participate in Internet chat rooms, you can create legal exposure. That is not to discourage you from taking advantage of technology. Just be aware of the legal concerns, and take simple protective measures such as clarifying in a signature line on your email that you are not giving professional advice.

If you decide to sponsor an interactive area on your website such as a chat room or blog, some legal exposure can come from third party comments (for example, defamation) so you may want to check with an attorney experienced in this area before setting up an interactive site. Website operators have been sued on a wide range of legal claims, including defamation and copyright infringement, based upon the remarks of third parties. Certain federal statutes offer website operators some legal protection for from the illegal postings of third parties. A federal law called the "Digital Millennium Copyright Act" offers a website operator some immunity from the copyright violations of third party posters. In order to be immune, the website operator must comply with various statutory requirements, including a procedure for promptly removing infringing material when it receives notice of a copyright violation.

Another statute, the "Communications Decency Act," offers interactive service providers some immunity for third party content. The immunity does not extend to claims based on copyright laws and there are certain other exceptions. An interactive service provider can itself be seen as an information content provider. As one judge stated, "Websites are complicated enterprises, and there will always be close cases where a clever lawyer could argue that something the website operator did encouraged the illegality."[9] For this reason, it helps to check with a lawyer experienced in Internet law, particularly prior to starting up a chat room or blog.

---

[9] Fair Housing Council of San Fernando Valley v. *Roommates.com*

Privacy Issues Related to Practice Websites and Social Media

Stories about possible violations of patient privacy through social media have appeared in the news. For example, news media have reported that:

- A hospital took away a doctor's privileges for an online post that included information that could be used to identify a patient[10]

- A hospital identified an incident involving employees who allegedly used social media to discuss patients[11]

- An emergency room worker posted a photo of her workstation, which included a computer screen displaying information about a patient. The patient subsequently notified law enforcement that she was the victim of identity theft[12]

Whether a dental practice posts a message or photo on the practice's social media site, or a member of the dental team makes a personal post, privacy laws may be violated if the post identifies a patient, or could be used to identify a patient, and the patient has not authorized the disclosure.

Successfully managing the risks through appropriate policies, procedures and training can help dental practices benefit from social media while protecting patient privacy in compliance with applicable federal and state laws. A dental practice's policies and procedures prohibiting improper disclosures of patient information should clearly apply in any context, whether inside or outside of the dental practice, and whether the disclosure is electronic, on paper, or oral.

The Security Rule under the Health Insurance Portability and Accountability Act of 1996 (HIPAA) requires covered dental practices to have reasonable safeguards in place to protect electronic patient information. The HIPAA Privacy Rule requires a covered dental practice to obtain patient authorization before disclosing identifiable patient information unless the disclosure is permitted by HIPAA, such as a disclosure for treatment, payment or health care operations. If patient information is disclosed in violation of HIPAA, the dental practice may be required to provide breach notification to the affected patient(s), the federal government, and, in some cases, the media. HIPAA violations can also result in substantial monetary penalties, where the state law and some HIPAA violations carry criminal penalties.

HIPAA covered dental practices must also comply with applicable state law where the state law is more stringent than HIPAA. Dental practices that are not covered by HIPAA must comply with applicable state law. State laws protecting patient information may include medical confidentiality laws, data security laws, and laws requiring breach notification when sensitive personally identifiable information is improperly acquired, accessed, used or disclosed. Violations of state privacy laws can result in fines, and some state laws allow individuals to take legal action.

Therefore, before posting on social media, a dental practice should carefully review the content to determine whether the content complies with applicable law. For example, a covered dental practice that wishes to post patient before-and-after photos on a social media site may be required to obtain HIPAA-compliant written authorization from the patients if the photos could be used to identify the patients. Under HIPAA, full face photos and comparable images are considered identifiers.

---

[10] Conaboy, Chelsea. "For doctors, social media a tricky case," The Boston Globe. April 20, 2011.
www.boston.com/lifestyle/health/articles/2011/04/20/for_doctors_social_media_a_tricky_case/?page=full.
[11] Stickney, R. "Hospital will fire workers in Facebook scandal," NBC San Diego. June 8, 2010.
www.nbcsandiego.com/newshe or health/Hospital-Fires-Emps-in-Facebook-Scandal-95794764.html.
[12] McCann, Erin. "Hospital Facebook post leads to ID theft," HealthcareITNews. October 21, 2013.
www.healthcareitnews.com/news/hospital-facebook-post-brings-id-theft.

Even if a patient has voluntarily made his or her health information public, HIPAA and certain state privacy laws still apply to the information. For example, if a patient discusses his or her health information with the news media, or in a social media post or online rating service, a covered dental practice must continue to protect the information in compliance with HIPAA and applicable state laws.

This is not to say that a dental practice can never respond to a patient's social media post, only that the dental practice must do so in compliance with applicable laws, and that such laws may prohibit disclosures that identify the patient. For example, in response to a patient's post stating that her questions were not answered to her satisfaction, a dental practice may be able to respond with a general statement that does not identify the patient, such as, "We encourage patients who have questions about their care to call our office right away so we can provide any follow up information they require." If a patient posts a complaint about wait time, a dental practice may be able to respond, "Occasionally a dental emergency requires us to alter our schedule, and we apologize to patients who are affected when this happens."

To help prevent privacy law violations on social media:

- Understand and comply with applicable federal and state privacy and data security laws

- Train staff never to disclose identifiable patient information or sensitive personal information via social media without proper patient authorization

- Keep in mind that patient information that is protected by privacy laws can extend beyond traditional patient records. Photo or videos of a patient, even just sitting in the waiting area, may be patient information that is protected by HIPAA. Merely revealing that an individual is a patient may violate privacy laws.

- HIPAA protects information that identifies a patient, or that could be used to identify a patient. Even if a patient's name is not disclosed, if other data elements are disclosed that make the information identifiable, then the information may still be protected by HIPAA.

- Even if a patient has publicly disclosed his or her health information, HIPAA still applies to that information. A covered dental practice must protect patient information even if the patient has willingly made the information public.

- Responding to a patient's comment on a social media site can result in a privacy law violation if the response includes information that identifies the patient, or that could be used to identify the patient. If a dental practice believes that it is prudent to respond to a post, restricting the response to a general statement that does not contain any information that could be used to identify a patient can help reduce the risk of a privacy law violation.

- Before posting patient photos, have the patient sign any authorization, consent or release forms required by HIPAA or any applicable state law. Applicable law may also require a dental practice to have staff members sign releases before posting their photos.

- Even photos depicting the interior of the dental practice should be screened to make sure they do not include any patient information. For example, make sure the photos do not include patient charts or computer screens displaying patient information.

In light of the importance of protecting patient privacy, and the risks associated with violating privacy laws, dentists may wish to have policies and procedures on privacy compliance when using social media.

Related References and Resources

- Question 121: What Effect Did the 2013 Omnibus Final Rule Have on HIPAA Compliance?

- Advertising Basics for Dentists and Dental Associations: A Guide to Federal and State Rules and Standards
  ADA.org/en/member-center/member-benefits/legal-resources

- The ADA Practical Guide to Creating and Updating an Employee Office Manual
  adacatalog.org or 1.800.947.4746

44. What Protective Measures Can I Build Into the Design of My Site to Help Avoid Liability?

Most websites use certain tools to protect against legal liability. The most common is the use of disclaimers. Disclaimers are typically housed in "Terms of Use" that explain and attempt to bind the user to the rules and limits of the site. Another tool is the "sign on" or "participation" agreement for particular site functions, which requires the user to specifically agree to certain additional rules, typically by clicking "I Accept" before accessing the desired Web page or function. These mechanisms usually purport to limit the user's ability to sue for information on the site, or for what happens on the site, or for the results of using the site. The likelihood that these limitations will be upheld in court is at least theoretically advanced if your lawyer is able to tell the judge things such as:

- The user could not use those portions of the website without first seeing the rules

- The user had to proactively "click" his mouse on the "I Accept" button and thereby accept an agreement to play by those rules in order to obtain access to those portions of the website

- The user could always easily review those rules through a simple click on a readily identifiable link

If you post rules or policies that state you will not collect, use, disclose or track certain site visitor information, make sure that you abide by these rules or policies. The Federal Trade Commission (FTC) considers it a deceptive trade practice not to abide by a privacy policy that was posted on your website when the information about an individual was collected, unless you have obtained the individual's consent to do otherwise. If your website may collect personal information you should take reasonable steps to protect the information.

Another legal concern has to do with website accessibility. The U.S. Department of Justice has stated that the websites of "public accommodations" must be accessible to individuals with disabilities under the Americans with Disabilities Act, a public accommodation is a business that is generally open to the public, including a dentist's office. If you are developing a website for your practice, it would be prudent to have your website developer assure that your website will be accessible to persons with disabilities in compliance with some recognized standard, such as Section 508 or W3C Web Content Accessibility Guidelines (WCAG) 2.0.

45. What Steps About Site Content Can I Take to Reduce My Legal Exposure?

The specific words, graphics, and sounds on your site can make a world of difference legally. For example, do you really want to stand behind an absolute claim, such as "Whiter teeth guaranteed in 30 days"? Might a softer claim be just as effective from a marketing perspective? Words like "may, could, and might" are probably more defensible in many cases than "will, always, and shall."

When developing your website's content, think through what you are really trying to accomplish, and find the right words (and perhaps graphics and sound) to fit your objectives, while attempting to minimize your legal risks. Keep in mind the following:

- Be careful not to engage in the practice of dentistry online, unless that is your intent and you are properly insured

- To minimize the chances of being sued for inaccurate information, make sure your content is "solid" (accurate, truthful, and substantiated)

- Avoid using absolute claims (consider softer language where appropriate)

- Regularly update your site (e.g., take down information that is no longer accurate)

- Date the content on each page, so viewers will know what information is older and potentially less reliable (e.g., "created on ...", "last modified on ...," etc.)

- Archive your site, so you have a defense based on proof of what was actually on it if you are sued

- Maintain security, privacy, and confidentiality as appropriate

- Adhere to any applicable state and federal requirements

- Comply with copyright laws when using third party content

- Use a "Terms of Use" agreement to help protect against liability for third party content

Legal issues related to digital Internet marketing are, by and large, the same legal issues and concerns that arise when marketing in any other medium. What makes the Internet different is its ease and immediacy — a person can quickly and easily download something from the Internet and post it to their site (possibly infringing on a third party's intellectual property), a dentist might quickly and easily (and knee-jerk emotionally) respond online to a negative review (possibly giving rise to HIPAA concerns as well as appearing insensitive forevermore to anyone seeing your response). By understanding that the same legal concerns that arise in any other marketing context are also present in the digital world, you and your practice will be better positioned to avoid legal challenges.

Related References and Resources

- Question 33: What Legal Limits Are There on Advertising My Practice?

- Question 44: What Protective Measures Can I Build Into the Design of My Website to Avoid Liability?

- Question 47: When Do I Need Permission to Use What's Not Mine on My Website?

46. Are There General Rules for Communicating Online?

Yes. The key is to communicate truthfully. Do not post anything false or misleading on your site and be sure any claims you make can be substantiated. Keep in mind that FTC and other consumer protection laws may govern your content. Make sure to adhere to all dental practice codes and ethics codes that may apply. Make appropriate disclosures, including posting and adhering to any online privacy policy statement. Protect patient privacy in compliance with applicable law.

Related References and Resources

- Question 33: What Legal Limits Are There On Advertising My Practice?

- Question 35: What Rules Apply to Dental Specialty Claims?

- Advertising Basics for Dentists and Dental Associations: A Guide to State Rules and Standards
  ADA.org/en/member-center/member-benefits/legal-resources

Legal issues related to digital Internet marketing are, by and large, the same legal issues and concerns that arise when marketing in any other medium.

47. When Do I Need Permission to Use What's Not Mine On My Website?

The first thing new website owners often do is to register an Internet address or "domain name." Securing the name is often easy to do for a small fee, but you must first make sure your domain name does not infringe on a third party's trademark rights.

When it comes to using third party material on your website, make sure you get appropriate permissions, including permission of the copyright owner for third party content you may wish to post, and even permission of the "subjects" (including staff or patient photos) for photographs you may wish to display. If you are linking to other websites, get permission before using the other sites' logos, or use a simple text link instead. Avoid "framing" another site without permission. Otherwise, you may be making it appear that the site framed within your site contains your content. As an example, "framing" the ADA site is specifically prohibited, though linking is permitted so long as the links only reference permitted ADA member logos and do not otherwise use the ADA trademarks or service marks.

Copyrights and Social Media

At times, copyright law has had difficulty keeping up with the explosive developments of the Internet. For example, the law wrestled for some time with the question of whether patents or copyright should be used to protect computer software programs. The answer is that, based on the circumstances, either one may apply. There are those who have argued that in the wide-open environment of the Web such intellectual property concepts are outmoded. It is so easy to download from or upload to the Internet, and there is so much content freely circulated on it that many people have been lulled into the false sense that if content can be accessed from their computers, then it is there for the taking and sharing.

Copyright law applies to Internet content pretty much the same way it applies to written content, music, radio and television broadcasts, photos, and any of the other sorts of works covered by the copyright statute. When you post an article, photo, or video clip on your Facebook page, your blog or your website, you are potentially publishing it to a large audience, including to third parties unknown to you. That is a qualitatively and quantitatively different act from copying an article putting it in an envelope along with a letter to a friend or loved one.

Many times the naïve poster will not be trying to exploit the work of another for commercial gain, and often the owner of the copyrighted work in question will be satisfied if the content is removed when requested. As discussed below, however, there are instances where a copyright owner who has registered his or her copyright may demand payment and may have grounds for doing so.

To be subject to copyright, a work must be reduced or "fixed" in a tangible medium. Ideas, facts, concepts, general themes, and the like cannot be protected by copyright, but specific recorded expressions of them can be and often are. A common misconception is that there must be something truly creative in the artistic sense for copyrights to come into play. Actually, the creativity bar with respect to copyrightability is set pretty low, so that all manner of what one might consider mundane and merely factual expression may well be subject to copyright. The law recognizes, however, that straightforward descriptions of fact-intensive subjects, such as a particular dental procedure or an accepted course of treatment, are bound to be similar. Two works may be similar, even identical, but there is no copyright infringement unless there has been copying.

When it comes to creating dental practice websites, certain Web design companies have sometimes decided that it is easier to appropriate existing content describing or explaining various procedures and treatments than it is to write new, original text. Even more unfortunate is that the purloined content has been the subject of a copyright registration, which gives the copyright owner the option of filing an action for copyright infringement in Federal Court and to seek enhanced damages, which can be anywhere up to $150,000 per infringement in cases of willful infringement, as well as for attorneys' fees and costs.

It is natural for the dentist purchasing Web design services to expect that the Web designer is either creating original content or obtaining appropriate permissions from copyright owners. That is not always a safe assumption. Some dentists are also surprised to learn that they can be liable for the infringement, even though they relied entirely on the Web designer. Of course, if a copyright owner makes a claim against a dentist, the dentist can turn around and make a claim against the designer. In the unfortunate instance where the copyright owner files a lawsuit against the dentist, the dentist can join the designer in the action and assert that the designer is liable to the dentist for whatever amount, if any, the copyright owner is awarded against the dentist. But if you have hired a college student or a business operated on a shoe string to design your site, you are likely to find it virtually impossible as a practical matter to recover anything from that quarter, and you will end up paying any damages award yourself.

One way to help insulate yourself from this situation is to work with an established design firm and make sure there is a written contract between you and the designer and that the designer expressly represents in the contract that the designer has the right to provide to you any of the text, photographs, audio, or video content that it incorporates in your site, free from any intellectual property rights or claims of any third party.

It is also important to remember that the copyrights in the underlying work are not necessarily transferred with the work itself. When you hire a Web design company you are hiring an independent contractor. Unless the designer, whether an individual or a company, assigns the copyrights to you, they will remain with the author. If this is the case, you may see numerous websites from the designer that look just like yours and you will have little or no legal basis to object.

As a communications and marketing tool, social media has no equal. Just remember that the copyright law applies to the Internet to the same extent it does to more traditional media.

Related References and Resources

- Question 36: Can I Use ADA Materials or Other Existing Material in Promoting My Practice?

- Question 37: Can I Use the ADA Logo to Market My Practice? How Can I Use the ADA Logo on My Website? What Rules Apply to the ADA Membership Logo?

48. How Can I Protect What's Mine on My Website?

Ask your lawyer about copyright, trademark, and other protection for the content of your website. Put appropriate copyright notices on your content, trademark notices on your logos, and include a thorough section on "Terms of Use." As an example, see how we've handled those protections on ADA.org. Be sure to obtain ownership of the domain name for your website, so you don't lose control of your domain name if you change website hosts. Your agreement with your website host should contain a provision that allows you to obtain the content of the website if you change hosts.

49. Should I Have Written Contracts With Professionals I Hire to Help Design My Website?

Written agreements with vendors who specialize in website design and management are not legally required (however, if the vendor will have access to patients' protected health information, the vendor must sign a business associate agreement if the dental practice is a covered entity under HIPAA). Nevertheless, written agreements with website design and management vendors can be very helpful to outline the expectations and obligations of the parties and to manage your legal risks.

A Web design expert, though potentially of great help in positioning your practice favorably online, can also harm you through poor service, project delays, or even in some cases disclosures of patients' protected health information. A written agreement (particularly one that is well crafted, carefully drafted and reviewed by your attorney) can maximize the chances that you will own the domain name of your website, as well as all copyrights and trademarks in the information, graphics, logos, etc. It may also provide you with a remedy in case there is any problem. A written agreement is a useful tool for project timelines and seamless transitions if you decide you would prefer to work with someone else. Sample contract clauses can help provide some helpful insights and suggest some issues you should consider before you work with a Web design expert. However, every situation is different. Consult with your personal attorney about what is right for you.

Related References and Resources

- Chapter 15: HIPAA, State Law and PCI DSS: Patient Information

- Appendix 7: Sample Website Development Agreement

- HIPAA 20 Questions
  ADA.org/DentistGuidetoLaw

50. Does My Dental Practice Website Need to Be Accessible to People With Disabilities, Such as Someone Who Is Blind or Hard of Hearing?

Some people with disabilities have difficulty using the Web. For example, an individual who is blind may have "screen reader" software that uses a speech synthesizer to read the text on a computer screen. However, if the website features photos and does not include alternative text for the photos, then the screen reader cannot convey the information that is in the photos. Including alternative text in images is an example of a way to remove a barrier to accessibility on a website.

The U.S. Department of Justice (DOJ), which enforces the federal Americans with Disabilities Act (AwDA), has interpreted Title III of the AwDA to require businesses to make their websites accessible to individuals with disabilities. Some plaintiffs' lawyers have also alleged that businesses have denied access to the disabled because the businesses' websites are inaccessible in some respect. Although the DOJ has not yet promulgated regulations with standards for website accessibility, DOJ settlements with businesses have required the businesses to comply with existing website accessibility standards, such as Website Content Accessibility Guidelines (WCAG) 2.0 Level AA.

This area of law is still developing, and a dental practice's legal obligation may vary from jurisdiction to jurisdiction. A qualified attorney could provide information about the application of federal, state and local disabilities laws to a dental practice's website.

In the current (as of this writing) absence of a final rule promulgating standards for website accessibility under Title III of the AwDA, a dental practice may wish to contractually require its website developer to ensure that the website meets certain existing standards, such as WCAG 2.0 standards, or the standards developed under Section 508 of the Rehabilitation Act of 1973, which apply to the public content of federal agencies' electronic and information technology.

For example, Appendix 7: Sample Website Development Agreement, includes the following provision:

> D. Accessibility. Designer represents and warrants that all Deliverables will be in conformity with all applicable regulatory requirements, including but not limited to conformance with applicable provisions of Web Content Accessibility Guidelines (WCAG) 2.0 Level AA.

Related References and Resources

- Appendix 7: Sample Website Development Agreement

- W3C Web Accessibility Initiative
  www.w3.org/WAI.

- Section 508.gov: Opening Doors to IT
  www.section508.gov

51. Do I Really Have to Worry About All This? Won't My Website Be Insured?

Don't assume your current insurance policies cover your website. Assess your current coverage. If your agent offers a cyberliability policy or rider that covers your website, it might make sense for you to consider obtaining the additional coverage.

Related References and Resources

- Question 115: What Are the Legal Concerns in Selecting an EHR Vendor? In Entering Into a Contract With Your Chosen EHR Vendor?

Employment Law

Chapter 9.
Introduction to Employment Law

As a dentist and employer — and even before you begin your hiring efforts — you'll need to become familiar with laws that affect the employer-employee relationship. This will help ensure compliance with employment laws at the federal, state and local levels that affect your practice, and allow for structuring your practice and various employment relationships in ways that will maximize value while minimizing undue legal risk.

The following simple, key concepts can help you keep out of legal harm's way:

- Know and act in compliance with employment laws

- Prepare your employees to do the same

- Treat all of your employees equally and do not participate in any discriminatory practices

- Document all of your actions regarding the management of your employees

- Consult with your personal legal counsel when appropriate

52. What Employment Law Issues Arise in a Dental Office?

Listed below are some of the laws and issues that may affect your practice. It is important for dentists to have a basic understanding of these matters.

- Age Discrimination in Employment Act (ADEA)
- Americans with Disabilities Act (AwDA)
- At-Will Employment
- COBRA Benefits
- Employee Retirement Income Security Act (ERISA)
- Equal Pay Act
- Fair Credit Reporting Act
- Fair Labor Standards Act (FLSA)
- Family and Medical Leave Act (FMLA)
- Federal Insurance Contributions Act (FICA)
- Federal Unemployment Tax (FUTA)
- HIPAA and the HITECH amendments
- Independent Contractor vs. Employee Distinction
- National Labor Relations Act (NLRA)
- Negligent Hiring and Retention

- OSHA
- Pregnancy Discrimination Act
- Title VII of the Civil Rights Act
- USERRA (Uniformed Services Employment and Reemployment Rights Act)
- State unemployment compensation laws
- State workers' compensation laws

Related References and Resources

- Question 121: What Effect Did the 2013 Omnibus Final Rule Have on HIPAA Compliance?

- Some Laws That Can Affect Dentistry
  ADA.org/DentistGuidetoLaw

53. What Law(s) Do I Have to Comply With — Federal, State or Local Law?

Ultimately, you'll have to comply with all laws applicable to your situation. Depending on the subject matter and statutes involved, this may mean some combination of federal, state and local law.

You may have noted that the above list is comprised mostly of federal law issues. That is so because, in many cases, Congress will pass a law on a particular subject that supersedes all similar state and local laws. Other times, Congress will pass a law that sets a minimum federal requirement and expressly establishes that more strict state or local laws on the subject may also apply. In the latter case, the AwDA being an example, federal laws establish a minimum compliance floor and state or local laws may establish stricter requirements. You must comply with the federal law and any stricter state or local requirements. In addition, state and local laws may be enacted in areas not covered by federal law. Such laws are numerous and vary from jurisdiction to jurisdiction, so the above list is necessarily incomplete and should not be considered exhaustive without further research or consultation with an employment law attorney in your area.

Many federal, state and local laws only go into effect if a business has a certain number of employees. Many dental practices have a small number of employees, so certain laws may not directly apply to your practice. Examples include the FMLA, which only applies to businesses with 50 or more employees, and the employment law provisions of the AwDA, which only apply to businesses with 15 or more employees. However, some states have enacted family and medical leave laws that apply to employers with fewer employees, and many states have discrimination statutes that cover businesses that have one or more employees. These state and local laws often rely heavily on the federal laws. Consult with your attorney to help you stay current with what is required.

Ultimately, you'll have to comply with all laws applicable to your situation. Depending on the subject matter and statutes involved, this may mean some combination of federal, state and local law.

54. What Is the Risk of Non-Compliance?

Violations of the employment laws can make your dental practice a target for employee litigation — and potentially even investigation or suit by the government. Laws, rules and regulations that affect the workplace vary widely from state to state and even locality by locality. They change constantly. A claim or suit by a current or former employee or by the government could deplete your practice of many of its resources — funds, time, emotional energy, and efforts that could better be spent elsewhere. Accordingly, it is prudent to seek legal advice from your personal attorney regarding employment laws and to keep current as these laws vary from jurisdiction to jurisdiction and change from time to time.

55. Who in My Office Needs to Know Employment Laws?

In addition to you, any employees who are responsible for the hiring, payment, firing, and management of personnel should be familiar with employment laws. Make it a part of your ongoing training to educate your staff on the legalities of all areas of the employment relationship — hiring, discipline, firing, promotions, wages, job assignments, fringe benefits, and other terms and conditions of employment. This provides quality control and consistency — both great defenses against discrimination liability. And keep in mind that everyone in the office will need to know about other laws as well.

Related References and Resources

- Chapter 15: HIPAA, State Law and PCI DSS: Patient Information

- HIPAA 20 Questions
  ADA.org/DentistGuidetoLaw

56. Are These Employment Lawsuits I Hear About for Real?

Yes. It's truly a misconception to believe that dental offices are too small to be sued, and there is good reason to stay current on trends and issues that are fueling litigation. For example, today a diverse workplace is of high importance. Many businesses have been subject to lawsuits that allege all types of discrimination — including discrimination based on race, sex, disability and age, and discriminatory harassment, such as sexual harassment.

It is prudent to seek legal advice from your personal attorney regarding employment laws and to keep current as these laws vary from jurisdiction to jurisdiction and change from time to time.

Chapter 10.
Office Manual and Policies

57. How Can I Protect My Practice?

One of the best ways to protect your practice is to know the laws in your jurisdiction. Not only do you need to become familiar with federal, state, and local employment laws, you should work hard to comply with these laws. By doing so, you can take preventive steps to protect your business against employment law issues by creating a workplace environment that is free of discrimination and harassment.

You should monitor labor laws and legal issues that affect the dental profession. With the help of your attorney, you should draft and adapt your dental office policies and procedures accordingly.

The following questions address some actions you can take as you begin the process of protecting your practice from legal pitfalls in the hiring and management of staff.

Related References and Resources

- *The ADA Practical Guide to Creating and Updating an Employee Policy Manual*
  adacatalog.org or 1.800.947.4746

58. Are There Special Concerns Dentists Should Have About Employment Lawsuits?

Small business employers are often hardest hit in terms of employment lawsuits. Why? Small businesses — and this includes dentists — tend to have few, if any, employment policies in writing. As a result, treatment of employees may be inconsistent.

For example, the hiring process can result in litigation if specific rules are not followed. Anyone in your office who is involved in interviewing job applicants should be trained in proper interviewing techniques. They should be aware of what questions to ask — as well as questions not to ask. In addition, it's a good idea to use the same questions for every applicant. For the average dentist, a lawsuit could be financially overwhelming. Engaging in sound office policy is key in preventing claims from occurring in the first place.

Small business employers are often hardest hit in terms of employment lawsuits. Why? Small businesses — and this includes dentists — tend to have few, if any, employment policies in writing. As a result, treatment of employees may be inconsistent.

59. Is Having an Office Policy Manual or Employee Handbook a Good Idea? Will It Take Care of My Legal Needs?

It's a great idea as long as it's drafted properly and you apply it consistently. Many dental practices have a dental office policy manual or employee handbook. Federal and state laws require that employers communicate to their employees regarding issues such as equal employment opportunities and workers' compensation. An employee office manual is an easy way to get this information to employees. A manual can provide consistent information on policies and procedures, job descriptions and specifications, benefit packages, and any other pertinent information. It can also let the dental team know what is expected of them in terms of performance, behavior, and attitude. Most importantly, an employee office manual can be an important tool for fostering communication, and for protecting both the practice and the employees from legal violations in employee hiring, firing, and supervision.

A manual can provide consistent information on policies and procedures, job descriptions and specifications, benefit packages, and any other pertinent information. It can also let the dental team know what is expected of them in terms of performance, behavior, and attitude.

It's also a good idea to have your employee office manual reviewed by an employment attorney. Among other things, the lawyer may have guidance about how to frame the manual so it does not become a contract that binds you, unless of course you wish it to be legally binding. You can discuss with your lawyer what should be detailed in the manual, and what might simply be referenced in the manual and established separately in a stand-alone office policy.

The bottom line: create an employee office manual, or handbook, that clearly explains all of your policies, or at least incorporates by reference any policies that remain stand-alone (such as your HIPAA Privacy policy). Once that's done, have your employees sign acknowledgement forms to signify that: they have reviewed the handbook; they realize they are at-will employees; they recognize that non-exempt employees must adhere to the rules about overtime; and anything else that you and your lawyer deem appropriate. Be sure to review, update, and re-circulate your employee handbook on a regular basis.

Related References and Resources

- *The ADA Practical Guide to Creating and Updating an Employee Policy Manual*
  adacatalog.org or 1.800.947.4746

60. What Office Policies Do I Need?

Your office policies should address employees' responsibilities and rights. Let's look at each side of the equation in turn. In each case, remember to keep your policies non-discriminatory.

The responsibilities part is key. As practice owners, dentists typically bear the legal burden of what may go wrong in the office. So it is important to have policies in place to make sure things go right! An office policy can make clear that the team works at the direction of the dentist, in accordance with all applicable laws. It can also specify any particular requirements, such as how the office will handle infection control issues (such as, "This office follows CDC guidelines and ADA recommendations on standard precautions and infection control."). Additional specific policies can help ensure compliance with applicable regulations.

In this day and age, important subjects for office policies establishing employee responsibilities include:

- Anti-Discrimination Policy. Discrimination can lead to lawsuits by employees and patients. It is thus important legally — and the right thing to do — to try to keep the practice discrimination-free. An anti-discrimination policy can be targeted to ensure compliance with all applicable civil rights laws, such as the AwDA and more stringent state or local laws that protect both employees and patients with disabilities.

- Anti-Harassment Policy. All employers are expected to provide their employees with a harassment-free work environment. A good anti-harassment policy is essential. Employers should prepare appropriate polices, monitor their effectiveness, update them as the laws change, and ensure that all office workers are aware of the policies and how they work. A well-written policy should protect against harassment by both office colleagues and patients. Please remember that a complaint-free workplace is not a guarantee of a problem-free workplace. Office workers who are being harassed may be afraid to complain because of fears of job loss, retaliation, or potential negative treatment by co-workers. Thus anti-harassment polices benefit your office workers while minimizing your legal exposure.

- Electronic Communications Policy. This policy can explain the risks created by electronic communications (including emails), define when electronic communications may and may not be used, state what protocols must be followed (existing rules for other means of communications may apply), and establish a records retention protocol.

- HIPAA Privacy Policy. Covered Entity dentists must develop written policies and procedures and train staff to safeguard the privacy of patient protected health information (PHI). These policies and procedures should include information such as how patient information will be dealt with in the office, what privacy forms will be used and how to use them, and how to handle privacy complaints. At a bare minimum, all staff should sign an acknowledgment that they received a copy of the policies.

- OSHA and Office Safety Compliance Policy. Under OSHA regulations, employers must comply with the Act and specific standards to provide a place of employment deemed to be free from recognized hazards to workers. Employers must see that employees comply with all occupational safety and health standards issued by OSHA that apply to their own actions and conduct on the job. Among the subjects this policy will cover are how your office will comply with OSHA's Bloodborne Pathogens and Hazard Communication Standards, and the requirements for an Emergency Action and Fire Prevention Plan.

On the other side of the coin, a number of policies can be used to spell out the scope of employee rights. Here are some to consider:

- Employment at Will policy. In states upholding the employment at will doctrine, an employer can terminate the employee at any time for any reason and the employee can quit at any time, with or without notice. On a practical level from the employer's perspective, the doctrine can be used to reinforce that the employee does not have a right to continued employment. This can be done in many ways, including by inserting language such as "Either [dental office] or employee may terminate the employment relationship at any time with or without notice or cause" in your employee handbook.

- Some additional possible subjects for written office policies include: Sick and Emergency Leave, Personal Days, Weather Closures, Election Day Absences, Jury and Witness Duty, and Leave of Absence.

Seek legal advice from your personal attorney while drafting your dental office policies.

Related References and Resources

- Question 76: What Issues Arise When Terminating an Employee? How Does Employment "At Will" Fit In?

- Chapter 14: OSHA

- Chapter 15: HIPAA, State Law and PCI DSS: Patient Information

- HIPAA 20 Questions
  ADA.org/DentistGuidetoLaw

- Sample Anti-Harassment Policy
  ADA.org/DentistGuidetoLaw

- Sample Electronic Communications Policy
  ADA.org/DentistGuidetoLaw

- Sample Employment Policies
  ADA.org/DentistGuidetoLaw

- The ADA Practical Guide to HIPAA Compliance: Privacy and Security Manual
  adacatalog.org or 1.800.947.4746

- The ADA Practical Guide to OSHA Compliance: Regulatory Compliance Manual
  adacatalog.org or 1.800.947.4746

- The ADA Practical Guide to Creating and Updating an Employee Policy Manual
  adacatalog.org or 1.800.947.4746

Chapter 11.

Hiring

61. When Hiring an Associate Dentist, Do I Need a Written Contract And, If So, What Should Be in It?

A written contract is a good idea. Hiring an associate will raise a number of considerations, and a written contract will help both parties sort through and agree upon the issues. Even though a written agreement may sound like extra work, it is worth it from the legal perspective, as well as from the standpoint of office relations. Two key considerations for the contract are: 1) should the associate be an independent contractor or an employee; and 2) will the employer-dentist be able to hold the associate to a restrictive covenant if the associate leaves the practice?

Related References and Resources

- Chapter 20: Common Dental Agreements.

- Question 121: Should the Associate Be an Independent Contractor or Employee?

- Question 150: Are Restrictive Covenants Enforceable?

- Appendix 3: Sample Employee Associateship Agreement

- Appendix 4: Sample Independent Contractor Associateship Agreement

- Appendix 5: New Employee Checklist.

62. What Is the Importance of the Exempt vs. Non-Exempt Distinction?

Employees are classified as "exempt" or "non-exempt." Non-exempt employees are those who are not exempt from (that is, they are covered by) the overtime provisions of the Fair Labor Standards Act (FLSA), a federal law administered by the U.S. Department of Labor which specifies wage and overtime requirements for employees. Exempt employees are exempt from (that is, they are not covered by) the FLSA overtime provisions (certain other provisions of the FLSA will apply to exempt employees). In practical terms, we think of this distinction as hourly (non-exempt) and certain salaried (exempt) staff.

Currently, exempt employees include executives, administrators and professionals who meet certain tests concerning specific job duties and are paid on a salary basis that meets or exceeds $455 per week (as of July 2008). Non-exempt employees often hold secretarial, clerical, technical, and building maintenance positions. With the possible exception of other dentists you employ and your office manager, most of your staff will likely be non-exempt. Therefore, their wages and overtime requirements are protected by the FLSA. However, stay abreast of the new FLSA regulations as well as your state wage and hour laws, and keep in mind that specific determination of exempt or non-exempt status requires a careful review of FLSA provisions and state regulations by your attorney.

63. Can I Conduct a "Working Interview" With a Prospective Employee?

Not unless you pay the candidate for his or her time. Some practices erroneously believe it is acceptable to ask a promising candidate or candidates to spend a few hours actually performing the duties of an open position to better understand a prospective employee's capabilities and "fit." The would-be employee is not paid, as the practice considers the time spent a so-called "working interview." However, federal and state wage-hour laws require that any person performing work for the practice must be paid for his or her time. Generally speaking, good interviewing techniques should surface potential "fit" issues that may arise, but if the practice wishes to have the individual perform actual work before making a hiring decision, the candidate must be paid for his or her time.

64. Can I Require Drug Testing of Applicants?

Maybe. If you are covered by the employment provisions of the Americans with Disabilities Act (you are covered if you have 15 or more employees), you may require drug testing of job applicants only after an employment offer has been made, subject to more restrictive state or local law. The employment offer may be contingent on verifiable results. Test results must remain confidential.

According to the EEOC, if an employee of an employer covered by the AwDA is medically cleared for return to work following a leave of absence for treatment due to drug addiction, provided he or she continues to attend a support program regularly, "the employer may for a reasonable period of time require periodic drug testing, verification from the employee that she is regularly participating in such a program, or other reasonable assurances that she is no longer engaging in the illegal use of drugs."

Current use of illegal drugs is not a disability under the AwDA, but an individual may be considered disabled under the Act if the individual: 1) has successfully completed a drug rehabilitation program or has otherwise rehabilitated and is no longer using illegal drugs; 2) is participating in a drug rehabilitation program and is no longer using illegal drugs; or 3) is erroneously perceived as using illegal drugs, but is not engaged in such use.

The employment provisions of the AwDA do not apply to private dental offices with fewer than 15 employees. Check your state and local requirements. In many cases, they will be similar to the federal approach and they may apply to employers with fewer employees. Because of the legal risks and complexities of this issue, check with your attorney before taking action.

65. What Information Should Be Included in a Background Check for a Potential Employee? Can a Credit Check Be Run Before Hiring a New Employee?

Background and credit checks may provide information that can help an employer make good hiring decisions. A background check can also help limit an employer's potential liability for "negligent hiring," which is a civil action alleging that an employer is responsible for an injury caused by an employee if the employer might have prevented the injury by making a reasonable inquiry into the employee's background.

Background and credit checks should be limited to information that is relevant to the position being filled. For example, a background check on applicants for a professional position should include verification of their academic credentials and licenses. If the professional's work will be billed to Medicare or Medicaid, the background check should include a determination of whether the individual has been excluded from those programs. If the job being filled may involve handling cash, claims, or accounts, a background check may determine whether an applicant has been convicted of fraud or embezzlement.

Federal laws, including the Fair Credit Reporting Act (FCRA), and certain state laws apply to employee background and credit checks. To conduct a credit check, many employers hire an outside company (referred to in the FCRA as a "consumer reporting agency" or CRA). While some employers personally check certain elements of an applicant's background (for example, calling references), hiring a CRA to conduct background checks can help ensure compliance with federal and state legal requirements. Before hiring a CRA for credit or background checks, it may be prudent to verify the procedures the CRA will undertake and confirm that its practices have been reviewed and are in compliance with federal and state laws. In some states, for example, it is illegal to inquire about criminal convictions on employment applications, and criminal background checks may only be undertaken after an offer has been made (subject to revocation if the background check turns up job-related issues).

The FCRA imposes a number of requirements on an employer who hires a CRA. For example, the employer must notify the applicant in writing that a report may be obtained and must obtain the applicant's written authorization. Before an employer takes any adverse action in reliance on the report such as denying the applicant a job (even if the report is only a minor factor in the decision), the employer must first give the applicant a pre-adverse action disclosure, with a copy of the report and a copy of the FTC document, "A Summary of Your Rights Under the Fair Credit Reporting Act." After taking the adverse action, the employer must give the applicant notice of the action along with the name, address and telephone number of the consumer reporting agency, a statement that the agency did not make the adverse decision and cannot give specific reasons for it, and a notice that the applicant has the right to dispute the accuracy or completeness of the report and to request an additional free report from the agency. An employer who fails to satisfy the requirements of the FCRA will have legal exposure in federal court by the unsuccessful job applicant.

Background and credit checks should be limited to information that is relevant to the position being filled.

In addition to the FCRA, certain federal and state laws govern employers' conduct when conducting background and credit checks of potential employees, including what an employer may ask (or say to) an applicant, what information may be obtained, and how that information may be used. Employers using background and credit checks must take care not to violate equal employment opportunity laws. For example, background and credit checks should be conducted uniformly on all applicants for a given position and an employer should not request information about an applicant's medical history. An employer who wishes to conduct a credit check or a criminal background check on job applicants must be able to demonstrate that an individual's credit rating or criminal record is job-related and consistent with business necessity, or an applicant may claim that the check was discriminatory. In addition, many states prohibit basing employment-related action based solely upon an arrest (as opposed to conviction) record. An employment lawyer can help you evaluate the risk of conducting credit or background checks on applicants for a given position.

An employer who uses a consumer reporting agency to conduct a credit or background check on a job applicant may be required to report under the federal government's "Red Flags Rule" if an applicant submits suspicious documents or information (for example, if the address on an employment application does not match the address on the consumer report). The Red Flags Rule was intended to help detect and prevent identity theft.

Related References and Resources

- Chapter 16: FACTA: Red Flags and Disposal Rules

- Some Laws That Can Affect Dentistry
  ADA.org/DentistGuidetoLaw

- OIG, Online Exclusions Database
  http://exclusions.oig.hhs.gov

- FTC Business Center
  www.ftc.gov/bcp/edu/pubs/business/credit/bus08.shtm

Chapter 12.
Managing the Dental Team

66. How Should I Approach Performance Appraisals?

Like many other employment decisions, performance appraisals are subject to federal, state, and local labor laws and regulations. The bottom line is this: an employer must administer appraisals in a fair manner to avoid discrimination claims. Performance appraisals should accurately reflect the individual's work performance and should be supported by objective evidence.

Here are some suggestions to follow when administering performance appraisals.

- Deal with performance issues as they arise. This shows the employer is ready and willing to remedy a problem. A well-written memorandum provides an employee with notice of the problem(s) and identifies the corrective action that needs to be taken. Down the road, these types of memoranda help support a dentist's claim that he or she acted fairly and in a non-discriminatory manner.

- Document both good and bad performance characteristics accurately, providing concrete, factually-supported examples. Avoid conclusory terms such as "bad attitude" or "not a team player." Instead, describe the conduct that leads to your conclusion. Give one copy of the appraisal to the employee, and file one in the employee file.

- Do not write discriminatory notes (e.g., "too old to perform assigned tasks in a timely manner") on appraisal forms

- Obtain the employee's signature on the appraisal form and provide a space for employee comment. The signature proves the employee received the appraisal; the comment section permits the employee an opportunity to respond. The employee does not have to agree with the rating. If the employee refuses to sign the appraisal, the employer or other employee who is conducting the appraisal should indicate this in writing, and sign the form.

- Be consistent with performance appraisals. Address performance issues consistently for all employees on a timely basis.

An effective evaluation program for small businesses has two components. One component is a formal performance appraisal on a yearly basis. The second component is giving feedback on performance on a regular, as-needed basis.

67. How Should I Handle Employee Discipline?

Many employers discipline their employees in steps, with documentation along the way. Handling discipline in this "progressive" manner provides notice to the employee that his or her performance needs to be improved and provides the practice with something to reference in arguing that the disciplinary process was fairly handled should termination ultimately be necessary. There are many reasons why an employee may be disciplined. Some of these reasons include: poor job performance, insubordination, stealing, violence, and using illegal drugs and alcohol on the job. An employee who is failing in his or her job performance should be confronted. If an employee's job is in jeopardy, tell him or her. Explain, document, and discuss poor performance to your failing employee. Be fair, and offer your employee an opportunity to improve. You could even provide training to strengthen problem areas. In simple terms, disciplinary warnings are basically ways to convince employees to bring their performance up to par.

Consider disciplining an employee in progressive steps (so-called "progressive discipline"): counseling, oral warning, written warning, probationary period (60-90 days) — and finally, termination. Written memoranda should indicate that the disciplinary process is subordinate to your at-will employment relationship with the employee if you are an at-will employer. Any progressive disciplinary policy should specifically state that steps in the process may be eliminated based upon the severity of the matter giving rise to discipline.

By taking these steps, not only are you giving your employee another chance — an opportunity to save his or her job — you are also protecting yourself against being accused of firing a person on a discriminatory basis. You are also showing your staff that you are a fair and just employer.

Here are the basic steps in a progressive disciplinary process:

- **Step 1: Talk to the Employee.** Discuss problematic areas and what changes must take place to improve. This is considered a verbal warning. A written verification of the incident should be put in the employee's file.

- **Step 2: Give a Written Warning.** Detail the nature of the problem, the measures the employee is expected to take to resolve it, and a time frame within which improvement is expected. Tell the employee you appreciate his or her efforts, but the efforts still do not reflect satisfactory job performance.

- **Step 3: Take Disciplinary Action.** If you feel the employee has not improved and you have provided enough assistance to help your employee, then provide the disciplinary action, such as a probationary period (60-90 days). The employee should be told that any further problems may result in more drastic disciplinary measures being taken, including termination. If you are an at-will employer, you may want to reiterate in your employee office manual that the disciplinary procedures are subordinate to both parties' rights to terminate with or without cause.

- **Step 4: Suspension. Possible suspension without pay.**

- **Step 5: Termination. Possible termination.**

68. What Should I Do If the Employee Is Engaging in Unlawful Acts, Such as Embezzlement, Theft, or Writing Prescriptions on Stolen Pads?

If you have evidence of employee wrongdoing, consult your attorney, who can advise you how to proceed and how to notify the proper authorities. An employee engaging in unlawful activities can be destructive to your practice. The ADA offers materials on how to help prevent this from happening, or at least minimize the harm should it occur (for example, by bonding employees as they are hired). Conducting pre-hiring background or credit checks, particularly for employees in sensitive positions, can be helpful.

If an employee is suspected of embezzlement, contact your accountant or your attorney immediately. Various options, such as an internal audit, could put your mind at ease. Of course, if those options confirm your suspicions, termination and even criminal charges are appropriate to consider.

Some employees may be more interested in drugs than money. If you suspect an employee of stealing drugs or falsifying prescriptions using office prescription pads, secure appropriate professional help to assess the situation. If you are correct, requiring treatment for chemical dependency may be an option; continued employment could be made contingent on completion of treatment, compliance with all treatment recommendations, and participation in a formal monitoring program. Applicable state law or regulations may impose testing or other standards with regard to substance-abusing health care professionals. Current use of illegal drugs is exempt from coverage under the Americans with Disabilities Act (AwDA); however, a person who no longer engages in the illegal use of drugs could meet the AwDA definition of disability if he or she has successfully completed a supervised drug rehabilitation program or otherwise been rehabilitated successfully, or if he or she is participating in a supervised rehabilitation program. The employment provisions of the AwDA applies to employers with 15 or more employees, but state and local discrimination laws may apply to employers with fewer than 15 employees. If you decide to terminate or take other action against an employee whom you suspect of stealing drugs, falsifying prescriptions, using illegal drugs, or related behavior, you should first seek the counsel of an experienced employment lawyer. In addition to any action you may consider with respect to the employee, you may have duties to report what happened to federal or state authorities, particularly if controlled substances are involved.

Related References and Resources

- Question 65: What Information Should Be Included in a Background Check for a Potential Employee? Can a Credit Check Be Run Before Hiring a New Employee?

- Question 70: What If I Suspect an Employee or Co-Worker Is Abusing or Taking Drugs From the Dental Office?

- ADA Dentist Health and Well-Being Program
  ADA.org/en/member-center/member-benefits/health-and-wellness-information
  1.800.947.4746 ext. 2622

- U.S. Drug Enforcement Administration
  www.usdoj.gov/dea

- The ADA Practical Guide to Creating and Updating an Employee Policy Manual
  adacatalog.org or 1.800.947.4746

69. I'm Concerned About a Disturbing Change in the Behavior of an Individual Who Works in My Dental Practice. What Should I Do?

An unexpected change in an individual's behavior can have many causes. Life stress such as the serious illness of a family member can cause people to act differently than usual. However, behavior changes can indicate other problems such as a physical or mental illness including a substance abuse problem or the side effect of medication. Sometimes unusual behavior can indicate wrongdoing such as embezzlement or drug diversion.

If the individual's behavior results in negligence, damage, or injury, your practice could be liable for failing to properly supervise his or her work, or for failing to eliminate a known hazard to patient safety. If your practice is a partnership and the individual is your partner, you could be personally liable for his or her actions. If patients are aware of the individual's behavior change, your practice may suffer from patient attrition.

An attorney can help you minimize the legal risks that can arise in these situations. The causes of behavior changes can involve very serious issues, and casting suspicions as fact can expose you to a lawsuit for libel or slander, particularly if your suspicions turn out to be inaccurate. If the individual is an employee, an employment attorney can advise you as to how best to evaluate, document, and respond to the problem. A first step may be to discuss your observations with the individual in question, express your concern, and ask for the individual's explanation.

When the behavior of an employee or professional in the practice is related to a physical or mental condition, the practice may be required to take action to comply the Americans with Disabilities Act (AwDA) or similar state or local laws (for example, affording unpaid time off or making a reasonable change in work schedules so the individual can access treatment). Note, however, that if your practice is subject to the AwDA or similar state laws, you may not make a "medical inquiry" of an employee who has not voluntarily shared such information. While you can say, "I am concerned that you are behaving erratically," you cannot ask if the person is suffering from a physical or mental medical condition. You can, however, ask if there is anything that you should know or if there is anything you might do to assist the employee. If the individual owns a portion of the practice, you may also be required to follow procedures set forth in your governing documents (for example, your board of directors may be required to discuss and act on the issue). If you believe patients are at risk due to the behavior of a professional in your practice, you may have a duty to contact your state's licensing board. You may need to contact law enforcement authorities in the event of suspected criminal activity. If the behavior change is caused by a treatable condition and the individual agrees to an evaluation and treatment program (and poses no risk to patients), you may wish to require periodic progress reports and documentation of adherence to treatment. If the individual fails to adhere to the treatment program, it may be necessary to terminate the relationship. Such documents may help defend against a lawsuit brought by the individual (for example, for wrongful termination or discrimination) or by a third party.

Contact your state dental society's well-being or rehabilitation committee for information about helping a dentist or dental hygienist who may be impaired by a physical or mental condition including alcoholism and other addictive disorders. The ADA Dentist Health and Wellness program offers personal assistance, including referral information on treatment facilities for alcohol and other drug dependence, evaluations, and state well-being committee contacts.

Related References and Resources

- Question 67: How Should I Handle Employee Discipline?

- Question 70: What If I Suspect an Employee or Co-Worker Is Abusing or Taking Drugs from the Dental Office?

- Some Laws That Can Affect Dentistry
  ADA.org/DentistGuidetoLaw

- ADA Dentist Health and Well-Being Program
  ADA.org/en/member-center/member-benefits/health-and-wellness-information
  1.800.947.4746 ext. 2622

70. What If I Suspect an Employee or Co-Worker Is Abusing or Taking Drugs From the Dental Office?

Drug abuse can occur among people from all walks of life, health care workers included. It is important to understand behavior that may indicate that a co-worker or employee is diverting or abusing drugs, as well as your responsibilities and options if you have concerns about an individual in your dental office. An employment lawyer can advise you as to how to proceed if you wish to investigate suspected drug abuse or diversion, to encourage a co-worker or employee to seek drug treatment assistance, or to discipline or terminate an employee for abusing or diverting drugs.

Substance abuse and drug diversion are extremely serious accusations and casting suspicions as fact can expose you to a lawsuit for libel or slander, particularly if your suspicions turn out to be inaccurate.

Dentists can use safeguards to reduce the risk that drugs in the dental office will be abused or diverted, and should be familiar with federal and any applicable state laws that mandate security procedures for health care practitioners who prescribe controlled substances. The DEA Practitioner's Manual discusses recordkeeping, inventory, and disposal requirements for controlled substances as well as steps that practitioners must take to guard against theft and diversion. For example, practitioners should store Schedule II through V controlled substances in a substantially constructed, securely locked cabinet, and practitioners hiring an employee for a position that involves access to controlled substances should not hire an individual with a felony conviction related to controlled substances or an individual whose DEA registration has been denied, revoked, or surrendered for cause. The DEA Practitioner's Manual recommends additional safeguards, such as using tamper-resistant prescription pads, minimizing the number of pads in use, and keeping them in a safe place where they cannot be stolen.

A dentist's DEA registration can be revoked if he or she fails to maintain effective controls against diversion of controlled substances. The DEA has revoked practitioners' licenses for offenses such as allowing an unauthorized individual to use the practitioner's DEA number to obtain drugs and for signing blank prescription forms. The DEA has also revoked the licenses of practitioners whom it deemed unfit to practice due to drug and alcohol abuse. Practitioners are required to notify the DEA of any thefts or significant losses of controlled substances. Failing to comply with DEA reporting requirements (including reporting inventories and reporting theft or significant loss of controlled substances) may also be grounds for revocation. If an employee's misconduct involving controlled substances results in a criminal investigation, it is possible that the DEA may consider failure to report the misconduct inconsistent with the goal of decreasing diversion and maintaining public health, which could be a factor in license revocation.

Theft of a controlled substance is a criminal act and should be reported to law enforcement authorities and state regulatory agencies so they can investigate and prosecute. If you contact law enforcement because you have evidence of criminal activity, review your HIPAA obligations and any state confidentiality and privacy laws before releasing patient health information. HIPAA allows certain communications to law enforcement authorities without patient authorization. Check with your attorney before releasing information to make sure the disclosure will not violate the law.

Your state dental society may offer a well-being or rehabilitation committee to help dentists and dental hygienists who may be impaired by addictive disorders, or another physical or mental condition. The ADA Dentist Health and Wellness program offers personal assistance, including referral information on treatment facilities for alcohol and other drug dependence, evaluations, and state well-being committee contacts.

According to the EEOC, a person who currently engages in the illegal use of drugs is excluded from coverage under the Americans with Disabilities Act (AwDA). However, a person who no longer engages in the illegal use of drugs may be considered "disabled" if he or she has successfully completed a supervised drug rehabilitation program or otherwise been rehabilitated successfully, or if he or she is participating in a supervised rehabilitation program. The employment provisions of the AwDA apply to employers with 15 or more employees. Similar state or local laws may apply to employers with fewer than 15 employees.

Related References and Resources

- Question 65: What Information Should Be Included in a Background Check for a Potential Employee? Can a Credit Check Be Run Before Hiring a New Employee?

- Some Laws That Can Affect Dentistry
  ADA.org/DentistGuidetoLaw

- DEA, Drug Addiction in Health Care Professionals
  www.deadiversion.usdoj.gov/pubs/brochures/drug_hc.htm

- DEA Practitioner's Manual
  www.deadiversion.usdoj.gov/pubs/manuals/pract/index.html

- ADA Dentist Health and Well-Being Program
  ADA.org/en/member-center/member-benefits/health-and-wellness-information
  1.800.947.4746 ext. 2622

- EEOC, Questions and Answers on the Notice of Proposed Rulemaking for the ADA Amendments Act of 2008 (Scroll down to question 16)
  www.eeoc.gov/policy/docs/qanda_adaaa_nprm.html

71. Must a Dentist Be Present When a Hygienist Is Working?

The answer depends on the level of supervision required by your state's dental practice act for the specific procedures that a dental hygienist can perform.

The law in your state may require that the dentist be present in the dental facility when a hygienist performs certain procedures. For example, a state that allows a hygienist who is trained and certified to administer anesthesia is likely to require the dentist to be present at the same time. State law may permit a dental hygienist to perform other listed procedures (such as oral health screenings) when the dentist is not present as long as various requirements are met. For example, the law may require that the patient be a patient of record whom the dentist has examined and diagnosed prior to treatment by the hygienist; the dentist may have to be near enough to the dental facility to return quickly if necessary; the dentist may be required to authorize the procedures by a notation in the patient's record; and the dentist may be required to examine the patient after treatment and prior to dismissal. It may also be necessary to inform the patient that the dentist may be out of the office during the procedure.

Some state dental practice acts provide exceptions for school-based oral health programs, for patients who are institutionalized or unable to travel, or for other specified situations. Consult your state dental society and your state's dental practice act for the specific requirements in your state. Your attorney can help you interpret your state's laws and any rules or regulations.

72. What Are My Obligations as an Employer When an Employee or an Associate Dentist in My Practice Has Been Called to Active Duty by the Military?

The Uniformed Services Employment and Reemployment Rights Act of 1994 (USERRA) protects employees who are voluntarily or involuntarily called to active military service (and certain types of service in the National Disaster Medical System).

While the employee is serving in the military, the employer's leave of absence policies apply. In addition, the employee on military duty has certain rights to continued employee health benefits, and his or her pension benefits are protected. Upon returning from military service the employee has reemployment rights under the "escalator" principal: the employer must reemploy the returning service member in the job he or she would have attained if not for the military service, and grant the employee the level of seniority, status, and pay that the employee would have qualified for if he or she had stayed. The employer may be required to provide reasonable retraining, as well as reasonable accommodations if the employee returns disabled.

USERRA contains a number of restrictions. For example, the employee must give the employer notice as required in the statute that he or she has been called to military service. At the end of the military service the employee must also comply with the statute's requirements when notifying the employer of the intent to return to work. With certain exceptions, reemployment rights are limited to a military service of five years (cumulative). A convalescing veteran may be granted additional time to apply for reemployment. To receive USERRA protection, the returning service member must have received a non-punitive discharge from military service under honorable conditions.

An employee may not be entitled to reemployment in certain cases. For example, if the employer's circumstances have changed, making reemployment impossible or unreasonable, or if re-employment would pose an undue burden on the employer.

USERRA only applies to employees: if the staff member or associate dentist who is called to military service is an independent contractor as defined under the USERRA regulations, he or she may not be entitled to USERRA protection.

USERRA prohibits an employer from discriminating against a job applicant based on military service or membership in any branch of the military. If an offer of employment has been extended to an individual who is then called to military duty, the employer cannot withdraw the offer.

Additional rights may also be available to returning military or their families if the practice is covered under the Family and Medical Leave Act (i.e., if the practice employs 50 or more employees within a 75-mile radius).

Due to the complexity of USERRA and other potentially-applicable laws and regulations, you should consult your attorney about your obligations if any questions arise in your practice.

ADA Dues Waiver for Military Service. Dentists called to active duty may apply for a waiver of their ADA dues.

Liability Insurance. The ADA Council on Member Insurance and Retirement Programs recommends dentists call their insurance agents to discuss canceling or suspending liability insurance coverage while serving on active duty.

Mutual Aid Agreements. Dentists sometimes develop mutual aid agreements to assist each other in the event one of them becomes unable to practice. A mutual aid agreement may provide for the assistance of a dentist called to active duty.

Related References and Resources

- ADA Dues Waiver for Military Service
  *ADA.org/en/member-center/join-or-renew-ada-membership/federal-dental-services/
  federal-dental-services-dues-installment-and-waiver-programs-faq*

73. What Do I Need to Document?

As a general rule, a dentist should document everything related to employee management. It is important to document all the good work you've done, such as keeping copies of policies on hand, having employees sign that they received your office manual and were trained in the various stand-alone policies, and so forth.

In terms of employee management, be sure you maintain comprehensive employee records including job descriptions, want ads, hiring interview notes, and documented discipline problems. If you ever conduct meetings outside of the workplace, be sure you convey the same level of professionalism as you would in-office. And in connection with employee discipline or termination, have thorough documentation describing and supporting your actions.

74. What Notices Must I Post About Employment Matters?

Federal law requires employers to post certain notices in a conspicuous place, such as an employee lounge bulletin board, to inform employees of their protection and rights under the law. Your state, county, or city may have additional posting requirements as well.

You may be required to post the following notices in your dental practice:

- OSHA Form 2203 — "Job Safety and Health" poster available from the U.S. Department of Labor

- OSHA Form 300 — Summary of recordable occupational injuries and illnesses posted between February 1 and March 1 annually (Dental offices with 11 or more employees). Available from the U.S. Department of Labor.

- Employment Discrimination — "Equal Opportunity is the Law" poster (for dental offices with 15 or more employees) available from Equal Employment Opportunity Commission offices

- Fair Labor Standards Act (FLSA) — Minimum Wage poster available from the U.S. Department of Labor

- Polygraph Protection — Wage-hour poster 1462 available from the U.S. Department of Labor

Related References and Resources

U.S. Department of Labor Workplace Posters
www.dol.gov/elaws/posters.html

U.S. Equal Employment Opportunity Commission
www.eeoc.gov
1.800.669.4000

U.S. Department of Labor
www.dol.gov
1.866.4.USA.DOL

Federal law requires employers to post certain notices in a conspicuous place, such as an employee lounge bulletin board, to inform employees of their protection and rights under the law.

75. Are There Employment Law Resources That Can Help Me?

In addition to the various ADA publications described in this chapter, there are a variety of resources that can help you manage your employees and understand the complex issues of employment law. Keep in mind that a competent employment attorney may be well worth his or her fee in setting you up safely or assisting in handling problems that do arise.

You can now find information and quickly access numerous U.S. employment laws, such as occupational safety and health and family and medical leave, at the Department of Labor's website. In addition, the Department has developed "elaws advisors" to help employees and employers understand their rights and responsibilities under numerous Federal employment laws. These advisors come complete with links to regulatory text, organizations, and other helpful publications.

The American Dental Association has numerous practice management resources designed especially for dental offices. You and your attorney can use ADA resources as tools when you work together, rather than having your attorney start from scratch. You may save considerable money on your legal fees and your employee handbook may be better designed to address your needs.

Related References and Resources

- Appendix 5: New Employee Checklist

- Appendix 6: Termination Checklist

- Valuable Federal Government Websites
  ADA.org/DentistGuidetoLaw

- U.S. Department of Labor
  www.dol.gov
  1.866.4.USA.DOL

- DOL, E-laws Employment Laws Assistance for Workers and Small Businesses
  www.dol.gov/elaws

- American Dental Association
  ADA.org

- *The ADA Practical Guide to Creating and Updating an Employee Policy Manual*
  adacatalog.org or 1.800.947.4746

Chapter 13.
Termination

76. What Issues Arise When Terminating an Employee? How Does Employment "At Will" Fit In?

You should be aware of federal, state, and local laws affecting termination. These laws are complex and subject to change. In addition, there is no simple rule that provides a clear and definite procedure for termination in every instance.

The general rule that governs most employment relationships is the "employment at will" doctrine. This rule simply states that an employer and employee have an employment agreement for an indefinite period of time and that either party can terminate the employment relationship at any time and for any reason or for no reason, so long as the reason is not unlawful. However, over the years, courts and legislatures have placed limits on an employer's ability to fire at-will employees.

Although in an employment-at-will relationship both the employer and the employee generally have the right to terminate the employment relationship, it is sometimes looked upon more harshly for an employer to terminate an employee abruptly than for an employee to unexpectedly quit. Therefore, it can be helpful if you have proof and records that you followed fair and logical steps during a termination process, and that the termination was based upon lawful, non-discriminatory reasons.

One important limit to firing employees is found in anti-discrimination and human rights laws. Under a variety of federal, state, and local human rights acts, employees cannot be terminated on the basis of such characteristics as race, gender, religion, age or disability.

In addition, most states recognize "public policy exceptions" to the employment at will doctrine. These exceptions provide that an employer cannot discharge an employee if the termination would violate a fundamental public policy in the particular state. For example, a staff member cannot be fired for reporting practice breaches in OSHA standards. Similarly, if an employee refuses to break a law, he or she cannot be fired for that refusal. For example, a dental hygienist fired for refusing to perform a procedure that state law says only a licensed dentist can do may be able to assert an employment claim against the employer. Likewise, a public policy exception exists when an employer fires an employee in retaliation for filing a legally assertable claim. An example would be a worker discharged for making a valid worker's compensation claim.

Another exception to the employment at will doctrine may exist when there is an employment contract, either expressed or implied, between the employer and employee. In this situation, an employer usually has a written or oral contract with the employee. This contract usually specifies certain terms and conditions of employment. However, some courts have held that an implied contract of employment may exist when the employer provides a worker with an employee handbook or manual. Often this involves interpretation of the language of the handbook or manual.

If you decide to use an employee handbook or manual, have your lawyer carefully review it to avoid inadvertently forming either an expressed or implied contract. You may want to include a statement indicating:

> This employee handbook is not an expressed or implied contract of employment.

> [Dental office] reserves the right to change, modify or delete any provision of this employee handbook at its sole discretion with or without notice. Either [dental office] or employee may terminate the employment relationship at any time with or without notice or cause.

When an expressed or implied employment contract exists, the employer may be permitted to terminate the contract — and the employment — for "good cause." Courts have found implied employment contracts to exist in cases where employers provided assurances of continued employment, designations of employees as "permanent" after initial training periods, letters setting forth an "annual" salary and thus inferring a one-year contract, and clauses in employee handbooks implying discharge occurs only for unsatisfactory performance.

As you can see, it makes sense to practice good management. Be fair to your employees. The worst type of termination is one that comes by surprise. Be fair and give a warning. Be sure you've tried to help your employee improve before you terminate his or her employment. If an employee is failing in his or her job performance, he or she should be confronted — promptly. Do not wait until an annual review.

Explain, document, and discuss poor performance to your failing employee. Offer your employee an opportunity to improve. You could even provide training to strengthen problem areas.

Accurate, detailed performance appraisals can validate a termination, for they serve as excellent documentation of an employee's performance. On the other hand, remember that an employee who has received good appraisals and who is later terminated may be able to prove to a court that the employer's claims of "poor performance" are unfounded.

There are many valid reasons for a termination. Some of these include:

- Absenteeism not protected by leave laws or policies
- Conviction of a job-related crime
- Damage to practice property
- Illegal drug use on the job
- Incompetence
- Insubordination
- Low productivity
- Misrepresentations on job applications
- Negligence
- Practice rule violations
- Safety violations
- Theft

An employee can also be discharged when the position is no longer necessary to the practice, or because the practice suffers a significant loss of patients or revenue.

Avoid terminating an employee who has not had a "warning" and who has received good performance appraisals. For example, consider disciplining an employee in steps: counseling, oral warning, written warning, probationary period (90 days, six months) — and finally, termination. This is called progressive discipline. Your documentation should state that your progressive discipline process is subordinate to your at-will employment status.

According to employment law experts, you should be careful about the timing of an employee termination. For example, try to avoid discharging an employee during times when they are experiencing health or personal problems, or right before a holiday. It is best not to discharge an employee right before he or she is supposed to receive a raise. Even if you have valid reasons for the dismissal, other people will see that as being the main reason for the firing. A jury may see it that way, too, if the incident were to ever end up in a courtroom. In addition, a termination may be questioned if the employee has recently received a commendation, award, or merit increase.

Related References and Resources

- Question 60: What Office Policies Do I Need?

- Question 66: How Should I Approach Performance Appraisals?

- Appendix 6: Termination Checklist

77. Can I Terminate an Employee Who Has HIV? What About an Employee Who Has Hepatitis C?

It depends, and this gets a little complicated. Persons with infectious diseases may have protections under the AwDA or similar state or local laws. The employment provisions of the AwDA apply to employers with 15 or more employees, and similar state or local laws may apply to employers with fewer employees. The first question is whether the person has a "disability" and is thus covered by the law. There are no per se disabilities under the AwDA; rather, a case-by-case determination is made as to whether the person has a disability, which is generally defined as a physical or mental impairment that substantially limits a major life activity, a record of an impairment that substantially limited him or her in the past, or is regarded by an employer as having a substantially limiting impairment. The AwDA Amendments Act of 2008 (the AwDAAA), enacted on September 25, 2008 and effective as of January 1, 2009, significantly broadened the AwDA definition of "disability.

According to the EEOC, HIV is an example of an impairment that will consistently meet the definition of "disability."

Although hepatitis C (HCV) is not considered as impairing as HIV, an individual with HCV may also have a disability as defined by the AwDA. Assuming that an HIV-positive individual has a "disability" for legal purposes, it is important to note the legal protections he or she may have are not absolute. Indeed, under the AwDA, an employer is likely to be able to terminate the employee if he or she poses a "direct threat" to patients or the dental team. The scientific question in such a case is whether the risk of transmission can be eliminated by standard precautions and infection control.

Notwithstanding CDC guidelines and ADA and AMA policies that infected workers can in many cases safely treat if proper precautions are taken, some courts that have examined this issue in the context of employed health care workers have ruled against the employee (holding that termination or reassignment to a non-clinical position was allowable). The core of these cases is that precautions cannot eliminate all risk of transmission. Some states have adopted laws and regulations concerning the definition of an invasive procedure and restrictions that must be imposed on an infected health care worker. Check with your attorney about the laws in your jurisdiction.

The EEOC has indicated that HIV-positive health care workers who perform certain exposure-prone invasive procedures specially defined by the Centers for Disease Control and Prevention (CDC) may pose a safety risk. The EEOC has indicated that infected health care workers performing certain other procedures do not pose a direct threat to patients (such as a phlebotomist at a blood bank who is responsible for drawing blood and who adheres to standard precautions). The EEOC has filed lawsuits under the AwDA on behalf of some HIV positive workers. To minimize the risk of an employment discrimination lawsuit, it is important to consult an attorney prior to terminating or restricting the duties of an employee who has tested positive for a disease such as HIV/AIDS or HCV.

Your state's dental practice act, department of professional regulation, or department of public health may impose disciplinary action on dentists and dental hygienists who practice while knowingly having infectious or communicable diseases, and may also require certain diseases to be reported. Consult your personal attorney and state dental society for the requirements in your state.

A related question is whether the dentist can or must disclose (or compel the infected employee to disclose) his or her health status to patients. In addition to the issues noted above, state law may require disclosure in order to secure informed consent. A prudent health care provider knows he or she may be held accountable if a transmission were to occur, especially if the dentist was aware of the employee's condition. A number of states have adopted laws and regulations concerning an HIV-positive health care worker's responsibility to notify patients and staff. It is important to discuss these issues with your personal attorney to determine your state's requirements, and to weigh the risk of a malpractice/consent suit against a possible charge of discrimination. Your State Board may have specific requirements for you to consider in this regard as well.

Related References and Resources

- Some Laws That Can Affect Dentistry
  ADA.org/DentistGuidetoLaw

- EEOC, Questions and Answers on the Notice of Proposed Rulemaking for the ADA Amendments Act of 2008
  www.eeoc.gov/policy/docs/qanda_adaaa_nprm.html

To minimize the risk of an employment discrimination lawsuit, it is important to consult an attorney prior to terminating or restricting the duties of an employee who has tested positive for a disease such as HIV/AIDS or HCV.

78. Can I Terminate a Staff Person Who Is Continuously on Sick Leave?

Before making a decision to terminate a staff person for excessive absenteeism due to illness, an employer should consider a number of factors, including:

- Whether the staff person is an employee or an independent contractor

- Whether there is a written or oral contract between the employer and the staff person (and if so, what are the terms of the contract)

- The provisions of any applicable policies, procedures, employee handbook or manual (and whether those provisions have been applied consistently with regard to all similarly situated staff persons)

- Whether the individual has exhausted any leave to which he or she is entitled (such as paid or unpaid sick days, vacation, personal days, or any medical leave of absence)

- The facts and circumstances of the staff person's employment (not limited to those that give rise to the employer's wish to terminate)

- Whether those facts and any relevant communications with the staff person have been appropriately documented

- Any applicable laws or regulations such as the Family and Medical Leave Act or similar state medical leave legislation or the Americans with Disabilities Act or state or local disabilities laws, or workers compensation laws (if the sick leave is for a work-related medical condition)

Terminated staff persons sometimes bring lawsuits arguing, for example, that the termination breached a written or oral contract or that the termination was discriminatory or retaliatory. Before making a decision to terminate for excessive absenteeism due to illness, the employer should review any relevant contracts, policies, procedures, handbooks or manuals to determine whether any provisions govern termination, sick leave, leave of absence, absenteeism, and the like. The employer should make sure that the policies and procedures have been communicated to employees and enforced in a consistent and nondiscriminatory manner. The employer should also determine whether progressive discipline has been followed and documented with respect to the excessive absenteeism due to illness. The employer should consider whether the termination is likely to result in a claim of employment discrimination or retaliation.

The employer should also determine whether it has any obligations under the Americans with Disabilities Act or similar state or local laws (for example, to make reasonable accommodations so a disabled employee can return to work or otherwise perform the essential functions of his or her position). Depending upon the particular circumstances, reasonable accommodations may include a temporary change or reduction in the employee's work hours, or time off without pay (even if the employer is not subject to the Family and Medical Leave Act or a state-law version).

Consulting an employment attorney prior to terminating a staff person can help prevent lawsuits (and help defend any lawsuits that do arise).

Related References and Resources

- Question 67: How Should I Handle Employee Discipline?

- Some Laws and Issues that Can Affect Dentistry
  ADA.org/DentistGuidetoLaw

79. Can I Terminate an Employee for Reporting to Authorities What He or She Perceives as a Legal Violation?

Be very careful about terminating an employee for reporting appropriate information to authorities. To encourage employees who know of unlawful activity to feel safe reporting it to authorities, some laws provide specific protection for "whistleblowers." Further, even if an individual is not protected by such a law, and even if the termination was for reasons wholly independent of any report of a violation (real or perceived), an employer may have a difficult time defending a wrongful termination or "retaliation" lawsuit should the whistleblowing become an issue.

To encourage employees who know of unlawful activity to feel safe reporting it to authorities, some laws provide specific protection for "whistleblowers."

Compliance: OSHA, HIPAA, FACTA, COPPA, and the Physician Payments Sunshine Act (Open Payments)

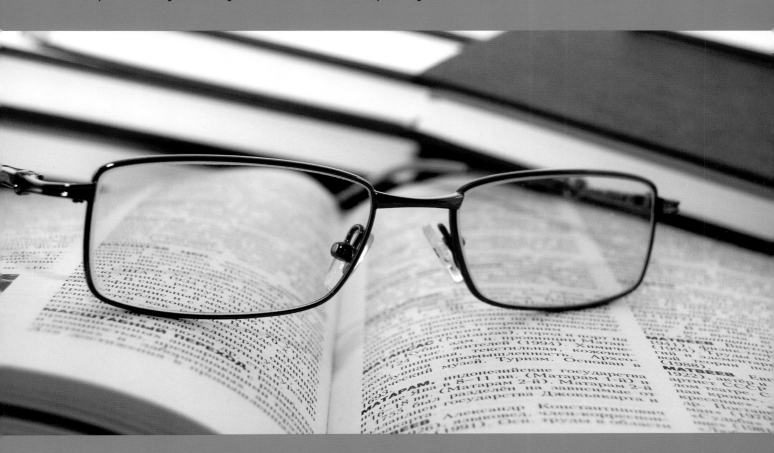

Chapter 14.

OSHA

The practice of dentistry involves many activities that are regulated under the Occupational Safety and Health Act. Despite the fact that small dental offices are not frequently inspected by OSHA compliance officers, it is important for dentists to understand their rights and responsibilities in this area. Failures to comply with OSHA regulations can result in stiff penalties.

The questions below focus on the federal OSHA program. Much of this guidance applies to state OSHA programs as well, but differences do exist. Dentists in states with state-run programs should consult with their state dental societies or their personal attorneys, as appropriate.

Related Resources and References

- Some Laws That Can Affect Dentistry
  ADA.org/DentistGuidetoLaw

- Occupational Safety and Health Administration (OSHA)
  www.osha.gov

- The ADA Practical Guide to OSHA Compliance: Regulatory Compliance Manual
  adacatalog.org or 1.800.947.4746

80. I Am Just a Small Business. Does OSHA Really Apply to Me?

OSHA applies to any employer that has even a single employee. For a professional corporation, the single employee requirement might be met by the dentist/owner who is paid a salary and is considered an "employee" of the corporation. Of course, even a practice operating as a sole proprietorship is covered if, for example, it includes a hygienist or receptionist.

81. I Never Hear From OSHA, But I Do Hear From a State Agency. Why Is That?

OSHA has jurisdiction over about half the states. The other half operate their own OSHA programs. In most cases, state-run programs simply incorporate federal OSHA standards, but procedural rules will vary. Some states have unique safety and health standards. California is one example.

Related References and Resources

- List of OSHA State Plans
  www.osha.gov/dcsp/osp/index.html

82. Does OSHA Regulate My Relationships With My Patients?

No. OSHA only regulates matters affecting the employment relationship. Of course, many safety related issues that affect the employment relationship also affect patients.

83. What Are My Obligations Under OSHA?

Employers have two basic obligations under OSHA. First, employers must comply with the Act's "general duty clause." Second, employers must comply with safety and health standards issued pursuant to the Act.

84. What Is the "General Duty Clause?"

Section 5(a)(1) of the Act requires employers to maintain a workplace "free from recognized hazards that are causing or are likely to cause death or serious physical harm..." This is a catch-all provision, which applies only when there is no specific OSHA standard in place. Ergonomics is one type of hazard presently addressed by OSHA under the general duty clause, because there is no ergonomics standard. A hazard is recognized if the employer or the employer's industry is aware of it or if the hazard is otherwise generally recognized. Thus, a dentist must protect employees not only with respect to issues specifically addressed in standards (such as bloodborne pathogens) but also with respect to any other hazardous condition which is generally understood as posing a risk, or understood by the dentist or the dental profession to pose a risk. A hypothetical example of the "catch-all" provision's scope might be that if an OSHA inspector finds that a coat hook, because of its location within the office and the height at which it is installed, poses a significant risk of eye injury, the inspector may require that the hook be removed.

85. What Is My Duty With Respect to OSHA Standards?

The Act requires employers to comply with applicable safety or health standards. There are hundreds of such standards, many of which could apply to dentistry. Two of the most important standards applicable to dentistry are the bloodborne pathogen and hazard communications standards. Both of these standards require comprehensive written programs to address all aspects of the hazards addressed by each standard. Thus, for example, a dentist's bloodborne pathogen program (known as an exposure control plan) would have to address how the dentist will comply with the standard's requirements for how to respond to an exposure incident involving needle sticks. It would also have to address standard precautions, exposure assessments, how to deal with contaminated laundry and a host of related requirements.

The regulations can change from time to time, so it is important to be aware of OSHA updates. Within the last few years, for example, labeling requirements for certain medical devices and containers have been revised. Another recently added regulation is OSHA's requirement for a written emergency action plan (EAP) for dental offices. EAP compliance is simple, and can be easily accomplished.

The regulations can change from time to time, so it is important to be aware of OSHA updates.

Related References and Resources

- OSHA Emergency Action Plan Standard
  www.osha.gov/pls/oshaWeb/owadisp.show_document?p_id=9726&p_table=STANDARDS

- The ADA Practical Guide to OSHA Compliance: Regulatory Compliance Manual (Contains an Emergency Action Plan Template)
  adacatalog.org or 1.800.947.4746

86. How Do I Prepare Generally for OSHA's Required Written Programs?

There are many resources available to you, such as OSHA online materials, the ADA, consultants, and private attorneys. The ADA offers a number of products to assist dentists in complying with their OSHA obligations. A dentist could also rely upon the standards themselves for guidance, but dentists should understand that these standards may be confusing and may not appear to be helpful, at least not without significant expenditure of effort. OSHA also has sample programs and other guidance, either available at *www.osha.gov* or from the local OSHA Area Office. Finally, a dentist can retain a consultant or an attorney who can prepare a written program tailored specifically to the dentist's office.

87. Do I Have to Voluntarily Let an OSHA Compliance Officer Inspect My Office?

No. OSHA may inspect a workplace only with the consent of the employer or after obtaining a warrant from a court. Thus, an employer is always free to demand a warrant before admitting an OSHA inspector to the office. It is important to understand, however, that it is not particularly difficult for OSHA to obtain a warrant and that voluntary permission may make sense in many, if not most, situations. Demanding that the OSHA inspector obtain a warrant may unnecessarily antagonize the OSHA inspector, who will probably be able to obtain the warrant fairly easily.

88. What Should I Do If an OSHA Inspection of My Office Is Taking Place?

First, find out why the compliance officer is there; he or she has to tell you. Based on what you learn, try to limit the scope of the inspection to the subject of the inspection. In other words, try to prevent the compliance officer from engaging in a fishing expedition.

Second, do not let the compliance officer wander around the office unattended. You have the right to accompany the compliance officer at all times, except during employee interviews.

Third, avoid admitting error or problems. As they say on TV, "What you say can and will be used against you." If the compliance officer points out a potential violation, take note of it and say nothing more than you will look into it. Of course, if the compliance officer points out a simple and obvious problem which can be easily corrected on the spot, do so.

Fourth, listen and take contemporaneous notes. If the compliance officer points out an alleged violation, write it down. If the compliance officer suggests ways to correct a problem, write them down. If the compliance officer makes a statement indicating a lack of understanding, or even bias, write it down. All of this may be useful to you if a citation is issued and you decide to fight it.

Finally, and of the greatest importance, tell the truth. A "panicky" false statement will often get the employer in more trouble than the truth.

Related References and Resources

- Question 90: The Compliance Officer Wants to Interview Me! Do I Agree to Be Interviewed?

89. The Compliance Officer Wants to Interview My Employee, Should I Allow It?

You have no choice on this, but your employee does. An OSHA compliance officer has the right to conduct interviews of employees. Employees, however, are free to refuse or to insist on someone else, including the employer, being present. Be aware that OSHA's very strong preference is for such interviews to be conducted in private. You should be careful to avoid even the suggestion that you are discouraging cooperation by your employees. Instead, in front of the compliance officer, tell the employee that OSHA would like to interview him or her and that you encourage cooperation. Also tell the employee that he or she is free to ask for anyone else to be present during the interview.

90. The Compliance Officer Wants to Interview Me! Do I Agree to Be Interviewed?

It's up to you. Management and ownership have a right to have an attorney present during any OSHA interview. If you are uncomfortable for any reason, simply tell the compliance officer that you need to consult with an advisor before being interviewed. (Of course, you can also simply refuse to be interviewed, but this may cause matters to escalate; the compliance officer may seek to then compel your formal testimony through a subpoena.)

91. No OSHA Compliance Officer Is Trying to Inspect My Office, but OSHA Sent Me a Letter and Expects a Response. What Do I Do?

Investigate and promptly respond to OSHA. Most often, OSHA will not inspect a dental office. Instead, it will send a letter by fax (sometimes preceded by a telephone call) stating that information has been received indicating the presence of a hazardous condition. The letter will also state that an inspection is possible. A dentist receiving such a letter should investigate the underlying facts and promptly send a complete response back to OSHA. If additional time is needed to respond, call the OSHA office before any deadline and ask for a short extension.

92. OSHA Issued a Citation. What Do I Do?

Respond before the deadline. Any employer receiving an OSHA citation has 15 working days to respond. This is construed to mean three weeks, excluding federal holidays. If a dentist has any question whatsoever about when this deadline expires, the dentist should call the OSHA office and ask when the "contest date" is. Make a note of the day and time you call and the name of the person who provided the information. Under no circumstances may this time period be extended.

93. Can I Get an Extension of the 15-Day Period?

No! This is essential to know. This time period is set by statute and OSHA simply has no authority to give an extension. Many employers have made the mistake of ignoring the deadline.

94. What Happens If I Do Nothing?

After 15 days, the citation becomes final and unappealable. The fine, if any, and the obligation to fix any alleged violations are then enforceable by OSHA in court.

95. What Are My Options After Receiving a Citation?

Generally, you have three options. 1. You can do nothing, which means you have accepted the citation, will do what OSHA says and pay any fine. 2. You can schedule an "informal conference." Or, 3. You can send a "notice of contest."

An "informal conference", option 2, is a chance to meet at the local OSHA offices to try to settle the citation. Typically, OSHA will reduce the proposed penalty at such a conference. It is also possible that parts of the citation could be altered or even dropped altogether. If agreement is reached, OSHA will prepare an "informal settlement agreement" setting forth the terms agreed upon. Scheduling an informal conference does not extend the fifteen-day period for responding to the citation. Any party may be represented by counsel at an informal conference.

Your third option is to send a "notice of contest" within 15 working days of receiving a citation. This is simply a letter stating that the employer wishes to contest, or appeal, the citation. This is the only way, other than a settlement agreement, to prevent the citation from becoming final.

The notice of contest is a letter, addressed to the local OSHA Area Director, as indicated in the papers accompanying the citation. It should list the OSHA citation number or numbers — there may be more than one (from the citation) and state that the employer is contesting the citation or parts of it. In general, when in doubt about what to contest, the safer course is to contest the entire citation, each item listed in the citation, the proposed penalties, the abatement dates, the proposed abatements and all things subject to contest. The notice of contest must be sent before the fifteen-day deadline (or "contest date"). Hand deliver the contest, if convenient, or fax it and mail a copy by registered mail.

Upon receipt of a notice of contest, the local OSHA office loses jurisdiction. No informal conference can be held. Instead, the file will be sent to OSHA's lawyers who will file a formal complaint with the Occupational Safety and Health Review Commission. An administrative law judge will be assigned to the case and it will proceed through the Commission in a manner similar to a civil lawsuit. In the meantime, the employer does not need to pay the penalty or take other steps to satisfy the requirements of the citation.

96. Do I Need a Lawyer?

Depending on the level of knowledge of the dentist or dental office staff, as well as the time available to devote to compliance, a dentist may wish to consult a knowledgeable attorney or consultant to assist with program development and other compliance issues. Legal guidance from an attorney familiar with OSHA procedures can also be helpful in the event of an inspection or to prepare a response to a letter or citation.

A dentist may be represented by an attorney at an informal conference and at proceedings before the Review Commission. Although a dentist is not required to have an attorney present at an informal conference or a Review Commission proceeding, it is a good idea to consult with an attorney in advance, and to consider having an attorney present during either of these proceedings, particularly if the dentist is not very familiar with the procedures and requirements involved.

Although a dentist is not required to have an attorney present at an informal conference or a Review Commission proceeding, it is a good idea to consult with an attorney in advance, and to consider having an attorney present during either of these proceedings, particularly if the dentist is not very familiar with the procedures and requirements involved.

Chapter 15.

HIPAA, State Law and PCIDSS: Patient Information

Dental practices collect, use and disclose information about patients in order to provide good patient care and to do the business of dentistry. Dental practices must decide which information to collect, record the information properly, secure the information, and determine how the information can be used and disclosed. Not surprisingly, these activities are governed by federal and state laws. But protecting patient information is not just required by law; it is also good risk management and the right thing to do.

97. How Does HIPAA Affect How I Manage Patient Information?

If a dental practice meets the HIPAA definition of a "covered entity" or "business associate," the dental practice risks substantial penalties if the dental practice is not in compliance with the four HIPAA Rules. There is also a risk of reputational harm, since the federal government makes public certain data breaches and violations through online postings or media releases. A dental practice that has agreed contractually to comply with HIPAA (for example, in a participating provider agreement) risks liability under the contract for failure to comply.

The Four HIPAA Rules

Dental practices that are covered by HIPAA must comply with the HIPAA Privacy Rule, Security Rule, Breach Notification Rule and Enforcement Rule, and also with applicable state laws that are more stringent than HIPAA. Some of the requirements of the various HIPAA Rules overlap. For example, the Privacy and Security Rules both require a covered dental practice to designate personnel to be responsible for certain HIPAA-related tasks, to have written policies and procedures in place, to train workforce members and document the training, and to apply appropriate sanctions if a workforce member fails to comply. Both the Privacy and Security Rules require compliant written agreements with "business associates," which are generally defined as outside entities and individuals who do something for or on behalf of the dental practice that requires access to patient information.

Here are examples of requirements in each of the HIPAA rules:

The Privacy Rule applies to patient information in any format, such as electronic, hard copy (e.g., paper, films, and other physical items) and oral. It also:

- Gives patients certain rights over their information, such as the right to see information and obtain a copy, the right to an accounting of disclosures of their information, and the right to ask for changes to the information. Each of these rights has certain limitations. A dental practice that does not comply with the rules on patient rights can be subject to penalties.

- Tells a covered dental practice when HIPAA permits patient information to be used or disclosed without getting the patient's written authorization.

- Includes certain other standards and requirements to protect patient privacy, such as the "minimum necessary rule," which generally requires using, disclosing and requesting the minimum amount of patient information necessary for the purpose of the use, disclosure or request.

The Security Rule applies only to electronic patient information. The Security Rule requires covered dental practices to assess the risks to the confidentiality, integrity and availability of patient information and document the risk assessment, and to update the risk assessment as appropriate (for example, when the dental practice buys new technology or learns of a new risk). The Security Rule requires covered dental practices to have certain safeguards in place to protect electronic patient information.

The Breach Notification Rule requires covered dental practices to notify affected individuals, the federal government, and in some cases the media, of any breach of unsecured patient information, unless the dental practice can demonstrate that there is a low probability that the information is compromised by performing a written analysis of all relevant factors, including four required factors. Many states have adopted breach notification laws that may impose breach notification obligations on dental practices whether or not the dental practice is covered by HIPAA, and whether or not the breached information is patient information. For example, a state breach notification law may apply to a breach of a Social Security number that a dental practice has collected from an employee. Some breaches may require notification under both HIPAA and state law.

The Enforcement Rule contains provisions relating to government investigations, penalties for HIPAA violations, and procedures for hearings. For example, the Enforcement Rule requires covered dental practices to cooperate with investigations and compliance reviews, and to permit the U.S. Department of Health and Human Services to access to the dental practice's facilities, books, records, accounts and other sources of information, including patient information, that are pertinent to ascertaining compliance with HIPAA.

Related References and Resources

- Question 98: Do I Have to Comply With HIPAA?

- ADA Resources on HIPAA Privacy and Security
  ADA.org/HIPAA

- The HIPAA/HITECH Breach Notification Rule
  ADA.org/en/member-center/member-benefits/legal-resources/publications-and-articles/hipaa-and-data-security/the-hipaa-hitech-breach-notification-rule

- ADA Center for Professional Success
  success.ada.org/en

- U.S. Department of Health and Human Services Office for Civil Rights Health Information Privacy
  www.hhs.gov/ocr/privacy

- OCR, The HIPAA Enforcement Rule
  www.hhs.gov/ocr/privacy/hipaa/administrative/enforcementrule/index.html.

98. Do I Have to Comply With HIPAA?

Yes, if you are a HIPAA "covered entity" or "business associate," or if you have agreed in a contract to comply with HIPAA.

A dental practice is a HIPAA covered entity if the practice has sent patient information electronically using a format established by the HIPAA transaction standards (or if another entity has done so on behalf of the dental practice). Many dental practices become covered by HIPAA when they submit claims electronically or have a billing company do so on their behalf.

The submission of an electronic claim is often the transmission that makes a dental practice subject to HIPAA. HIPAA applies to dental practices that have submitted claims electronically or have used other HIPAA regulated electronic transactions, like eligibility inquiries and claim status inquiries. HIPAA also applies to entirely paper dental offices that submit paper claims to a billing service that converts the paper into electronic format and submits the claims to a dental plan electronically for the dental practice. The simple use of a typical, stand-alone fax machine by an otherwise all paper office does not trigger HIPAA, because traditional (e.g., non-digital) faxes are not HIPAA standard transactions.

A dental practice must also comply with HIPAA if it is a "business associate" of a HIPAA covered entity. HIPAA generally defines "business associate" as an outside individual or entity that does something for or on behalf of a covered entity that involves access to patient information.

Both covered and non-covered dental offices may bind themselves contractually to comply with HIPAA (for example, by signing a participating provider agreement with an insurance company that requires HIPAA compliance).

Dentists who are not HIPAA covered entities must comply with applicable state laws, such as state patient privacy and data security laws. Covered dental practices must comply with both HIPAA and with applicable state laws that are more stringent than HIPAA (e.g., where a state requires notification of a breach in a shorten time period than allowed under HIPAA). A qualified attorney can help determine which laws apply to a dental practice, and how appropriately to comply with those laws.

Related References and Resources

- CMS, Are You a Covered Entity?
  www.cms.gov/Regulations-and-Guidance/HIPAA-Administrative-Simplification/HIPAAGenInfo/AreYouaCoveredEntity.html

- CMS, Covered Entity Charts
  www.cms.gov/Regulations-and-Guidance/HIPAA-Administrative-Simplification/HIPAAGenInfo/Downloads/CoveredEntitycharts.pdf

99. What Do I Have to Do in Order to Comply With HIPAA's Privacy Rule?

Some of the key requirements of the Privacy Rule are:

- Designate a "privacy official" for your dental practice

- Develop and implement appropriate written privacy policies and procedures

- Have in place appropriate administrative, technical, and physical safeguards to protect the privacy of patient information in all formats (e.g., electronic, paper, and oral)

- Develop the necessary documents, such as the Notice of Privacy Practices (NPP) (and acknowledgment of receipt of the NPP), and business associate agreements.

- Provide your NPP to patients on their first visit, and ask them to sign written acknowledgement that they received your NPP. Prominently display your NPP in your office and make copies available to patients upon request.

- Obtain written patient authorization prior to any use or disclosure not permitted by HIPAA

- Respond appropriately if a patient exercises his or her rights under HIPAA; e.g., by requesting an accounting of disclosure, access to records, an amendment to records, for confidential communications, or for restricted disclosures. Each of these patient rights has certain limitations and requirements.

- Adhere to HIPAA's "minimum necessary" rule. When patient information must be used, disclosed, or requested, limit the information to the minimum necessary for the purpose of the use, disclosure or request (the minimum necessary rule does not apply to disclosures for treatment purposes).

- Implement reasonable safeguards to limit incidental uses or disclosures of patient information that result from any use or disclosure permitted under the Privacy Rule

- Train your staff about your office's privacy policies and procedures and document the training. Apply appropriate sanctions for violations of your policies and procedures, and document any sanctions applied.

- Enter into compliant business associate agreements

- Maintain documentation of HIPAA compliance for the time period required under HIPAA. Each document must be retained for at least six years from the date of the document's creation, or at least six years from the date when it is no longer in effect, whichever is later.

Note: Keep in mind that HIPAA's privacy rule covers more than just the traditional written patient record. It extends protection to information about the patient, including demographic information, that identifies (or that could be used to identify) the patient and that pertains to the patient's past, present or future:

- Physical or mental health

- Health care

- Payment for health care

This can include records such as patient charts and billing records, and includes information in any format, such as paper, photos and films, oral information, and electronic information.

Related References and Resources

- Question 121: What Effect Did the 2013 Ominbus Final Rule Have on HIPAA Compliance?

- *The ADA Practical Guide to HIPAA Compliance: Privacy and Security Manual* *adacatalog.org* or 1.800.947.4746

100. If I Give a New Patient Our Notice of Privacy Practices and the Patient Won't Sign the HIPAA Acknowledgement, Should I Still Provide Treatment?

You cannot refuse to provide care solely because a patient refuses to sign the form. Your obligation is to make a good faith effort to secure patient acknowledgment of receipt of your Notice of Privacy Practices. If the patient signs the form you are good to go. However, patients have a right not to sign the form, and you should not refuse treatment simply because they exercise that right. If the patient refuses to sign the acknowledgement form, you must document your good faith effort and the reason why acknowledgement was not obtained.

101. Is Following HIPAA Enough, or Should I Follow State Law (Too)?

Both federal and state law may come into play when it comes to managing patient information. The federal HIPAA law requires covered entity dental practices to take a number of steps to protect patient privacy and the security of electronic protected health information, to control the use and disclosure of protected health information (PHI) (that is to say, a patient's individually identifiable information), and in the case of a breach of unsecured patient information, to provide notice to affected individuals, the federal government, and in some cases the media.

HIPAA establishes a federal "floor" for covered dental practices and states are free to enact more stringent standards than those established by HIPAA. A covered dental practice must comply with both HIPAA and with any more stringent state laws (e.g., where a state requires notification of a breach in a shorten time period than required by HIPAA). Dental practices that are not HIPAA covered entities must comply with applicable state laws, such as privacy and data security laws. Many such laws have been around for years (for example, some states require patient consent to release health care information, even for consultation with another health care provider).

A qualified attorney can provide guidance on compliance with HIPAA and state privacy statutes. State dental societies may also have information about applicable state laws.

102. Can the Outside Cover of the Record Contain Patient Information?

Displaying patient information on the outside cover of a patient's chart can make that information accessible to unauthorized individuals. Using the cover to display only the patient's name or the account number, unless more is required by state law, can help prevent impermissible disclosures. Flagging a chart on the outside cover, using an abstract, in-office system (color or symbol coding), can help restrict information about patients to the office staff members trained to decipher the flag. A flag or sticker on the outside cover can alert the team to look on the inside for important information regarding allergies, medications, antibiotic pre-medications, and clinical conditions that might affect dental treatment.

103. Who Can Make Entries in the Record?

The dentist is ultimately responsible for the patient's chart, and often takes on the responsibility of making record entries. Some entries may be delegated to office staff if allowed by state law. A dentist who opts not to make his or her own entries should dictate the entries to the assistant.

104. Are There Rules About How to Write in the Record?

Yes. Applicable laws may require certain entries in the record and may dictate how entries should be written. In addition, it is important to keep in mind that the record is an important source of evidence in a liability claim. Always think before you make an entry, especially if the remarks are complex in nature. But don't delay. It is best to document while the patient is still in the office or shortly thereafter.

Make sure all of your entries are objective in nature. Record what happened. Confine your comments to necessary information about the patient's treatment. Do not make unnecessary comments. Under HIPAA and many state laws, a patient has a right to request to see his or her record (including "personal notes" you may keep in a separate chart). If the record ever appears in a court case, disparaging remarks could alienate the judge and the jury.

Always think before you make an entry, especially if the remarks are complex in nature. But don't delay. It is best to document while the patient is still in the office or shortly thereafter.

105. Is It OK to Alter the Record?

There are times when it is appropriate to make a correction in the record. There is nothing wrong with a correction if handled properly. Unless state law dictates the specifics of what must be done, a prudent approach is to append corrections to the record. If you remember something you wish to record at a later date, just make the entry chronologically, and refer to the date of the visit in question. In contrast, altering or concealing a record could make it appear that you have hidden the truth. Do not delete or obliterate an entry by using markers or "white-out" on paper records. Some states may allow you to use a thin line to simply cross out the erroneous entry and make the appropriate change. Date and initial the change. The important factor is that the original wrong entry must still be readable.

HIPAA covered dental practices must comply with HIPAA regulations concerning patients who request an amendment to a record.

106. Who Owns the Record? What Rights Do Patients Have?

Ownership of the record is governed by state law. In many states, the dentist owns the physical record of the patient. This includes radiographs.

Nevertheless, patients have numerous rights concerning their dental records under HIPAA and certain state laws. For example, with limited exceptions, HIPAA gives patients the right to inspect and obtain copies of their records. The dental team should be trained to comply with applicable law, such as laws governing when and how patients have the right to access their records.

Related References and Resources

- *The ADA Practical Guide to HIPAA Compliance: Privacy and Security Manual*
adacatalog.org or 1.800.947.4746

Ownership of the record is governed by state law. In many states, the dentist owns the physical record of the patient. This includes radiographs.

107. What Permission, if Any, Must a Patient Give for Me to Transfer His or Her Records?

This depends on several factors, such as whether your dental practice is covered by HIPAA, the requirements of your state law, and the specifics of the situation.

Transfers to the patient. HIPAA permits covered dental practices to disclose patient information for certain purposes without obtaining the patient's written authorization. For example, with very limited exceptions, patients have the right to see and get copies of their records. HIPAA permits a covered dental practice to require such requests to be in writing as long as the dental practice informs individuals of this requirement.

Transfers to a person designated by the patient. If a patient asks a covered dental practice to send a copy of the patient's information directly to another person, the request must be in writing, signed by the patient, and must clearly identify the designated person and where to send the copy of the patient's information. The covered dental practice must provide the copy to the person designated by the individual.

Permitted disclosures. HIPAA does not require covered dental practices to obtain the patient's authorization in order to disclose a patient's information for certain purposes, such as treatment, payment or health care operations (as defined by HIPAA). Disclosures generally must be limited to the "minimum necessary" amount of information that must be shared in order to accomplish the intended purpose of the disclosure. However, the minimum necessary rule does not apply to disclosures for treatment purposes.

Patient authorization. If a disclosure is not "permitted" by HIPAA, a covered dental practice must obtain "valid authorization" from the patient (or the patient's personal representative). For example, if a covered dental practice wanted to use a full face photo of a patient on the dental practice website, the dental practice may first need a valid authorization. The valid authorization must be in writing and must contain certain information specified in the HIPAA Privacy Rule.

State law. States may have more stringent requirements that may apply whether or not a dental practice is covered by HIPAA. For example, state law may require patient consent before a dental practice transfers the patient's records to another health care provider. All dental practices whether or not covered by HIPAA, must comply with applicable state law.

Restricted disclosure. HIPAA also gives patients the right to ask a covered dental practice to restrict disclosure of their records. A covered dental practice is generally not required to agree to such a request; however, a covered dental practice must agree if a patient asks the practice not to disclosure information to a health plan for purposes of payment or health care operations as long as the dental practice has been paid in full for the item or service from a source other than the health plan.

Recording transfers. Making a notation in the patient's chart as to the date, where, and to whom copies were sent facilitates collection of this information if necessary at a later date. For example, HIPAA covered dental practices are required to provide an accounting of certain disclosures of patient information if requested by a patient or the patient's personal representative. With certain exceptions, the accounting must include disclosures made during the prior six years and need not include certain disclosures, such as disclosures made for treatment, payment, or health care operations (as defined by the HIPAA).

108. How Does HIPAA Affect Dealing with Patient Surrogates or Representatives Who Request Information in, or Copies of, the Record (Such as Non-Custodial Parents)?

Parents

HIPAA generally allows parents to have access to the dental records of their children, unless such access is inconsistent with state law. If you are dealing with minor children, HIPAA defers to state law to determine who is the "personal representative" authorized to access and make decisions about the minor's protected health information (PHI). If two parents who are not married are involved in a dispute over access to information about their child's health care, you should defer to your state's law. If there is a court order that establishes custodial or parental rights, including rights to the child's health information, it would be a good idea for you to request a copy of that order before proceeding to disclose.

There are situations when a child's parent may not be considered a minor's personal representative under HIPAA, such as when a minor obtains health care at the direction of a court. However, even in such exceptional situations, state law may require or permit parental access. According to the Office for Civil Rights (the federal agency that administers HIPAA):

> If State or other applicable law is silent on a parent's right of access in these cases, the licensed health care provider may exercise his or her professional judgment to the extent allowed by law to grant or deny parental access to the minor's medical information.

Finally, as is the case with respect to all personal representatives under the Privacy Rule, a provider may choose not to treat a parent as a personal representative when the provider reasonably believes, in his or her professional judgment, that the child has been or may be subjected to domestic violence, abuse or neglect, or that treating the parent as the child's personal representative could endanger the child.

HIPAA generally allows parents to have access to the dental records of their children, unless such access is inconsistent with state law. If you are dealing with minor children, HIPAA defers to state law to determine who is the "personal representative" authorized to access and make decisions about the minor's protected health information (PHI).

Family, Friends and Others

If a person other than the patient's personal representative brings the patient in for an appointment, it is sometimes less clear whether the patient's health information may be discussed with that person. Generally, it would be best to obtain permission from the legal representative before talking to a third party about patient's health care. However, the U.S. Department of Health and Human Services Office for Civil Rights has stated:

> If the patient is present and has the capacity to make health care decisions, a health care provider may discuss the patient's health information with a family member, friend, or other person if the patient agrees or, when given the opportunity, does not object. A health care provider also may share information with these persons if, using professional judgment, he or she decides that the patient does not object. In either case, the health care provider may share or discuss only the information that the person involved needs to know about the patient's care or payment for care...

> If the patient is not present or is incapacitated, a health care provider may share the patient's information with family, friends, or others as long as the health care provider determines, based on professional judgment that it is in the best interest of the patient. When someone other than a friend or family member is involved, the health care provider must be reasonably sure that the patient asked the person to be involved in his or her care or payment for care. The health care provider may discuss only the information that the person involved needs to know about the patient's care or payment.

Personal Representatives

HIPAA defers to state law to determine when an individual is a patient's personal representative. Unless the patient is an unemancipated minor, an adult for whom a court has appointed a guardian, or an individual for whom another person has been legally designated to make health care decisions on his or her behalf, the patient generally has the right to make decisions about his or her health information, even if the patient has a disability or communication difficulties. Of course, if you feel that it would be helpful to involve a family member or friend in discussions of the patient's health information, ask the patient if this would be acceptable and proceed if the patient agrees. However, never assume that merely because a patient is older or is facing some challenges it is permissible to disclose that patient's health information to a relative, friend or caregiver. In an emergency or other unusual situation in which the patient is incapacitated or not present, dentists can use their professional judgment to determine whether it would be in the patient's best interest to disclose a limited amount of the patient's health information that is directly related to the person's involvement with the patient's care.

Related References and Resources

- OCR, Does the HIPAA Privacy Rule Allow Parents the Right to See Their Children's Medical Records? *www.hhs.gov/ocr/privacy/hipaa/faq/right_to_access_medical_records/227.html*

- OCR, Personal Representatives *www.hhs.gov/ocr/privacy/hipaa/understanding/coveredentities/personalreps.html*

- OCR, Communicating with a Patient's Family, Friends, or Others Involved in the Patient's Care *www.hhs.gov/ocr/privacy/hipaa/understanding/coveredentities/provider_ffg.pdf*

109. What If the Patient's Spouse, or an Adult Patient's Parent, Is Responsible for Paying the Patient's Bill? What Information Can I Disclose to the Person Responsible for Payment?

Generally, as little as necessary for the purpose of the disclosure, which is payment. HIPAA does not require health care providers to obtain patient authorization before disclosing patient information for payment purposes, as long as the disclosure is limited to the minimum amount of information necessary for the purpose of the disclosure. In making such disclosures, health care providers also must honor any reasonable request by the patient for confidential communications. Moreover, if a covered dental practice has agreed to any restriction on the use or disclosure of the patient's information, the dental practice must honor such restriction as well. Keep in mind that HIPAA now requires a covered dental practice to agree to a request to restrict disclosure to a health plan for purposes of payment or healthcare operations as long as the dental practice has been paid in full from a source other than the health plan. Your Notice of Privacy Practices can state that if a patient designates another person as responsible for payment, you will disclose the minimum amount of patient information necessary to obtain payment from that person. A patient who objects to a disclosure for payment purposes may need to choose between allowing you to disclose information in order to obtain payment, or paying for the services out of pocket. Finally, covered dental practices must comply with applicable state law that is more stringent than HIPAA. A dental practice that is not covered by HIPAA must comply with applicable state law on this issue.

110. Someone Has Subpoenaed a Patient's Record. What Should I Do?

Check with a qualified attorney about what is required. Under HIPAA, there are certain times when a covered dental practice is permitted to disclose patient information in response to a subpoena without first obtaining the patient's authorization.

If the form of the subpoena is not listed in the HIPAA provision on permitted disclosures, or if the subpoena is insufficient under applicable state law, your attorney may advise you to ask your patient to sign a HIPAA valid authorization allowing you to release the information to the party requesting it. In some states, specific items may need to be included in an authorization or consent form.

HIPAA does not preempt more stringent state law, so even if HIPAA would permit a disclosure in response to a subpoena, applicable state law may prohibit the disclosure. A qualified attorney can provide information about both HIPAA and applicable state law.

111. Should I Release Original Records or Is It Better to Make Copies?

Do not release original records to anyone. There is one exception: if you are required to do so by a government agency with proper authority, such as a court order, or in some states, a subpoena. If this situation occurs, you should make copies of the original records for your office.

112. Can I Charge Patients for Copying Their Records?

Unless limited by state law, a HIPAA covered dental practice may impose a "reasonable, cost-based fee." This fee must be limited to the cost of supplies for and labor of copying, the cost of postage (if the patient agrees that the copies are to be mailed), and the cost of preparing an explanation or summary of the records, if the patient agreed in advance to receive a summary or explanation of the records and has agreed in advance to the fee for its preparation. Note that pursuant to HIPAA, covered dental practices may not charge for time spent locating, searching or retrieving records. In addition, state law may also address what can be charged for copies of records. If applicable state law requires dentists to provide copies at a lower cost or no cost, dentists must follow state law.

A dental practice that provides an electronic copy may charge a reasonable, cost-based fee, and the fee can include certain costs associated with labor and supplies for creating an electronic copy, including the cost of electronic media (for example, a blank CD-ROM or USB drive) if the patient agrees to receive the copy on electronic media supplied by the dental office. However, the dental practice may not include fees associated with maintaining systems, retrieval cost, or the infrastructure costs in the fee charged for electronic copying. When providing electronic copies, the fee may include the labor for copying the information, but not the labor cost of retrieving the information. The labor costs may include skilled technical staff time spent to create and copy an electronic file such as compiling, extracting, scanning and burning the information to the electronic media and distributing the media.

Keep in mind that the HIPAA provision that gives patients the right to see and get copies of their records does not permit a dental practice to refuse to release a patient's record just because a dental bill has not been paid.

Dental practices that are not HIPAA covered entities must comply with applicable state law.

113. How Long Must I Retain Patient Records?

There is no one-size-fits-all answer, and a number of factors may come into play. State laws generally specify the time following the last patient visit that records must be maintained. There is usually a different requirement for the retention of records of children; in many states, those records must be kept for a certain period after the child reaches the age of majority. Your malpractice carrier may have recommendations about retention, perhaps suggesting that you keep records even longer than the minimum required by law.

In the event of the sale of a dental practice, state law may specify the obligations of buyer and seller regarding record ownership, maintenance and retention. The contract between the buyer and seller may spell out the terms for record retention and access (for example, the selling dentist may request access to records for a specified period of time). Of course, such an arrangement would reflect the contractual obligations of the parties and would not relieve either party of legal obligations under state law.

There is usually a different requirement for the retention of records of children; in many states, those records must be kept for a certain period after the child reaches the age of majority.

114. Are There Legal Issues in Making the Transition to a Paperless Office?

Yes. Electronic patient records are an increasingly common practice management tool and can offer certain advantages over paper records. Nevertheless, the transition to "paperless records" is not seamless, totally safe or problem-free, and may not eliminate the need to keep paper records due to legal requirements in some states. A number of legal issues may arise in connection with electronic records, such as:

- Selecting an EHR vendor

- Negotiating contract terms for acquiring technology

- HIPAA business associate agreements

- Complying with HIPAA Security or applicable state data security law

- Using appropriate encryption to secure data

- Breach notification requirements

- Providing electronic copies of patient records

- Insurance coverage for data security incidents

115. What Are the Legal Concerns in Selecting an EHR Vendor? In Entering Into a Contract with Your Chosen EHR Vendor?

Adopting an Electronic Health Record (EHR) is a complicated process — often one of the larger challenges that a dental practice will face. Selection of the right system is critical, and time spent on due diligence will be time well spent. You will want to consider a number of factors (e.g., the track record and reliability of the vendor, whether the platform works well with those third party payers to whom you will be supplying information for payment purposes).

The federal government also provides useful resources with respect to negotiation of the contract with your vendor, such as the Health Resources and Services Administration's (part of the U.S. Health and Human Services) (see Related References and Resources below). Your EHR vendor will almost certainly be your HIPAA "business associate," so make sure that they are willing to sign an appropriate Business Associate Agreement. Finally, considering that this is generally a large financial investment (as well as a large investment of staff time), it would be wise to have your attorney review the vendor's proposed contract. Remember, despite any promises made by sales personnel or in sales material, it's what is in the contract that you sign that will likely control the vendor's and your obligations, so make sure that any promises that you receive (e.g., interoperability, connection to HIEs, support and maintenance, pricing, upgrades, training) are clearly, fully and accurately addressed in the contract.

A dental practice that is negotiating the purchase of technology such as electronic health records should carefully consider the terms of the purchase agreement before signing. A qualified attorney can explain various contract terms and associated risks. Examples of contractual terms that could involve costs or risks to the dental practice include indemnification and insurance provisions, terms of support or service, and provisions concerning what happens if the agreement is terminated.

HIPAA Business Associates

An EHR vendor or support company may meet the definition of a HIPAA "business associate." In general, a HIPAA business associate is an outside individual or entity that performs a service for or on behalf of a covered entity involving access to patient information. HIPAA requires a covered dental practice to have a compliant "business associate agreement" in place before permitting a business associate to access patient information.

The HIPAA Security Rule

The HIPAA Security Rule may require a covered dental practice that intends to purchase technology to take certain compliance steps. For example, the Security Rule requires covered dental practices to conduct a written risk assessment and to update the risk assessment as necessary, and to implement and document certain safeguards to protect electronic patient information. The Security Rule also requires a covered dental practice to take other steps such as training workforce members to comply with the dental practice's security policies and procedures (and document the training).

Securing Data Through Appropriate Encryption

Dentists with electronic records should consider securing electronic data through the use of appropriate encryption, both for data "at rest" and data "in transit." Encryption can help protect patient information from unauthorized access. Moreover, a HIPAA covered dental practice is not required to provide breach notification if properly encrypted patient information is lost, stolen, or accessed by an unauthorized individual as long as the encryption key is not compromised. State data breach laws may also provide that breach notification is not required for encrypted data.

Breach Notification

The HIPAA Breach Notification Rule requires covered dental practices to notify patients, the U.S. Department of Health and Human Services, and, in some cases, the media of a breach of unsecured patient information, whether the information was in electronic, hard copy, or oral format. Notice to patients must be provided without unreasonable delay and in no case later than 60 days after discovery of the breach. Covered dental practices must have written breach notification policies and procedures, and must train workforce members to comply. Covered dental practices must comply with state breach notification laws that are more stringent than HIPAA, or that are not contrary to HIPAA. A dental practice that is not covered by HIPAA must comply with applicable state breach notification laws.

A dental practice transitioning to electronic patient records may need to update existing breach notification policies and procedures and training to take into account the risks and requirements of the new technology.

Electronic Copies of Patient Records

HIPAA allows patients to request access to their patient information in electronic form if the dental practice is covered by HIPAA and maintains the patient records electronically. A dental practice transitioning to electronic patient records may need to determine how best to respond to such a request.

Insurance Coverage for Data Security Incidents

A dental practice's general liability policy may not cover liability for data security incidents. Some insurance companies offer "cyberliability" policies that provide some coverage in this area. Whether or not a dental practice chooses to purchase such coverage, the dental practice may find that even simply investigating and applying for cyberliability coverage can help the dental practice better understand cybersecurity risks and ways to decrease the likelihood of a data security incident.

Related References and Resources

- Appendix 11: Sample Business Associate Agreement

- HIPAA Privacy and Security
  ADA.org/HIPAA

- FAQ on HIPAA Business Associates
  ADA.org/en/home-cps/practice/operations/regulatory/faqs-on-hipaa-business-associates

- HIPAA Business Associates: Am I One?
  ADA.org/en/home-cps/practice/operations/regulatory/hipaa-business-associates-am-i-one

- HIPAA Security Rule FAQ
  ADA.org/en/member-center/member-benefits/legal-resources/publications-and-articles/hipaa-and-data-security/hipaa-security-rule-faq

- How HIPAA Can Apply to You; How to Comply if it Does
  ADA.org/en/member-center/member-benefits/legal-resources/publications-and-articles/hipaa-and-data-security/how-hipaa-can-apply-to-you-how-to-comply-if-it-does

- OCR, HIPAA Security Rule, including a link to a HIPAA Security Risk Assessment Tool
  www.hhs.gov/ocr/privacy/hipaa/administrative/securityrule/index.html

- The HIPAA/HITECH Breach Notification Rule
  ADA.org/en/member-center/member-benefits/legal-resources/publications-and-articles/hipaa-and-data-security/the-hipaa-hitech-breach-notification-rule

- OCR, Breach Notification Rule
  www.hhs.gov/ocr/privacy/hipaa/administrative/breachnotificationrule/index.html

- OCR, Health Information Privacy: Business Associates
  www.hhs.gov/ocr/privacy/hipaa/understanding/coveredentities/businessassociates.html

- OCR, Health Information Privacy: Sample Business Associate Agreement Provisions
  www.hhs.gov/ocr/privacy/hipaa/understanding/coveredentities/contractprov.html

- OCR, EHR Contracts: Key Contract Terms for Users to Understand
  www.healthit.gov/sites/default/files/ehr_contracting_terms_final_508_compliant.pdf

- *The ADA Practical Guide to HIPAA Compliance: Privacy and Security Manual*
  adacatalog.org or 1.800.947.4746

- HRSA, How to Select an EHR Vendor *http://www.hrsa.gov/healthit/toolbox/healthitimplementation/implementationtopics/selectcertifiedehr/selectacertifiedehr_7.html*

- HRSA, EHR Contracts: Key Contract Terms for Users to Understand
  http://www.healthit.gov/providers-professionals/implementation-resources/ehr-contracts-key-contract-terms-users-understand

116. Can I Get in Trouble If My Business Associate Violates HIPAA?

If your dental practice is covered by HIPAA, then vendors who have access to patient information must also comply with HIPAA. HIPAA calls these vendors "business associates." Examples of business associates include accounting firms, lawyers, document disposal companies, tech firms — provided they have access to identifiable information about your patients. A covered dental practice must enter into compliant "business associate agreements" with each of the dental practice's business associates.

Here are some ways that a dental practice can be implicated if a business associate violates HIPAA:

If there's an agency relationship. A covered dental practice can be directly liable for the HIPAA violations of a business associate if the business associate is deemed to be an "agent" of the dental practice. Whether or not the business associate is deemed to be an agent depends on the facts, and will take into consideration the terms of the agreement with the business associate and the extent of the dental practice's control over the business associate (the more control, the more likely that an agency relationship will be found).

If the dental practice knew of the violation. Whether or not the business associate is an agent of the dental practice, if the dental practice knows that the business association is in violation of HIPAA, the dental practice must take reasonable steps to end the violation, and if that is not successful, the dental practice must terminate the business associate agreement, if that is feasible. The dental practice must also take steps to mitigate harm resulting from the violation. A dental practice may be deemed in violation of HIPAA if it knows of a business associate's HIPAA violation and fails to take the necessary steps.

Breach notification. If a business associate discovers a breach of unsecured patient information, HIPAA requires the business associate to notify the covered dental practice. The dental practice is responsible for notifying affected individuals, the federal government, and, in some cases, the media. A covered dental practice is in violation of HIPAA if the dental practice fails to provide timely notification after being notified by a business associate of a reportable breach. "Timely" notification can depend on the circumstances:

- If the covered dental practice discovers the breach, the dental practice must provide notice without unreasonable delay, and in no case later than 60 calendar days after discovery of the breach (note that state law may require faster notice and may apply whether or not the practice is covered by HIPAA)

- If a business associate discovers the breach, *and the business associate is not an agent of the covered dental practice,* then the business associate must notify the dental practice of the breach without unreasonable delay and in no case later than 60 calendar days after discovering the breach. The dental practice must, in turn, provide notification to the affected patients, the federal government,[13] and, in some cases the media, without unreasonable delay, and in no cases later than 60 days after learning of the breach from the business associate. Therefore, a total of 120 calendar days may elapse between the business associate discovering the breach and the dental practice providing notice, provided the delay is reasonable (and again, unless state law requires faster notice; state law may apply whether or not the dental practice is covered by HIPAA).

---

[13] This timeframe applies to breaches affecting 500 or more individuals. However, if a breach of unsecured protected health information affects fewer than 500 individuals, the covered dental practice is required to notify the federal government of the breach within 60 days of the end of the calendar year in which the breach was discovered, although the dental practice may choose to report the breach to the federal government sooner. State law may require a dental practice to notify a state government official of a breach, whether or not the dental practice is covered by HIPAA.

- However, *if the business associate is deemed to be an agent of the covered dental practice,* then the dental practice must provide notification to patients, the federal government,[13] and, in some cases, the media, without unreasonable delay and in no case later than 60 calendar days *after the business associate discovered the breach.* Therefore, it may be prudent for a dental practice to negotiate a provision in the business associate agreement requiring the business associate to provide prompt notice of any security incident or suspected breach, particularly if the business associate may be deemed to be an agent of the dental practice.

HIPAA does not require covered dental practices to conduct due diligence when selecting business associates, but a prudent dental practice may wish to conduct proper due diligence to help determine whether a business associate is likely to protect the dental practice's patient information. Examples of due diligence questions that a dental practice might ask a potential business associate include "Is your company HIPAA compliant?" "Have you trained all your workforce members to protect patient information?" "Has your company ever had a data breach? What happened? Did you improve your security practices afterward?" "Will your subcontractors have access to our patient information? Have you entered into compliant business associate agreements with each of your subcontractors?"

Related References and Resources

- Appendix 8: Business Associate Checklist
- Appendix 11: Sample Business Associates Agreement

117. A School Has Contacted Us to Ask About a Doctor's Note That Appears to Be From Our Dental Practice. Our Dental Practice Did Not Provide That Doctor's Note. Does HIPAA Prohibit Us from Responding to the School Without the Patient's Authorization?

HIPAA does not prohibit a covered dental practice from telling a school that the dental practice did not provide a certain document, such as a doctor's note, as long as the dental practice does not impermissibly disclose a patient's "protected health information" to the school.

It may help to think of it this way: the HIPAA Privacy Rule requires patient authorization before disclosing "protected health information" unless the disclosure is permitted by HIPAA (HIPAA permits disclosures for treatment, payment, health care operations, and a number of other purposes). "Protected health information" is generally defined as information about an individual's past, present or future physical or mental health, treatment, or payment for health care, that identifies (or could be used to identify) the individual.

A dental practice staff member is not disclosing protected health information when he or she says "that doctor's note did not originate at our dental practice" or "that is not my signature." However, HIPAA may prohibit providing the school additional information about the patient without the written authorization of the patient or the patient's personal representative (e.g., parent or guardian), such as information about the patient's dental treatment or appointment dates.

118. If a Patient's Employer or School Calls Our Dental Practice Directly and Asks Us for Information About the Patient, Can We Provide It, or Do We Need the Patient's Authorization?

In most cases, if a patient's employer or school asks a covered dental practice directly for information about the patient, the dental practice cannot disclose the information in response without the patient's authorization. However, there may be exceptions, such as if the requested disclosure were permitted by HIPAA (e.g., a disclosure for treatment purposes).

119. We Will Have Some Dental Interns in Our Office. Is There a Form the Interns Will Need to Sign for HIPAA? Do We Need to Get the Patient to Sign a Consent Form to Allow the Interns to Observe or Assist the Doctor?

In many cases, an intern can be treated, for HIPAA purposes, the same as any other member of the dental team and patients need not sign an authorization form to allow the intern to observe, assist, or otherwise access the patient's information.

If a dental intern fits the HIPAA definition of a "workforce" member, then a covered dental practice should treat the dental intern, for HIPAA purposes, the same as the practice treats its other "workforce" members (e.g., provide training and document the training, grant appropriate access to patient information, impose appropriate sanctions for failure to adhere to HIPAA policies and procedures and document any sanctions imposed, etc.).

HIPAA defines "workforce" as follows:

> Workforce means employees, volunteers, trainees, and other persons whose conduct, in the performance of work for a covered entity or business associate, is under the direct control of such covered entity or business associate, whether or not they are paid by the covered entity or business associate.

If the definition of "workforce" does not apply, the dental practice should determine what kind of relationship the dental practice has with the intern. For example, if the intern meets the definition of a business associate (generally, an outside individual or entity that performs a service for or on behalf of a covered dental practice), the intern and the dental practice should sign a compliant business associate agreement.

In many cases, an intern can be treated, for HIPAA purposes, the same as any other member of the dental team and patients need not sign an authorization form to allow the intern to observe, assist, or otherwise access the patient's information.

If patient information will be disclosed to the intern for a purpose that is not permitted by HIPAA, then the patient would need to sign an authorization form. However, HIPAA permits a covered dental practice to disclose patient information without patient authorization for a number of purposes, such as treatment, payment and health care operations. If an intern's access to patient information falls into one of these categories, patient authorization is not required under HIPAA.

Keep in mind that HIPAA does not preempt more stringent state laws (e.g., laws that give patients more rights or more protection), so a covered dental practice must also comply with any applicable state laws that are more stringent than HIPAA. A dental practice that is not covered by HIPAA must comply with applicable state law regarding the use and disclosure of patient information and other topics covered by HIPAA, such as data security and breach notification.

120. If a Patient Brings a Friend Along to a Dental Appointment, Do I Need the Patient to Sign an Authorization Form Before Disclosing Information in Front of the Friend?

Covered dental practices are permitted, in most circumstances, to communicate with the patient's family, friends, or others involved in their care or payment for care, if the patient is present and has the capacity to make health care decisions. In such a case, the dentist and dental team may discuss the patient's health information with a family member, friend, or other person if the patient agrees or, when given the opportunity, does not object. In addition, the dentist or member of the dental team may share information with these persons if, using professional judgment, he or she decides that the patient does not object.

If the patient is not present or is incapacitated, the Office for Civil Rights explains that "a health care provider may share the patient's information with family, friends, or others as long as the health care provider determines, based on professional judgment, that it is in the best interest of the patient. When someone other than a friend or family member is involved, the health care provider must be reasonably sure that the patient asked the person to be involved in his or her care or payment for care. The health care provider may discuss only the information that the person involved needs to know about the patient's care or payment."

Related References and Resources

- OCR, A Health Care Provider's Guide to the HIPAA Privacy Rule: Communicating with a Patient's Family, Friends, or Others Involved in the Patient's Care
  www.hhs.gov/ocr/privacy/hipaa/understanding/coveredentities/provider_ffg.pdf

121. What Effect Did the 2013 Omnibus Final Rule Have on HIPAA Compliance?

On January 25, 2013, the federal government published the 2013 Omnibus Final Rule, which changed the HIPAA rules to embody certain enhancements in the 2009 Health Information Technology for Economic and Clinical Health Act (the HITECH Act). The HITECH Act was part of the 2009 federal stimulus act known as the American Recovery and Reinvestment Act of 2009 or ARRA.

Covered dental practices were required to comply with most of the changes in the Omnibus Final Rule as of September 23, 2013. The following summarizes some of the changes in the Omnibus Final Rule that are most likely to affect dental practices. In the summaries below, the "new rule" refers to the Omnibus Final Rule.

Notice of Privacy Practices

Covered dental practices must update their Notice of Privacy Practices to include information required by the new rule.

Breach Notification Rule

The new rule replaced the old "harm standard" with a new "compromise standard." Under the old rule, notification was not required unless the impermissible use or disclosure of patient information posed a significant risk of financial, reputational or other harm to the individual. The new compromise rule requires a covered dental practice to send notice unless the dental practice can demonstrate that there is a low probability that the patient information was compromised based on an assessment of the relevant factors including, at a minimum, the following four required factors:

1. The nature and extent of the patient information involved, including the types of identifiers and the likelihood of re-identification

2. The unauthorized person who used the patient information or to whom the disclosure was made

3. Whether the patient information was actually acquired or viewed, and

4. The extent to which the risk to the patient information has been mitigated

Under the old rule, a covered dental practice was required to perform a risk assessment to determine whether breach notification was required. The new rule gives the dental practice the discretion to provide the required breach notifications without performing a risk assessment. However, if the dental practice does not provide notification because the dental practice determined that there was a low probability of compromise, the dental practice must document why the practice reached this determination.

Business Associates and Subcontractors

The new rule requires covered dental practices to update their business associate agreements to include new required provisions. Business associates and their subcontractors are required to comply with many parts of HIPAA. The government can directly impose penalties on business associates and subcontractors for noncompliance.

Restricted Disclosures to a Health Plan

The new rule gives patients the right to ask a covered dental practice to restrict disclosures to a health plan for purposes of payment or health care operations as long as the dental practice has been paid in full from a source other than the health plan. A dental practice must agree to and honor such a request and may not terminate the restriction unless the patient agrees.

Patients' Right to See and Get Copies of Their Records

Under the old rule, a covered dental practice had to act on a patient's request to see or get copies of records within 30 days (60 days if the information was off-site). The dental practice could get one 30-day extension. Under the new rule, the dental practice must act on such a request within 30 days whether the information is on-site or off-site. The dental practice may still get one 30-day extension.

The new rule also gives patients the right to get electronic copies of their patient information if a covered dental practice maintains the information electronically. The dental practice must provide the information in the form and format requested by the patient if the information is "readily producible" that way. The new rule adds requirements for permissible reasonable, cost-based fees for electronic copies.

Subsidized Marketing Communications

Under the new rule, if a covered dental practice or its business associate receives from a third party any "financial remuneration" (dollars) for making a marketing communication (a communication that encourages someone to buy a product or service), the dental practice must have the patient sign an authorization form before the dental practice makes the communication, and the authorization form must contain certain information. There are several exceptions, such as face-to-face communications and promotional gifts of nominal value.

Sale of Patient Information

Even if a disclosure is permitted by HIPAA, the new rule prohibits a covered dental practice from exchanging patient information for remuneration from or on behalf of the recipient without a signed authorization from the patient that states that the dental practice will be remunerated for the disclosure. There are several exceptions to this requirement.

Decedents

Under the new rule, HIPAA no longer applies to information about a patient who has been deceased for 50 years or more. Also, the new rule permits a dental practice to disclose certain information about a deceased patient to family members and others who were involved in the patient's care or payment for care without first getting the written authorization of the personal representative.

Enforcement

Under the new rule, the federal Office for Civil Rights (OCR) will formally investigate if a preliminary review indicates a violation due to willful neglect. If the OCR finds a violation due to willful neglect, it will very likely impose civil money penalties. If the facts indicate a degree of culpability less than willful neglect, the OCR has discretion as to whether or not to investigate.

Penalties

The new rule has tiered penalty amounts for increasing levels of culpability, up to an annual cap of $1.5 million for all violations of the same HIPAA requirement or prohibition. If a violation was due to willful neglect and was not corrected within 30 days, there is a minimum penalty of $50,000 per violation.

Fundraising

New opt-out requirements apply to a covered dental practice that wishes to use patient information in connection with a fundraising campaign (for example, if the dental practice is a nonprofit entity that wishes to send fundraising communications to patients). It is a HIPAA violation to send a fundraising communication to someone who has opted out. Certain information must appear in each fundraising communication and the opt-out process must not create an undue burden on the patient or cost more than a nominal amount.

Immunization Records

The new rule permits a covered dental practice to send proof of immunization to a school without a signed authorization form in states that have school entry or similar laws, as long as the patient (or a parent or guardian) agrees. If the agreement is oral (e.g., over the telephone), the dental practice must document the agreement (for example, by making a notation in the dental record). If the agreement is in writing (such as by letter or email), the letter or email is sufficient documentation. A signature is not required. A dental practice may still require a signed authorization form if the dental practice wishes. Note that the new rule applies only to immunization records. A covered dental practice must generally require a signed authorization form before disclosing any other patient information to a school.

Genetic Information

The new rule expressly provides that "genetic information" is protected health information under HIPAA. The new rule has a broad definition of "genetic information" that includes:

- Information about a patient's genetic test

- Information about the genetic test of a patient's family member (including a fetus carried by the patient or a family member, or an embryo legally held by a patient or family member utilizing an assisted reproductive technology)

- The manifestation of a disease or disorder in a patient's family member

- Any request for, or receipt of, genetic services by a patient or a patient's family member ("genetic services" means a genetic test, genetic counseling, or genetic education)

- Any request for, or receipt of, participation in clinical research that includes genetic services by a patient or a patient's family member

Research

The new rule made certain changes to the HIPAA rules for using and disclosing patient information for research purposes, such as changing requirements for authorization forms and addressing future use of patient information permissibly obtained for research.

122. What Happens to the Patient Records of a Deceased Practitioner?

Patient records are generally considered an asset of the dental practice, so the answer may vary depending on the legal nature of the dental practice, the legal relationship between the deceased practitioner and the dental practice, and relevant provisions of any applicable contracts (such as a partnership agreement).

For example, if a group dental practice is a professional corporation and the deceased practitioner was an employee, the records of the deceased practitioner's patients may remain the property of the corporation. If a dentist practices solo as the sole proprietor of the dental practice, and upon his or her death the assets of the practice are acquired by another dentist or dental practice, the patient records would likely be part of that transaction. A qualified attorney can provide information about applicable laws that govern the sale or transfer of patient records, including laws that apply to access to records for purposes of due diligence prior to purchase.

If the patient records are the property of the deceased practitioner's estate, and the records are not acquired by another dentist or dental practice, the executor of the deceased practitioner's estate must determine what to do with the records. The records may be necessary to defend against a malpractice claim, which can be filed after the practitioner's death as long as the applicable statute of limitations has not expired. A qualified attorney can provide information about the relevant retention period, patient rights concerning their records, and confidentiality laws that apply. The dentist's professional liability carrier may also be a source of information about record retention and access.

Even if the estate does not own the records, the estate may wish to request permission of the owner to make copies of the records for purpose of defending against potential malpractice claims. A qualified attorney can provide information about laws that apply to the copies, such as statute of limitations and confidentiality laws, and any rights patients may have to information in the copies. The deceased practitioner's professional liability carrier may also be able to provide guidance on these topics.

Secure Disposal of Records

At a certain point it will be legally permissible to dispose of patient records or copies of patient records (for example, when the statute of limitations for any potential malpractice claim has expired and the retention period is past under applicable state law regarding the retention of dental records). When it is appropriate to dispose of patient records or copies of patient records, using a secure destruction method can help reduce the risk of a breach of confidentiality or reportable data breach.

For example, under HIPAA, paper records, film and other hard copies are "secured" when they have been shredded or destroyed such that the information cannot be read or otherwise reconstructed. Electronic media must be cleared, purged, or destroyed consistent with NIST

Special Publication 800-88, *Guidance for Media Sanitization,* such that the information cannot be retrieved, in order to be "secured" under HIPAA. If the owner engages a document destruction firm to dispose of patient records or copies, the owner may wish to choose a firm that warrants that it is in compliance with applicable federal and state privacy and security laws, and to obtain a certificate from the firm with information such as the date the documents were destroyed and the destruction method employed. If HIPAA applies, the document destruction firm may be required to sign a compliant business associate agreement before it can access the records.

Estate Planning

A qualified attorney can help a dentist make decisions and lay plans for the transition of the dental practice and management of practice assets in the event of death or incapacity. Careful planning can help ease the burden on surviving family members, facilitate continuation of patient care, and preserve the value of the dental practice's assets, as well as decrease the risk of improper management or untimely disposal of patient records.

123. Can My Dental Practice Apply for Incentive Payments From the Federal Government if We Buy a New Electronic Dental Record System or Upgrade Our Existing One?

The federal government established the Medicare and Medicaid Electronic Health Record (EHR) Incentive Programs (also known as "Meaningful Use") to provide incentive payments to certain eligible professionals and hospitals as they adopt, implement, upgrade or demonstrate meaningful use of certified EHR technology.

To be eligible for the Medicaid program, a dentist must meet the applicable state's eligibility criteria, which generally requires having a dentist to have a minimum 30 percent Medicaid patient volume. Medicare providers who are eligible but decide not to participate are subject to payment adjustments beginning in 2015.

The Medicare and Medicaid incentive programs have different requirements and different timelines.

Related References and Resources

- CMS, My EHR Participation Timeline
  http://cms.gov/Regulations-and-Guidance/Legislation/EHRIncentivePrograms/Participation-Timeline.html

- CMS, EHR Incentive Programs: The Official Web Site for the Medicare and Medicaid Electronic Health Records (EHR) Incentive Programs
  www.cms.gov/Regulations-and-Guidance/Legislation/EHRIncentivePrograms/index.html

124. Before I Hire Someone, I'd Like to Make Sure That He or She Has Not Been Excluded From Participation in Federal Health Care Programs. Can I Look Them Up? Can I Also Periodically Check on the Status of My Current Staff?

Yes. The federal government lists excluded individuals and entities on a public website that is updated monthly.

With limited exceptions, a dental practice that hires an excluded individual such as a dentist, dental hygienist, or office manager risks nonpayment for certain dental items and services covered by Medicare, Medicaid or other federal health care programs. The U.S. Department of Health and Human Services Office of Inspector General (OIG) maintains a public, searchable and downloadable "List of Excluded Individuals and Entities" (LEIE).

According to the U.S. Department of Health and Human Services Office of Inspector General:

> The effect of an exclusion is that no payment will be made by any Federal health care program for any items or services furnished, ordered or prescribed by an excluded individual or entity. No program payment will be made for anything that an excluded person furnishes, orders, or prescribes. This payment prohibition applies to the excluded person, anyone who employs or contracts with the excluded person, any hospital or other provider for which the excluded person provides services, and anyone else. The exclusion applies regardless of who submits the claims and applies to all administrative and management services furnished by the excluded person.

There is a limited exception to this payment prohibition for the provision of certain emergency items or services not provided in a hospital emergency room.

Related References and Resources

- OIG, Exclusions FAQ
  https://oig.hhs.gov/faqs/exclusions-faq.asp

- OIG, Using the Exclusions Online Database Video
  http://oig.hhs.gov/exclusions/online.asp)

- OIG, List of Excluded Individuals and Entities (LEIE)
  https://oig.hhs.gov/exclusions/exclusions_list.asp

- OIG, To Receive Email Notices of LEIE Updates and Other OIG information
  https://oig.hhs.gov/exclusions/index.asp

125. I Keep Hearing About Data Breaches Involving Credit Card Numbers and Social Security Numbers. My Dental Practice Collects This Kind of Information. What Are Some of the Laws That I Should Be Aware of?

Many states have enacted breach notification laws that require businesses, including dental practices, to notify affected individuals of a breach of certain categories of sensitive data. One purpose of breach notification laws is to enable individuals to take steps to protect themselves against identity theft if their sensitive personal information is accessible to unauthorized individuals.

Generally, these state laws pertain to an individual's name (first and last, or first initial and last name) along with either the individual's Social Security number, driver's license number or state ID number, credit or debit card number, or account number along with a PIN or other information that would allow access. Some states protect additional categories of information. A qualified attorney can provide information about which categories of information are protected in your state, any steps that a dental practice must take to protect the information, and when breach notification is required.

The HIPAA Breach Notification Rule requires covered entities to provide notice of a breach of unsecured "protected health information" (PHI). PHI is generally defined as information that identifies an individual (or could be used to identify an individual) and pertains to the individual's past, present or future physical or mental health, health care, or payment for health care. A dental practice that is covered by HIPAA must comply with both HIPAA and with state law that is not contrary to HIPAA, or that is more stringent than HIPAA. A dental practice that is not covered by HIPAA must comply with applicable state law.

A HIPAA covered dental practice that discovers a breach may be required to comply with HIPAA and/or applicable state breach notification law. For example, if the dental practice discovers a breach of patient information that includes the patient's name and Social Security number, both HIPAA and state law may apply. If state law requires notification in a shorter period of time than HIPAA, the dental practice would likely be required to comply with the state law, which is "more stringent" than HIPAA.

State data breach laws are generally not limited to patient information. Thus, if a dental practice discovers a breach of its employment records resulting in unauthorized acquisition of an employee's name and Social Security number, the dental practice may need to provide notification under state law, but not under HIPAA.

Applicable law will determine whether a breach has occurred and whether notification is required, and, if so, the deadline for providing notice and the contents of the notice. In some states, notification must also be provided to the state attorney general. HIPAA requires notification to affected individuals, the federal government, and in some cases the media.

Breaches can be expensive and time-consuming. A dental practice can reduce the likelihood of a breach by complying with applicable privacy and data security laws, such as HIPAA and state laws, complying with the Payment Card Industry Data Security Standards if relevant, encrypting sensitive electronic data and locking up sensitive hard copy data, and training staff to follow the dental practice's privacy and security policies and procedures.

Related References and Resources

- Question 127: My Office is Considering Whether to Accept Credit Card Payments and Was Told by a Card Payment Processor That Our Office Would Need to Be "PCI Compliant." Is This Really True?

- Protect Yourself From Identity Theft
  success.ada.org/en/practice/operations/risk-management/protect-yourself-from-identity-theft

- PCI Security Standards Council FAQ
  www.pcisecuritystandards.org/faq

126. Will My Liability Insurance Cover the Financial Loss Caused by a Data Breach?

General liability insurance may not cover liability due to a data breach. Some insurance companies offer "cyberliability" policies that may help provide some coverage. Investigating and applying for a cyberliability policy may help a dental practice better understand data security risks involved and some safeguards that can help prevent a data breach, whether or not the dental practice makes a decision to obtain a cyberliability policy. Check with a qualified professional advisor.

127. My Office is Considering Whether to Accept Credit Card Payments and Was Told by a Card Payment Processor That Our Office Would Need to Be "PCI Compliant." Is This Really True?

Payment processors and banks often require dental practices that accept credit and debit cards to agree to comply with a set of security standards known as the "Payment Card Industry Data Security Standards," or PCI DSS. The dental practice's contract with the bank or payment processor frequently contains a provision requiring PCI DSS compliance.

PCI DSS is a set of 12 security standards developed by the PCI Security Standards Council. The Council was founded by five global payment brands: American Express, Discover Financial Services, JCB International, MasterCard, and Visa, Inc.

A dental practice that accepts credit and debit card payments and that is not PCI compliant risks penalties under the applicable agreement.

Under PCI DSS, dental practices that accept credit and debit card payments are considered "merchants."

Some of the PCI Data Security Standards are technical, and others are administrative or legal. Examples of technical standards include standards that pertain to firewalls and passwords. Other examples of PCI standards are those that pertain to data retention and secure disposal, staff training, and agreements with service providers.

Related References and Resources

- PCI Security Council's Resources for Merchants (includes a series of short training videos)
  www.pcisecuritystandards.org/merchants

128. How Do I Respond to an Investigatory Letter From the U.S. Department of Health and Human Services Office for Civil Rights, the Federal Agency That Administers HIPAA?

A dental practice that receives a letter from the Office for Civil Rights (OCR) must act quickly and appropriately in order to minimize the risk of potential penalties. A qualified attorney can provide information about the OCR inquiry and help the dental practice respond appropriately within the applicable timeframe. In some cases, a dental practice may not be permitted to supplement its response by providing additional information or documents at a later date.

Failure to respond to an OCR investigation can result in penalties. For example, OCR imposed a civil monetary penalty of $4.3 million on a HIPAA covered entity, Cignet Health, for violations of the HIPAA Privacy Rule, including Cignet's refusal to respond to OCR's investigation of certain patient complaints.

Dental practices that are selected by OCR for a HIPAA audit must also respond appropriately within the applicable timeframe. During the pilot audit program, OCR sent the selected covered entities notification letters that included, among other information, a description of the initial document and information requests and specified how and when to return the requested information to the auditor. OCR expected the selected covered entities to provide the requested information within 10 business days of the request for information.

Because the timeframe for response may be short, covered dental practices would be prudent to keep their HIPPA compliance documentation organized and easily accessible. Examples of HIPAA compliance documentation include:

- Designations of the dental practice's Privacy Official and Security Official

- Security risk assessment

- Privacy, Security and Breach Notification policies and procedures

- Workforce training documentation

- Documentation of sanctions applied for failure to comply with policies and procedures

- Executed business associate agreements (OCR may also request a list of the dental practice's business associates)

- Notice of Privacy Practices and signed acknowledgments of receipt

- If the dental practice has experienced a breach of unsecured patient information, copies of the notification letters that the dental practice sent to the affected individual(s)

Covered dental practices must retain HIPAA compliance documentation for at least six years from the date the document was created, or at least six years from the date the document was last in effect, whichever is later.

Related References and Resources

- OCR, Civil Money Penalty, Cignet Health Fined a $4.3M Civil Money Penalty for HIPAA Privacy Rule Violations
  www.hhs.gov/ocr/privacy/hipaa/enforcement/examples/cignetcmp.html

- OCR, Audit Pilot Program
  www.hhs.gov/ocr/privacy/hipaa/enforcement/audit/auditpilotprogram.html

129. A Law Enforcement Official Has Asked My Dental Practice for Information About One of Our Patients. What Should We Do?

This is a complicated question that can depend on both federal and state law as well as the facts of the particular case. A qualified attorney can evaluate a law enforcement request for patient information and advise the dental practice on whether the dental practice is permitted or required to provide the information, and, if so, any conditions that may apply. The following information may help a dental practice better understand some of the laws that may come into play when a law enforcement official requests patient information.

HIPAA

HIPAA permits a covered dental practice to disclose patient information in response to a request from a law enforcement official without first obtaining patient authorization as long as certain conditions are met. These rules are generally found in Section 164.512(f) of the HIPAA Privacy Rule.

Locating a Suspect, Fugitive, Material Witness or Missing Person

For example, HIPAA permits a covered dental practice to disclose limited information when a law enforcement official's request is for the purpose of identifying or locating a suspect, fugitive, material witness, or missing person. The dental practice may disclose only the following information:

- Name and address

- Date and place of birth

- Social Security number

- ABO blood type and Rh factor

- Type of injury

- Date and time of treatment

- Date and time of death, if applicable, and

- A description of distinguishing physical characteristics, including height, weight, gender, race, hair and eye color, presence or absence of facial hair (beard or moustache), scars and tattoos.

Except as permitted by the above list, this HIPAA provision does not permit a covered dental practice to disclose, for purposes of identification or location, any patient information related to the individual's dental records, or typing, samples or analysis of body fluids or tissue, DNA or DNA analysis.

Other Law Enforcement Requests for Patient Information

Other provisions in Section 164.512(f) permit certain limited disclosures, as long as specific conditions are met, in response to other types of requests from law enforcement officials, such as subpoenas. This section also sets forth conditions that apply to law enforcement requests for information about patients who are, or who are suspected to be, victims of a crime, information about criminal conduct that occurred on the premises of the covered entity, and the rules concerning reporting crimes in emergencies. A qualified attorney can help a dental practice determine when HIPAA and state law permit providing information to law enforcement officials in response to such requests.

Verifying the Identity and Authority of the Person Requesting Patient Information

With limited exceptions, the HIPAA Privacy Rule requires a covered dental practice to verify the identity of a person requesting patient information and the authority of such person to have access to patient information, if the person's identity or authority is not known to the dental practice. The HIPAA rules for verification, including rules concerning the authority of public officials, are in Section 164.514(g) of the Privacy Rule.

State Law

A HIPAA covered dental practice must comply with both HIPAA and with any applicable state law that is either (1) not contrary to HIPAA, or (2) is contrary to HIPAA and more stringent than HIPAA. Therefore, even if HIPAA permits a certain disclosure in response to a request from a law enforcement official, or in response to a document such as a court order or subpoena, if an applicable state law is more stringent than HIPAA and prohibits the disclosure, the dental practice must comply with the state law. A dental practice that is not covered by HIPAA must comply with applicable state law.

Related References and Resources

- USGPO, Section 164.512(f) of the HIPAA Privacy Rule
  www.ecfr.gov/cgi-bin/text-idx?SID=e7c006d716d2167cb15dfd16490d9f72&node=se45.1.1 64_1512&rgn=div8)

- USGPO, Section 164.514(g) of the HIPAA Privacy Rule
  www.ecfr.gov/cgi-bin/text-idx?SID=e7c006d716d2167cb15dfd16490d9f72&node=se45.1.1 64_1514&rgn=div8)

- OCR, Health Insurance Portability and Accountability Act (HIPAA) Privacy Rule: A Guide for Law Enforcement
  www.hhs.gov/ocr/privacy/hipaa/understanding/special/emergency/final_hipaa_guide_law_ enforcement.pdf

- How HIPAA Can Apply to You; How to Comply if it Does
  ADA.org/en/member-center/member-benefits/legal-resources/publications-and-articles/ hipaa-and-data-security/how-hipaa-can-apply-to-you-how-to-comply-if-it-does

Chapter 16.

FACTA: Red Flags and Disposal Rules

130. What Is FACTA and How Will It Affect My Practice?

The Fair and Accurate Credit Transactions Act (FACTA) amended the federal Fair Credit Reporting Act by adding new requirements intended primarily to help consumers fight identity theft, such as requiring credit bureaus to provide free credit reports and requiring that social security, credit card and other identifying numbers be truncated. Although some dentists still contact the ADA from time-to-time with questions about the so-called "Red Flags Rule," which arises under FACTA, the fact is that the Rule does not affect dentists in their practices. One aspect of FACTA that may be of some importance to dentists is the "Disposal Rule."

131. What Is the Red Flags Rule?

FACTA was enacted in 2003. In 2007 the Federal Trade Commission (FTC) issued regulations based on FACTA. Collectively, a group of these FTC regulations are referred to as The Red Flags Rule, which requires financial institutions and "creditors" to develop a written program that identifies, detects, and responds to the relevant warnings signs or "red flags" of identity theft in connection with a "covered account."

From the very beginning, the ADA opposed the application of the Red Flags Rule to dental practices, and especially to smaller practices. The Rule's requirements for written plans and other measures intended to guard against identity theft were overly burdensome and did not make sense in the context of dental practices or, for that matter, other professional practices. The ADA succeeded in delaying implementation of the Rule several times.

Eventually, supported by numerous health care organizations and other professions, the ADA spearheaded a legislative effort that resulted in the Red Flag Program Clarification Act of 2010. The legislation made it clear was that in adopting FACTA the Congress had not intended dentists and other professional practices to be reached by regulations such as the FTC's Red Flags Rule and it explicitly exempted dentistry and other professions from operation of the Rule. Both houses of Congress passed the bill and it was signed into law by the President.

132. What Does the Disposal Rule Require?

The Disposal Rule requires covered entities to take reasonable and appropriate steps to prevent the unauthorized access to, or use of, information in a consumer report. The rule appears flexible as it allows entities to determine and implement "reasonable" disposal measures by taking into consideration the costs and benefits of different disposal methods.

Examples of appropriate manners of destroying applicable consumer report information include:

- Burning, pulverizing, or shredding papers containing consumer report information so that the information cannot be read or reconstructed

- Destroying or erasing electronic files or media containing consumer report information so that the information cannot be read or reconstructed

- Conducting due diligence and hiring a document destruction contractor to dispose of material specifically identified as consumer report information consistent with the rule

133. Does the Disposal Rule Apply to All Dentists?

No. The Disposal Rule applies only to businesses and persons who obtain consumer reports for conducting business. This could include a dentist who obtains a patient's credit history for financing options. A dentist should contact a qualified attorney if he or she is unsure whether the requirements of the Rule apply.

134. When Does the Disposal Rule Take Effect?

The Disposal Rule is already in effect (as of June 1, 2005).

Chapter 17.

COPPA

135. My Dental Practice Wants to Create a "Kids' Corner" on Our Practice Website. Someone Mentioned "COPPA Requirements." What Is COPPA and Does It Apply to Dental Practices?

According to the Federal Trade Commission (FTC), the primary goal of the Children's Online Privacy Protection Act (COPPA) is to place parents in control over what information is collected from their young children online.

COPPA is a federal law that applies to websites and online services (such as apps) that are directed to children under 13, or that have actual knowledge that they are collecting, using, or disclosing "personal information" from children under 13.

COPPA defines a child's "personal information" broadly. The definition includes things like a child's name, address (or even just the names of the child's street and city), photo, video, audio file of the child's voice, screen name or user name, telephone numbers, etc. But the definition also includes "persistent identifiers" that can be used to recognize a user over time and across different websites or online services. A dental practice may not be aware whether its website collects persistent identifiers from visitors to the website.

If your dental practice wishes to have a website or online service directed to children under 13, or your dental practice has actual knowledge that it has collected, using, or disclosed "personal information" from a child under 13, then your dental practice may be required to comply with COPPA requirements such as posting particular information in an online privacy policy, providing direct notice to parents and obtaining verifiable parental consent before collecting personal information online from children.

Related References and Resources

- FTC, Complying with COPPA: Frequently Asked Questions, A Guide for Business and Parents and Small Entity Compliance Guide
  www.business.ftc.gov/documents/0493-Complying-with-COPPA-Frequently-Asked-Questions

136. How Do I Know Whether My Website Is Directed at Children Under 13? Does COPPA Provide a Test or Definition?

The COPPA statute does not give a clear definition of what constitutes a website directed at children under 13. It also fails to provide a bright line test for determining whether a website is directed at children under the age of 13. The Federal Trade Commission (FTC) has stated:

> The amended Rule sets out a number of factors for determining whether a website or online service is directed to children. These include subject matter of the site or service, its visual content, the use of animated characters or child-oriented activities and incentives, music or other audio content, age of models, presence of child celebrities or celebrities who appeal to children, language or other characteristics of the website or online service, or whether advertising promoting or appearing on the website or online service is directed to children. The Rule also states that the Commission will consider competent and reliable empirical evidence regarding audience composition, as well as evidence regarding the intended audience of the site or service...

> ...the amended Rule also considers a website or online service to be "directed to children" where it has actual knowledge that it is collecting personal information directly from users of another website or online service that is directed to children.[14]

---

[14] Source: Complying with COPPA: Frequently Asked Questions, A Guide for Business and Parents and Small Entity Compliance Guide, at *www.business.ftc.gov/documents/0493-Complying-with-COPPA-Frequently-Asked-Questions*

Chapter 18.

The Physician Payment Sunshine Act (Open Payments)

137. How Can I Find Out About the Physician Payment Sunshine Act and "Open Payments," the New Federal Government Website That Has Information About Industry Relationships With Doctors and Teaching Hospitals?

The federal government "Open Payments" website (*www.cms.gov/openpayments*) is a public website with information about relationships that certain manufacturers and group purchasing organizations (GPOs) have with doctors and teaching hospitals. Examples of these relationships include gifts, speaker fees, meals, travel, and manufacturer supported research activities, as well as ownership interests held by doctors or their family members. Open Payments was created under the Physician Payment Sunshine Act, a part of the Affordable Care Act.

Related Resources

- The Sunshine Act FAQ
  ADA.org/en/member-center/member-benefits/legal-resources/publications-and-articles/other-legal-issues/the-sunshine-act-faq

- CMS, Open Payments
  www.cms.gov/openpayments

138. Do I Have Any Choices About Information About Me That Might Appear on the Open Payments Website?

If a dentist receives a reportable payment or other "transfer of value" (such as a reportable meal, book or device) from an applicable manufacturer, the manufacturer must make a report to the federal government and the payment or transfer must appear on the Open Payments website. An "applicable manufacturer" is generally defined as an entity that manufactures a drug, device, biological, or medical supply covered by Medicare, Medicaid or CHIP.

Similarly, if a dentist or family member has a reportable ownership interest in an applicable manufacturer or applicable GPO, the manufacturer or GPO must report the interest on Open Payments.

Perhaps the best way for a dentist to control information on Open Payments is to ask about reportability prior to accepting any payment or transfer from a manufacturer, and declining to accept payments and transfers that the dentist does not wish to appear on Open Payments.

A dentist who accepts a reportable payment or transfer may ask the manufacturer to add to the report a brief statement of "contextual information" about the payment or transfer. However, a manufacturer is not required to agree to such a request.

To help ensure that reported information is accurate, Open Payments permits doctors and teaching hospitals to register to review reports before they are made public on Open Payments. A dentist who believes a report is inaccurate may initiate a dispute with the reporting manufacturer.

Related References and Resources

- CMS, Review and Dispute for Physicians and Teaching Hospitals
  www.cms.gov/OpenPayments/Program-Participants/Physicians-and-Teaching-Hospitals/Review-and-Dispute.html.

139. What Can I Do to Help Make Sure That Information About Me Is Accurate on "Open Payments"?

A dentist who registers on Open Payments is able to review reports and dispute inaccuracies before the reports are made public. If a dentist reviews reports and initiates a dispute with the appropriate manufacturer within the review-and-dispute time frame, the report may be corrected before it is made public. If a dispute is not resolved before the information is made public, Open Payments will indicate that the report is disputed. Disputes can be initiated after the review-and-dispute time frame, but data is not corrected until the database is refreshed.

Related Resources

- CMS, Review and Dispute for Physicians and Teaching Hospitals
  www.cms.gov/OpenPayments/Program-Participants/Physicians-and-Teaching-Hospitals/Review-and-Dispute.html

140. A Dental Manufacturer's Representative Provided Lunch for My Staff and Me. The Lunch was Great, but Why Is the Rep Asking for My NPI Number and Other Information?

To fulfill their reporting obligations under the Physician Payment Sunshine Act, applicable manufacturers will ask dentists who receive reportable payments or other transfers for information such as the dentist's name, business address, National Provider Number (NPI) and license number. Reportable payments and transfers are made public on the federal government's "Open Payments" website.

For purposes of Open Payments, a meal provided to a dentist may be treated differently than a meal provided to a non-dentist employee of a dental practice. In general, meals provided to non-dentist employees are not reportable, but there are exceptions. For example, a meal would have to be reported if the dentist requested the manufacturer to provide the meal to the employee.

Also, payments and transfers worth less than $10 are not reportable unless the manufacturer gives the dentist payments and transfers that add up to more than $100 in a given year. These dollar amounts are adjusted annually for inflation.

A dentist may wish to speak to manufacturers' reps in advance to clarify whether or not a meal will be reportable, and may also wish to keep track of payments and transfers from manufacturers. One option for keeping track is a free app created for this purpose by federal government.

Related Resources

- Question 138: Do I Have Any Choices About Information About Me That Might Appear on the Open Payments Website?

- CMS, FAQ for Open Payments Mobile for Physicians & Open Payments Mobile for Industry *www.cms.gov/Regulations-and-Guidance/Legislation/National-Physician-Payment-Transparency-Program/Downloads/Mobile-App-Public-FAQs.pdf*

141. What Is Teledentistry and What Are Some of the Regulatory and Legal Concerns?

Teledentistry, a component of telehealth, is the electronic exchange of dental patient information from one geographic location to another for interpretation or consultation among authorized healthcare professionals. Teledentistry utilizes both information and communication technologies and includes the electronic exchange of diagnostic image files, including radiographs, photographs, video, optical impressions and photomicrographs of patients.

Regulatory/legal considerations include the following:

- Licensure is one of the biggest concerns with teledentistry. Each state sets its own licensure requirements. A dentist who is licensed in one state may not be authorized to practice in another state via teledentistry.

- The next issue is patient privacy and security. For example, HIPAA may require a covered dental practice to include information that is being transmitted electronically in the practice's written risk assessment and develop and implement policies and procedures to protect the confidentiality, integrity, and availability of the information.

- The next issue is informed consent. In general, a dentist is required to obtain informed consent from a patient before any form of patient contact is established, although in some situations consent may be implied. Depending on the nature of the procedure, informed consent may require the dentist to advise the patient that teledentistry will be used and of any risk associated with the technology involved.

- Before performing teledentistry, a dentist would be wise understand the parameters of his or her malpractice coverage for teledentistry, including services crossing state lines. Also, in the case of a lawsuit, the dentist will want to know what state law applies to him or her.

- Lastly, a dentist will want to know what reimbursement options are available for teledentistry services.

In addition, ADA encourages dentists to consider conformance with the Digital Imaging and Communications in Medicine (DICOM) standards when selecting and using imaging systems.

Business Considerations

Chapter 19.
Contracts

As professionals and business people, dentists are routinely faced with a wide array of business decisions. Often these decisions involve contracts, such as a buy/sell of a practice, a partnership or associateship agreement, a lease of office space, or a contract to participate in an insurance plan. As with any practice option, these are all individual business decisions that will raise practical, legal, ethical and other considerations. There will be "pros" and "cons" to each. Some will be more important to certain dentists than to others; some may be critical considerations to some dentists, while others may not be important at all.

142. Should I Sign This Contract?

It's up to you. Whether to sign a contract is an individual business decision. As you begin assessing whether a particular contract is right for you, in most cases it is prudent to start with practice considerations. Does the proposal in question fit your practice preferences and long-range goals? If so, evaluate the economics of the deal, with the help of your financial and business advisors as appropriate. If the proposal does not make financial sense, stop there — there's no reason to hire an attorney at that point.

143. How Do the Legal Considerations Fit in?

If the proposal is attractive financially, then turn to the legal considerations. For starters, does the contract reflect the actual proposal that was of interest to you? Does it reflect your understanding of the deal? Does it include all the terms that you expect and need? We have heard numerous anecdotal stories about dentists signing contracts based on a sales pitch, but later finding that the actual contract language did not include what they expected.

Once you're comfortable that the contract properly captures your business arrangement, consider whether the contractual terms impact its financial attractiveness. For example, is there a way to quantify the financial implications to you of a hold harmless, restrictive covenant, or non-assignment clause? Also, what business risks may the contract language create for you, particularly if the contract does not lead to the benefit you hoped for or if the contract comes to a sudden end? Many dentists have reported being stuck financially on the contractual hook long after purchasing a product or service that was no longer being used or providing value. Even where the deal appears to be attractive, always consider and understand your right to terminate the agreement, as well as the potential cost (charges) in exercising your termination right. And beware of automatic renewals!

A qualified attorney can help you assess these and other issues. This process can help you decide whether to pursue the deal and, if so, it can position you or your attorney to negotiate the terms that are important to address your needs and priorities. Of course, your ability to negotiate will turn, in part, on marketplace considerations, such as how much the party you may contract with needs your business.

Related References and Resources

- Caution Ahead: Contractual Auto-Renew Clauses
  http://success.ada.org/en/practice/operations/efficient-systems/contractual-auto-renew

144. Do I (Still) Have to Do What the Contract Says?

Yes, subject to certain limited exceptions. Contracts are legally binding documents. The law presumes that each party to a contract has read, understood, and agreed to its terms prior to signing the agreement. Once you sign a contract you become legally bound to the agreement even if the terms are inequitable (and even if the contract terms do not conform to what you believed you agreed to — the signed agreement will almost always prevail over anything that was said or promised in the pre-contract discussions), although there may be times (albeit rare) when you need no longer honor your contractual obligations (for example, if the other party has materially breached the agreement). There are reasons why qualified legal counsel should be consulted prior to signing a contract.

Chapter 20.
Common Dental Agreements

Dentists will typically sign a number of agreements over the course of their practice lives. Let's look at some of them in general terms, from various perspectives.

145. What Are Some of the Issues Involved in a Buy–Sell Agreement?

As with most other contracts, the beauty of a buy-sell agreement is in the eye of the beholder. The seller will often establish what he or she believes to be a fair market price by providing a thorough, documented valuation. The seller will want the contract to include a firm commitment for the date of the closing and assurance that the purchaser has the means to close on that date. At the outset of negotiations, the parties will probably consider entering into a confidentiality agreement and may be required to sign a HIPAA Business Associate Agreement.

A prudent buyer will compare the cost of purchasing an existing practice to the time and expense of building up a new practice. Making this comparison will probably require some due diligence to determine the existing practice's real worth and outstanding liabilities. It may be wise for the buyer to insist on some assurances regarding the continuity of value prior to the sale (for example, with respect to the transfer of patient lists and records and the like). If the selling dentist will remain affiliated with the practice, additional issues regarding his or her role will need to be negotiated.

It is important to remember that many factors are involved in buying and selling a practice. A prudent dentist will review the situation carefully and seek the advice of a financial or business consultant to assess the financial aspects of the deal, and rely on legal counsel for advice about the sales contract and related issues.

Related References and Resources

- Chapter 15: HIPAA, State Law and PCI DSS: Patient Information

- Appendix 2: Buy-Sell Agreements (Background)

- HIPAA 20 Questions
  ADA.org/DentistGuidetoLaw

- Are You a HIPAA Business Associate?
  ADA.org/en/member-center/member-benefits/legal-resources/publications-and-articles/ hipaa-and-data-security/are-you-a-hipaa-business-associate

146. How Should I Evaluate a Contract With an Insurance Plan?

Before signing any agreement, including a contract with an insurance plan, do your homework to be sure the proposed agreement makes business sense to you, make sure you understand all of the provisions, and consult with your attorney as necessary. Remember that a decision as to whether to enter into an agreement is an individual business decision, based on your practice preferences and needs. Start with the practice and financial considerations. If you join a PPO to fill empty chair time, do you stand to profit? If you run the numbers and believe you will lose money on each PPO or HMO patient, don't expect to make it up on volume!

The ADA has an array of resources to help you assess whether and how to participate in a particular plan. Start with the practice resources first. The ADA's informational legal resources can help you get a feel for the legalities involved. As a rule of thumb, there is no need to get a lawyer's advice on the legal aspects of the transaction if a deal does not make business sense to you in the first place.

Perhaps the best known ADA practice resource is the Contract Analysis Service. This service analyzes provider contracts before they are signed, including contracts from managed care companies, and informs members in clear language about the provisions of the contracts so they can make informed decisions about the implications of participation. The service is available free to members through their state societies. It is not a substitute for legal advice, but can be of great help to you and your attorney when considering legal issues in plan participation.

Another key resource is the Model Contract for Third-Party Dental Service Agreements (*ADA. org/en/member-center/member-benefits/legal-resources*). The Model Contract offers examples of contractual language that would be fair to dentists and their patients. The Model Contract is designed as an educational tool for dentists contemplating contracts with third party dental benefit organizations, and is intended to assist members in their negotiations with those organizations, which generally offer contracts that have been drafted to favor the company.

In addition to offering sample contractual language, the Model Contract also contains commentary on each provision. These comments point out differences between the model language and terms sometimes found in agreements offered by dental benefit organizations. The commentary also highlights issues raised by certain provisions.

Before signing any agreement, including a contract with an insurance plan, do your homework to be sure the proposed agreement makes business sense to you, make sure you understand all of the provisions, and consult with your attorney as necessary.

Lastly, What Every Dentist Should Know Before Signing a Dental Provider Contract (*ADA. org/en/member-center/member-benefits/legal-resources*) provides additional information on provider contracts. This document addresses the following:

- Stop, read and consider before you sign

- Term and termination

- Modification clause

- Amendment/Modification clause

- What documents make up the contract? Obtain and carefully review all attachments, exhibits, appendices and undisclosed documents before signing the contract.

- Liability: consult a qualified attorney and professional liability insurance carrier before signing a contract with risk shifting clauses, like a hold harmless provision.

- Referrals: you have an obligation to your patients to make sure that treatment is not compromised, regardless of any restrictions in the contract.

- Utilization review: will the utilization review process influence or control the way in which you practice dentistry or compromise your professional judgment?

- Peer review

- Grievance system

- Arbitration

- Insurance: confirm exactly what your obligations are so you will know if you need to purchase additional insurance or change carriers.

- Compensation and services

- "Most favored nation" clause: will you be required to give XYZ Company the benefit of any "better price" that you give to another dental benefit organization?

- Noncompetition clause

- Assignment/delegation

- Assignment clause

- Liquidated damages: consult with counsel about liquidated damages provisions.

- Entire understanding: if it isn't in the contract, it probably is not enforceable.

- Governing law

The "Model Contract" and "What Every Dentist Should Know" (*ADA.org/en/member-center/member-benefits/legal-resources*) are intended as supplements to the tailored, informational analyses of contracts offered by the ADA Contract Analysis Service. While none of these resources constitute legal advice, we hope they are of great help to you and your attorney. Remember, the decision regarding whether or not to enter into an insurance plan agreement is up to you, the individual dentist.

Related References and Resources

- Model Contract for Third-Party Dental Service Agreements
  ADA.org/en/member-center/member-benefits/legal-resources

- What Every Dentist Should Know Before Signing a Dental Provider Contract
  ADA.org/en/member-center/member-benefits/legal-resources

147. Do I Need Employment Agreements With My Staff?

No, but they can be very useful. Written employment agreements are not essential for a harmonious and rewarding employee-employer relationship, but they can often improve the dentist's ability to effectively manage the dental office and communicate with staff.

Employment contracts with staff can clarify each party's rights and obligations, and help confirm that the employee is aware of and agrees to follow the office's policies and practices. It is a good idea to use an associateship agreement when retaining dentists who will not have an ownership interest in the practice, because of potential issues such as "whose patients are they?" With respect to other employees, practice owners may wish to rely on employee handbooks rather than written employment agreements.

If you elect not to use written employment agreements, it is prudent to have your staff acknowledge their receipt of (and perhaps even their agreement to uphold) your policies. And of course, an employee handbook can clarify employees' rights and obligations. To avoid potential confusion, employee handbooks frequently include a prominent and clear statement that they do not constitute a contract of employment.

Related References and Resources

- Question 148: How Can I Get the Most Mileage Out of an Associate Agreement?

- Chapter 10: Office Manuals and Policies

- *The ADA Practical Guide to Creating and Updating an Employee Policy Manual*
  adacatalog.org or 1.800.947.4746

Employment contracts with staff can clarify each party's rights and obligations, and help confirm that the employee is aware of and agrees to follow the office's policies and practices.

148. How Can I Get the Most Mileage Out of an Associate Agreement?

A written contract can be a big help. Practice owners and prospective associates may share common goals, such as the eventual transfer of the practice, and thus have an incentive to structure mutually beneficial contractual relationships. Still, their business interests are not identical. Negotiations are common over business issues such as compensation, whether the associate will be an independent contractor or employee, the formula for determining eventual sale price, the scope of any restrictive covenants, patient care considerations after the agreement ends, and patient records. A dentist–associate relationship may hold great promise, but it is a business relationship nonetheless, and an important one for both parties.

A written contract between the parties considering an associate relationship is valuable for a variety of practical and professional reasons. Written agreements enable both parties to fully discuss the fundamental components of the relationship. Putting an oral understanding in writing reduces the risk of a future disagreement or misunderstanding. Sometimes there is an urge to save money by having one lawyer draft a contract for both parties. This is not recommended. Each party should retain separate counsel.

Among the issues that can be addressed contractually are:

- Length of the contract

- Use of facilities (rights and privileges, time and extent)

- Confidentiality of patient information

- Compensation (terms of payment, possible offsets)

- Expenses (who pays office expenses)

- Management (who has management responsibility, including over staff)

As always, consult with your attorney about your specific needs.

Related References and Resources

- Appendix 3: Sample Employee Associateship Agreement

- Appendix 4: Sample Independent Contractor Associateship Agreement

149. Should the Associate Be an Independent Contractor or Employee?

It depends on your needs, though in most instances, dental associates will be employees for tax purposes. For practice owners and prospective associates, it is important to carefully review the advantages and disadvantages of being an independent contractor or employee. Doing so will help ensure that a mutually agreeable arrangement is achieved. It will also shed light on a very important tax consideration.

Selecting the proper arrangement can have far-reaching effects on a dental practice. For example, if an associate is an independent contractor seeking to build his or her own patient base, it may be inconsistent to include a restrictive covenant in the agreement. Dentists should also be aware that employees enjoy certain rights that independent contractors do not, such as protections under employment laws, employee benefits, minimum wage requirements and overtime rights.

If an associate dentist is deemed an employee for federal employment tax purposes, the employer becomes responsible for payroll taxes and withholding taxes under the Federal Insurance Contributions Act (FICA), the Federal Unemployment Tax Act (FUTA), and the income tax withholding provisions of the Internal Revenue Code. In contrast, if the associate dentist is considered an independent contractor, the associate is responsible for his or her own income taxes and self-employment taxes.

Generally, a worker such as an associate is classified as an employee when the employer (in this case, the hiring dentist) has the "right to control" the way in which the worker's services are performed. Employers have the right to control and direct the work of an employee, not only in terms of what will be done, but also how and when it will be done. In contrast, an independent contractor is subject to the hiring party's control only as to the end results of the work. The true nature of the relationship is not determined by the label. The question is whether an employer-employee relationship exists in fact.

The IRS has established a three-part test to determine whether the required control exists to establish an employer-employee relationship for federal employment tax purposes. The test includes an assessment of 1) the behavioral control (including, for example, how extensive instructions are, who controls what, when, and where to work, and the tools to be used), 2) financial control (such as who pays for business expenses, how much the person providing services has invested), and 3) the relationship of the parties (whether there is an agreement, whether benefits are provided, and so forth). In assessing your particular arrangement, it is important to look at all of the factors carefully. Doing so will help you avoid what seems to be a common trap in dentistry: automatically thinking that an associate (or hygienist or other team member) is an independent contractor, when in fact that individual falls squarely within the employee classification. Incorrectly classifying an associate or other worker can have serious consequences. Using its criteria, the IRS may decide that a worker you've classified as an independent contractor is really an employee. If that happens, you as the employer could be assessed back taxes and interest. In some cases, re-classification could create personal liability for the person responsible for deducting and withholding payroll taxes.

Specific regulations such as the IRS "safe harbor" regulations, which may provide relief from employment tax liability in certain circumstances, are beyond the scope of this section but should be considered.

In addition, dentists as employers must comply with state laws on employment taxes and unemployment insurance contributions. For example, in some states the definition of independent contractor is highly restrictive and may differ from the definition under federal law. A dentist should consult a qualified attorney to confirm that the independent contractor relationship, if desired, meets the IRS requirements and also complies with state laws.

Related References and Resources

- Question 165: What Are My Responsibilities Regarding Payroll Taxes?

- IRS, Independent Contractor or Employee?
  www.irs.gov/pub/irs-pdf/p1779.pdf

150. Are Restrictive Covenants Enforceable?

Restrictive covenants can be an effective method of protecting a dentist's interests when another dentist leaves the practice or is terminated. Dental associateship agreements frequently include a restrictive covenant. The restrictive covenant — or "agreement not to compete" — is a contract provision that may restrict the associate from practicing dentistry within a specific geographical area for a set period of time after leaving the employer's practice, and may restrict the ability of the associate to solicit or contact the dental practice's patients or employees after expiration of the employment agreement, or after his or her termination or resignation (agreements to refrain from soliciting patients or employees are sometimes referred to as "non-solicitation agreements"). Such a covenant is designed to prevent the associate from taking patients or employees away from the practice owner once the associateship is ended. The covenant is meant to protect an owner who has invested time, energy, and money in building a practice.

State laws vary greatly on the enforceability of non-compete agreements. Some states have held that such covenants are against public policy because they restrain trade. But many states will enforce "reasonable" covenant provisions that do not undermine public policy. In such states, courts that are asked to enforce such a covenant will examine the covenant carefully, based on the particular facts and circumstances presented. To be enforceable in these states, a court must deem the covenant "reasonable" as to duration (how long does the restriction last), scope (what specific activities are prohibited), and geographic area (the distance within which the departing dentist is prohibited from practicing). The court may also look to the duration of the dentist's tenure with the practice (for example, it might be deemed unreasonable to impose significant restrictions on a dentist who was only with the practice for a month). As a general rule, in a jurisdiction that will enforce a restrictive covenant, the more limited the restriction in the above-noted categories (duration of the restriction, scope of activities, and geographic), the more likely it is to be found "reasonable" (i.e., necessary to protect the practice) and enforceable. Because state laws vary considerably (and enforceability can turn on a nuanced basis) and because important interests are at stake for both parties, it is prudent to consult with an attorney before entering into a restrictive covenant.

The employer dentist must act in good faith to enforce a covenant. Say, for example, that an associate dentist signs an employment agreement that contains a restrictive covenant. The employment agreement provides that the associate dentist will become a full partner in the practice four years from the date of signing. After three and a half years, the group fires the associate dentist without cause and attempts to enforce the covenant against him or her. A court may refuse to enforce the covenant. On the other hand, a court is not likely to look favorably on an associate dentist who breaches his or her associateship agreement or does egregious things in the dental office in the hope of getting fired in order to get around the restrictive covenant.

Related References and Resources

- Appendix 3: Sample Employee Associateship Agreement (with sample restrictive covenant provisions)

- Appendix 4: Sample Independent Contractor Associateship Agreement (with sample restrictive covenant provisions)

151. What Should My Office Lease Contain?

Negotiating a lease for office space can be a frustrating and difficult experience for a dentist. However, with lease payments likely to be one of the largest practice expenses, directly affecting the dentist's bottom line profitability, it clearly makes sense to take the time and effort to negotiate the most favorable lease that market conditions make possible. To help in your negotiations, look for a lawyer experienced in negotiating commercial leases because commercial leases, when compared to standard residential leases, contain many more provisions imposing potential liability and expense on the tenant (for example, maintenance of common areas, insurance, taxes, repairs, and buildout costs). Therefore, consider using a lawyer at the outset of negotiations to assist in obtaining the most favorable lease terms that meet your needs. Commercial landlords often start with "form leases" which tend to favor the landlord's interests. Tenants who are not aware of the issues may find themselves stuck with some onerous lease terms.

A qualified attorney can provide assistance with lease clauses such as:

- Whether rental incentives or abatements are available

- Allocation of expenses (e.g., real estate taxes and maintenance) — tenant's proportionate share

- Whether the landlord will pay for all or part of tenant improvements (buildout costs)

- Waiving or avoiding giving any personal guarantees

- Option(s) to renew

- Right of first refusal on additional or adjacent space

- Right to assign and sublet

- Security deposit

- Grace period and notice of default

- Exclusivity for your dental practice

- Liability and indemnification

- Right to early termination (buyout)

In addition to the items discussed above, certain other key issues must be addressed in every office lease. Obviously, the amount of the rent and the rent increases will be of prime importance. But don't forget about other business issues, such as parking, signage, environmental and zoning concerns, and use restrictions. Make sure to consider the one question about which the ADA receives numerous inquiries: landlord-tenant issues concerning Americans with Disabilities Act compliance.

Related References and Resources

- Chapter 6: Dental Office Design

152. How Can I Be Sure That My Dental Laboratory Uses the Exact Materials Prescribed to Manufacture a Prosthesis?

You can take a number of steps to help ensure that the work you order from a dental lab conforms to your order and meets any relevant standards.

When selecting and working with a dental lab, find out whether the lab does all its work in-house, or if some or all of the work is outsourced to other labs. If a dental lab outsources work to a foreign laboratory, ask if the lab can provide its own registration number with the FDA as an "initial importer," "re-packager," or "re-labeler," as well as the FDA registration number of the foreign lab that will work on your order. Ask how the foreign lab was selected and whether individuals from the U.S. lab have actually visited the foreign lab to which your work will be outsourced.

Require that the lab provide documentation that the materials used in any work, whether or not outsourced, are FDA-approved and comply with all relevant ANSI and ISO standards. Ask for the lab's assurance that your detailed lab prescription will be filled as written, regardless of where the work is fabricated. When you write a dental prescription, be as specific as possible. Designate components and brands, and require the dental lab to inform you in advance of any substituted material. Require the lab to provide a document detailing the materials used in your work. Obtain safety data sheets (SDSs) from the lab for the stains that it uses.

If a dental lab cannot answer these questions to your satisfaction, investigate other labs. Place in the patient's chart any documentation and information received from a lab about sources and materials used in that patient's prosthesis.

Always write as detailed a prescription or lab order as possible. Your laboratory prescription form should contain a section for the lab to complete, indicating where the order will be fabricated (including the name and location of any U.S. or foreign lab that will supply all or part of the work) and the materials to be used in the fabrication. Require the lab to agree in writing that the work will conform to your order, that the lab will not substitute materials without your prior approval, and that the lab will indemnify you for and assume all liability arising from, claims for injuries allegedly caused by any of the lab's products that may contain adulterated, contaminated, or toxic materials or that do not conform to your lab prescription or any relevant standards. A qualified attorney can help you draft a document with terms and conditions that will help protect you in the event of a problem or lab error.

Carefully review any documents from the lab for terms related to matters such as outsourcing, materials substitution, disclaimer of warranties, or limitation of liability. Objectionable language can be crossed out and initialed by both parties. Talk to your lawyer about any language on the lab's forms that makes you uncomfortable.

A dental materials trade group has developed a sticker system called "IdentAlloy," which labs can use to inform dentists of the materials used for a case. The sticker is returned to the dentist with the product, and the dentist can file it in the patient's chart.

Related References and Resources

- IdentAlloy, The IdentAlloy and IdentCeram Certificate Program
  www.identalloy.org.

153. What Can I Do If I Have Been Charged for a Product or Service That I Received but Didn't Order?

If you receive unordered merchandise, you may not have to pay for it or send it back. In fact, you may be able to treat the merchandise as a gift. Under federal law and in many states, it is illegal for a seller to attempt to collect a bill for merchandise that its recipient did not order. It is also illegal for a seller in such situations to require the return of the merchandise, even if the seller will pay the shipping. Unordered services, and unauthorized substitution of an item in an order, can be treated in the same way you would treat an unordered item. Of course, if the order involves a legitimate shipping mistake, you may wish to contact the seller and offer to return the merchandise, so long as the seller pays the shipping. If you get into a dispute with the seller that cannot be resolved directly, contact your state or local consumer protection office, local U.S. Postal Inspector, or local Better Business Bureau. You may also file a complaint with the Federal Trade Commission.

Related References and Resources

- USPS, U.S. Postal Service's Mail Fraud Complaint Center
  https://postalinspectors.uspis.gov/forms/MailFraudComplaint.aspx
  1.800.372.8347

- NAAG, National Association of Attorneys General
  www.naag.org

- BBB, Better Business Bureau
  www.bbb.org.

- How to Steer Clear of Telemarketing Sales Scams
  success.ada.org/en/practice/operations/efficient-systems/how-to-steer-clear-of-telemarketing-scams

- YouTube, Business Directory Scams
  www.youtube.com/watch?v=4SbKrPN9nF4

154. Can I Sell Merchandise From My Dental Office, Such as Vitamins and Minerals or Electric Toothbrushes?

There are several legal issues to consider when deciding whether to sell merchandise from the dental office. Starting with the contractual issues, it is important to carefully review the terms of all sales contracts and documents with the manufacturer or supplier, taking into consideration the issues raised in Chapter 19: Contracts. Consult a qualified attorney about any terms that make you uncomfortable or that you don't understand. Having an attorney review a sales agreement, especially one that involves a long-term commitment or a large dollar amount, can be an excellent investment if it saves you time, money and stress in the long run.

If you sell a product that turns out to be defective, you may be named in a products liability lawsuit. Investigate the products you choose to sell and their manufacturer to make sure the products are of the highest quality and the manufacturer is a responsible company, and check with your insurance advisor to make sure your business liability policy would protect you and your practice if such a claim arises from any merchandise you sell.

Check with your accountant to determine whether you are responsible for collecting sales tax when you sell the products. If so, you will be required to obtain a resale tax number from the state and submit periodic reports and remittances.

If you lease your practice facility, check the terms of your lease to make sure there is no restriction on selling merchandise or certain categories of products. A shopping center landlord will sometimes restrict tenants from competing with the other tenants by restricting the scope of their businesses. For example, if the anchor tenant is a pharmacy, other tenants may be restricted from selling health and beauty aids.

If you sell products such as dietary supplements or dental products, make sure the products you sell are over-the-counter and not prescription. The sale of prescription products is highly regulated under state and federal laws.

Be careful not to violate HIPAA, as amended by HITECH, in connection with product sales, particularly if you are considering sending marketing information to patients or allowing another entity to send information to your patients. HIPAA restricts the sale of patient contact information for marketing communications and imposes restrictions on marketing communications to patients without their prior authorization.

Related References and Resources

- Question 39: Can I Send Information About Products or Services to Patients, or Sell Patient Lists to a Company That Wants to Send Them Information?

- Chapter 15: HIPAA, and State Law, and PCI DSS: Patient Information

- Chapter 19: Contracts

Chapter 21.
Antitrust

Dentists, as health care providers and prudent business persons, typically want to set their own fees that are responsive to market conditions and at levels that will allow their patients to afford quality care. Dentists also wish to preserve their right to engage in a mode of practice of their choice, such as fee-for-service or managed care. When it comes to issues such as fee setting and practice mode, it is important that dentists have some grounding in the antitrust laws so as to be aware of the potential legal risks and to know when to seek advice from legal counsel. Violation of the antitrust laws can subject dentists and dental societies to significant financial penalties and even jail time.

The questions below address some of the core antitrust issues in dental practice. Keep in mind that this analysis is not intended to be exhaustive and that antitrust considerations may come into play in many other contexts (for example, in dealing with insurance companies, the subject of a subsequent chapter).

Related References and Resources

- Antitrust
  ADA.org/en/member-center/member-benefits/legal-resources/publications-and-articles/antitrust

- FTC, FTC Guide to Antitrust Laws
  www.ftc.gov/tips-advice/competition-guidance/guide-antitrust-laws

155. What Are the Antitrust Laws and What Do They Mean to Me as a Dentist?

The antitrust laws are a series of laws that protect the public by promoting competition, including assuring that business entities compete independently. Congress passed the Sherman Act, the first antitrust law, in 1890. The Sherman Act addresses practices of companies possessing substantial market power, sometimes amounting to monopolies that restrict competition and drive smaller competitors out of the marketplace. The Sherman Act, which prevents the improper acquisition or use of monopoly power, also prohibits joint action ("contracts, combinations or conspiracies") by competitors in restraint of trade. It is this latter prohibition which has the greatest application to health care providers and professional associations.

Other antitrust laws were enacted later to address particular anticompetitive practices. In 1914, Congress passed the Federal Trade Commission Act, which bans unfair methods of competition and unfair or deceptive acts or practice, and the Clayton Act, which prohibits such mergers and acquisitions that substantially lessen competition or tend to create a monopoly. The Clayton Act was amended in 1936 by the Robinson-Patman Act to ban discriminatory pricing and again in 1976 by the Hart-Scott-Rodino Antitrust Improvement Act to require advance government notice from companies that are planning large mergers and acquisitions.

The states also have antitrust laws which are based on these federal laws.

For dentists, the main concern is that the antitrust laws prohibit certain joint actions by competitors that unreasonably restrain trade or harm competition, such as:

- Price fixing, including express or tacit agreements relating to prices and fees

- Agreements to allocate markets or customers

- Agreements not to compete, except for certain legitimate purposes

- Boycotts, or joint refusals to deal, directed against third parties, or agreements to exclude competitors or potential competitors from the marketplace

- Joint efforts to influence rates or charges, as in the case of insurers

The antitrust laws are enforced by the U.S. Department of Justice, the Federal Trade Commission, and the state attorneys general. Private parties, including competing dentists and insurers, who are injured in their business or property, can also bring legal actions to seek recourse for their injuries.

Violations of the antitrust laws can result in severe sanctions and penalties, including treble damages for the harm caused (three times the actual damages), injunctive relief and consent judgments/decrees, penalties of up to $1 million per violation for individuals and up to $100 million for corporations, and imprisonment for up to 10 years. None of the financial costs are likely to be covered by an individual's malpractice or business insurance.

156. Can I Consult With Other Dentists When Setting My Fees?

As a general rule, discussions among independent dentists about the fees they will charge can lead to allegations of a violation of the antitrust laws, especially where those discussions are followed by the adoption of identical pricing. Dentists are viewed as competitors in the marketplace, and agreements between competitors to fix prices is presumptively illegal. Moreover, price fixing is regarded as a "per se" violation, meaning that liability is automatic, with no consideration of any justifications or offsetting circumstances.

To avoid creating significant legal risk — both criminal and potentially expensive civil liability exposure — sole practitioners should always set their fees independently, based on what they perceive to be the value of their services and what they believe the market will bear. Dentists in partnerships or joint or group practices, however, are regarded as participants in a single entity for antitrust purposes, and their collaboration is legitimate. Similarly, properly structured networks of dentists that share financial risks may be viewed on balance as pro-competitive and thus, within that network, not subject to the antitrust laws, but the parameters for such networks are strictly defined.

Related References and Resources

- FTC, Antitrust Guidelines for Collaborations Among Competitors
  www.ftc.gov/sites/default/files/attachments/press-releases/ftc-doj-issue-antitrust-guidelines-collaborations-among-competitors/ftcdojguidelines.pdf

157. Is There Anything the ADA Can Do to Stop Insurance Carriers from Taking Actions or Engaging in Practices That Create Difficulties for Dentists?

The ADA and its members can lawfully lobby and advocate for the passage or enforcement of laws, attempt to influence public officials, or engage in good faith efforts through the judicial process to address abuses, even though the requested relief may affect competition. These actions fall within the exceptions to the antitrust laws known as the Noerr-Pennington Doctrine. The ADA and its dental societies may properly express to insurance carriers the views of their members that particular fees and reimbursement levels should be raised. However, neither a dental society nor individual dentists may suggest, imply or threaten a joint refusal to participate unless reimbursement is increased. Such action may be viewed as conspiring to an illegal boycott. Moreover, neither a group of dentists nor an association acting on their behalf may collectively negotiate the level of reimbursement.

Whether and how to participate in insurance plans, including managed care or any particular plan, is a decision each dentist must make individually, and the ADA will not encourage or facilitate agreements among dentists as to participation in particular plans. To assist individual members, the ADA offers a wealth of educational information about practice options, including managed care, to help members make informed individual decisions about how to practice.

Related References and Resources

- DOJ, Statement 5: Department of Justice and Federal Trade Commission Enforcement Policy on Providers' Collective Provision of Fee-Related Information to Purchasers of Health Care Services *www.justice.gov/atr/public/guidelines/1791.htm*

158. Do the Antitrust Laws Prevent Me from Promoting Direct Reimbursement?

No. Direct Reimbursement (DR) can be safely promoted, provided that the promotion is conducted appropriately. However, DR promotional activities, if undertaken inappropriately (which usually means without legal advice), could potentially violate antitrust laws and open the door to actions for libel, slander, or commercial torts. For example, a DR promotion that is no more than a call for an unlawful boycott of an insurance plan is problematic.

Some good rules of thumb are: (1) it is always safest to promote what you or your dental society is for, rather than what some dentists may be against; (2) DR promotions should avoid linkage to inappropriate criticism of other benefit plans; and (3) promotional activities should not be a means of disguising boycott or price fixing activities. As DR promotions do not occur in a vacuum but are in the context of other dental society activities, problems can be avoided by having an attorney review the materials to be used in the promotional campaign, including seminars and educational programs for members and employers, as appropriate.

159. Can Our Association Establish a Code of Ethics That Restricts Advertising or Prohibits Unacceptable Practices?

As a general matter, advertising restrictions can raise issues as a restraint on the ability to compete. This is especially true if the restriction affects price advertising. On the other hand, there is little antitrust risk involved in prohibiting false, deceptive or untruthful advertising, provided that there are workable definitions of false, deceptive or untruthful, are reasonably and consistently enforced. The more challenging cases arise when professionals go further and try to ban all or substantially all advertising or specific kinds of advertising on the ground that it is inherently deceptive or otherwise unethical. Regulators view codes of ethics as a means reaching joint agreements to how competition can occur. The Federal Trade Commission has recently obtained consent decrees from associations whose code of ethics precluded members from:

- Soliciting clients from other members

- Competing against other members by cutting pricing

- Speaking disparagingly against another member

- Soliciting or hiring an employee of another member

Associations should seek legal advice from competent antitrust counsel when developing code of ethics provisions.

Related References and Resources

- FTC, Other Agreements Among Competitors
  www.ftc.gov/tips-advice/competition-guidance/guide-antitrust-laws/dealings-competitors/other-agreements-among

- FTC, To Settle FTC Charges, Two Trade Associations Agree to Eliminate Rules that Restrict Competition
  www.ftc.gov/news-events/press-releases/2014/12/settle-ftc-charges-two-trade-associations-agree-eliminate-rules

160. Can Dentists Refuse to Deal With Health Care Practitioners Who Engage in Unethical Conduct or Who Engage in the Practice of Dentistry Without a License?

Agreements among providers to deny market entry to prospective competitors may violate the antitrust laws, even where the competitors are arguably engaged in wrongful or unethical behavior. For example, in the 1980s, chiropractors brought an antitrust suit against the American Medical Association (AMA) over an ethics provision that made it unethical to deal with "unscientific practitioners", which included chiropractors. The case resulted in a ruling against the AMA. (See *Wilk v. AMA*). Tooth whitening entities may constitute competitors (See *N.C. Board of Dental Examiners v. FTC*), as may mid-level providers.

161. Do the Antitrust Laws Prevent Insurance Companies From Setting Low Reimbursement Rates? From Imposing Burdensome Contractual Provisions?

As noted above, the antitrust laws generally prohibit two or more competitors from taking concerted action that restrains or diminishes competition. The law ordinarily does not, however, with some narrow exceptions, prevent a single competitor from taking action that may be deemed anticompetitive. While proof of an agreement between two or more insurance companies to set or reduce reimbursement rates would likely constitute an antitrust violation, that proof is usually hard to come by. Because each insurance company is viewed as a single competitor for legal purposes, it is generally free to set its own reimbursement rates on a take it or leave it basis.

If, however, an insurer is so dominant in an area that it has monopoly power, that is, it is able to dictate prices (including reimbursement levels) and exclude competitors — its conduct could possibly violate the aspect of the antitrust laws that prohibits the use of anticompetitive conduct to maintain or acquire monopoly power. Note, however, that the law does not prohibit the possession of monopoly power itself. Typically, monopoly power is shown by a dominant share, usually over 70 percent, of a relevant antitrust (geographic and product) market. The ADA believes, based on market share data, that certain payers may have monopoly power in select markets. But a violation of this law would be very difficult to prove in most markets, and courts are generally careful not to condemn legitimate business activity as anticompetitive. Moreover, even if a violation were proven in a specific market, it would not change the reality that in the overwhelming majority of markets, insurance companies are free to set their own reimbursement rates.

162. Is There Anything That a Group of Dentists Can Do to Address Threats to Our Practice?

That depends on what you want to do. There are a number of exemptions to the antitrust laws. A key exemption for dentists is the one allowing for good faith lobbying. The First Amendment to the United States Constitution protects the right to petition the government, including the executive branch, legislature, courts, and administrative agencies. As explicated in the Noerr-Pennington Doctrine, this Constitutional protection permits dentists and dental societies to advocate collectively for government action, even if that action would harm competition, as long as the advocacy is in good faith. Dentists may, for example, lobby the legislature or an insurance commissioner for changes in the law or regulations that would increase reimbursement levels, even they are not allowed to negotiate as a group with the insurers.

When engaged in lobbying for increased reimbursement, it is often more effective to show how the lobbying effort is primarily directed towards improving patient care as opposed to dentists' pocketbooks. Also, dentists should never suggest, as part of a lobbying effort or otherwise, a threat to boycott any insurer or other third-party payer unless reimbursement is increased. It is essential to remember that what is safe in the legislative arena may not be protected when discussed in the context of the marketplace (for example, if good faith lobbying turns into a call for boycott in the marketplace).

Chapter 22.
Tax Issues

163. Is It OK for Me to Stay on Cash Basis Accounting or Must I Use Accrual Basis Accounting?

There are two basic methods of accounting for the income and expenses of a practice: cash and accrual, and current IRS rules allow for small businesses to elect to use either. Cash accounting recognizes revenue when it is received and expenses when they are paid. Most individuals and many small businesses use the cash method of accounting. In contrast, accrual accounting recognizes revenue when the services are rendered and expenses when they are incurred. (Prepaid expenses are considered assets and accrued expenses are therefore considered liabilities.) This method often results in taxpayers paying taxes on accounts receivable prior to actually receiving payment, unnecessarily complicating the tax payment process and potentially exacerbating cash flow problems.

According to the IRS, you must use the accounting method that clearly reflects your income and expenses. Moreover, you must maintain records that will enable you to file a correct return. Also, you must use the same accounting method from year to year (unless you receive approval from the IRS to switch accounting methods).

Dentists should contact their accountants for advice on which accounting method is best for their practices.

164. Can I Claim the Americans With Disabilities Act Tax Credit for Purchases of Intraoral Cameras, Panorex Machines, New Chairs, Etc.?

Probably not. The American with Disabilities Act (AwDA) tax credit applies paid or incurred by an eligible small business for the purpose of enabling such business to comply with applicable requirements under the AwDA. The statute excludes new construction, and requires that the expenditure be reasonable and necessary to accomplish compliance with the AwDA.

The question often arises whether high-tech dental equipment purchases can fall within this category. In many cases, the IRS has taken the position that the credit may not be taken in such instances because the principal benefit of the new equipment was to the dentist. For example, the purchase was made to increase business, rather than remove barriers to access; the patients who benefit are primarily not disabled; and some of the purchases do not benefit patients with disabilities (for example, a panorex may help older patients with visual impairments, but does wearing glasses amount to a disability in the first place?). Some dentists have, nevertheless, prevailed when challenging the IRS, either in whole or at least in part (for example, the IRS has reportedly allowed a pro-rata portion of a dental chair purchase to be claimed under the credit, when the dentist showed she served a high percentage of disabled patients, and would not have claimed the credit otherwise). Like all tax matters, a dentist considering claiming this credit needs to decide how aggressive or risk-averse a tax position to take, and should understand that claiming the credit for high-tech dental equipment purchases may lead to audit. Consult with your accountant to determine how these tax credits apply to your practice.

165. What Are My Requirements Regarding Payroll Taxes?

Your obligation as an employer is to make all payroll tax withholding payments due to the IRS (or to the state, as applicable) on time, and before paying any other creditor. Otherwise, a fine can be assessed up to 100 percent of the back payroll taxes, in addition to the requirement of returning the tax amounts themselves. The fine is assessed personally against the person(s) the IRS determines to be responsible for collecting, accounting for, and paying over these taxes, and who acted willfully in not doing so. IRS Publication 15, Circular E, and Publication 15-A Employer's Tax Guide, is available free at your local IRS District Office, and also can be accessed online at the IRS website, along with all the necessary forms you need to file and related instructions.

The Federal Insurance Contributions Act (FICA) tax includes two separate taxes. One is social security tax and the other is Medicare tax. Different rates apply for each of these taxes.

The 2015 tax rate for social security is 6.2 percent for the employer and 6.2 percent for the employee, or 12.4 percent total. The current rate for Medicare is 1.45 percent for the employer and 1.45 percent for the employee, or 2.9 percent total.

Only the social security tax has a wage base limit. The wage base limit is the maximum wage that is subject to the tax for that year. For earnings in 2015, this base is $118,500.

There is no wage base limit for Medicare tax. All covered wages are subject to Medicare tax.

Since January 1, 2013, an Additional Medicare Tax applies to an individual's Medicare wages that exceed a threshold amount based on the taxpayer's filing status. Employers are responsible for withholding the 0.9 percent Additional Medicare Tax on an individual's wages paid in excess of $200,000 in a calendar year, without regard to filing status. An employer is required to begin withholding Additional Medicare Tax in the pay period in which it pays wages in excess of $200,000 to an employee and to continue to withhold it each pay period until the end of the calendar year. There is no employer match for Additional Medicare Tax.

In addition, employers report and pay Federal Unemployment Tax (FUTA) separately from federal income tax, and social security and Medicare taxes. An employer pays FUTA tax only from its own funds. Employees do not pay this tax or have it withheld from their pay.

Related References and Resources

- IRS Publication 15 (2015) (Circular E), Employer's Tax Guide
  www.irs.gov/publications/p15/index.html

- IRS, Questions and Answers for the Additional Medicare Tax
  www.irs.gov/Businesses/Small-Businesses-&-Self-Employed/Questions-and-Answers-for-the-Additional-Medicare-Tax

Chapter 23.
Insuring Your Practice

Insurance helps you protect your practice and your personal assets in the event of mistake or events beyond your control. This chapter addresses some of the forms of insurance policies that are important in dentistry.

166. What Type of Professional Liability Insurance Should I Have?

Dental Professional Liability (malpractice) insurance protects against claim allegations arising out of dental treatment or services you and your employees provide, or should have provided, to patients. A professional liability insurance policy is intended to protect the dentist both from the costs of litigation and any awards for damages or settlements. Depending on a particular state's statute of limitations, malpractice suits can be brought years after treatment has been provided.

Malpractice insurance is required to practice dentistry in most jurisdictions, although licensing regulations and insurance requirements vary by state. Contact your state licensing board or local dental society to verify your state's requirements for health care providers before purchasing a policy.

There are two forms of professional liability policies, claims-made and occurrence policies. An occurrence policy covers claims for treatment or services rendered while the policy is in force, regardless of when the claim is made (for example, claims reported after the policy has terminated).

A claims-made policy requires that both the treatment or service and the claim be made while the policy is in force. If a claim is made against the dentist after the policy terminates, there is no coverage unless the insured purchased an "extended reporting endorsement" (commonly referred to as "tail" coverage). If a claims-made policy is being replaced with another claims-made policy, the "tail coverage" can be purchased from the successor insurer. In this case, the coverage is called a "prior-acts endorsement." The prior acts endorsement should have a "retroactive date" that is the date on which the dentist first became continuously insured under any claims-made policy or policies. If a dentist has purchased a prior-acts endorsement from his or her successor insurer, then the successor insurer will cover all claims arising from treatments rendered after the retroactive date that are first reported while the new claims-made policy is in effect.

A professional liability policy's "limits of liability" stipulate the total amount of losses for which an insurer will provide coverage. There are two limits of liability in a policy. The first limit is the maximum amount an insurer will pay for a single malpractice claim. The second limit is the total amount an insurer will pay for all claims incurred within a single year. For example, a policy providing a $1 million/$3 million limit of liability will provide coverage for up to $1 million for any single claim and not more than $3 million for multiple claims in a single year. In some cases, a policy's limit of liability includes only amounts paid in damages to the plaintiff. In other cases, the limits may include the insurer's expenses in defending the claim or reaching an out-of-court settlement.

There are no firm guidelines as to what is considered appropriate limits of liability for dentists. The ADA believes that a majority of practitioners carry policies having $1 million per occurrence/$3 million aggregate limits of liability. In the vast majority of cases, these limits are more than sufficient. However, there have been cases where dental malpractice lawsuits against dentists, including general practitioners, have resulted in jury awards or pre-trial settlements that exceed $1 million. Therefore, the decision as to what constitutes appropriate limits of liability will depend upon the individual dentist's tolerance for assuming risk and the cost of purchasing a policy having high limits of liability. Dentists who are performing relatively complicated procedures, providing general anesthesia or conscious sedation, and practicing in major metropolitan areas or litigious areas may wish to err on the side of caution and purchase policy limits in excess of $1 million/$3 million.

Another consideration in purchasing professional liability insurance policies is the policy's "consent to settle" provision. This provision sets forth the conditions, if any, under which the insurance company can settle a malpractice claim without the dentist's consent. In some cases, the attorney assigned by the insurer to represent the dentist may conclude that it is more economical to settle a claim out of court, regardless of the merits of the plaintiff's case. This judgment may be based upon factors that are unrelated to the quality of the treatment rendered. For example, the trial may take place in a venue that has historically been unfavorable for doctors accused of malpractice. Or it may be the defense attorney's judgment that the dentist would not make a good witness for some reason, or that the dentist's records of the treatment are insufficient to document the quality of care provided. In such situations, the dentist may disagree with his or her defense attorney and may wish to proceed with a court trial to protect his or her professional reputation. The consent to settle feature of the dentist's policy will stipulate whether the dentist has the right to refuse to agree to a settlement offer and, if so, whether the dentist has to personally cover payments in excess of the proposed settlement offer if he or she is subsequently found liable for malpractice by the trial court.

There are other matters that should be considered in selecting a professional liability policy, including exclusions, other covered persons (such as employees or partners), the insurer's financial strength and experience in dental professional liability, and so forth. For these reasons, a dentist should work with a knowledgeable licensed insurance agent to evaluate his or her exposures and secure the necessary coverage.

Keep in mind that your state law may set certain requirements regarding malpractice coverage. In addition, if you are a participating provider in an insurance plan (such as a managed care network), the plan may impose certain requirements contractually as well.

Although the ADA does not endorse or evaluate professional liability insurance companies, the Council on Members Insurance and Retirement Programs does maintain a list of insurers available in each state with links to the insurers' websites.

Related References and Resources

- Directory of Professional Liability Insurers
  ADA.org/en/member-center/member-benefits/insurance-resources/directory-of-professional-liability-insurers

167. What About Liability Other Than Malpractice?

Business liability insurance, also called commercial general liability insurance, protects the dentist for non-practice related losses sustained as a result of bodily injury or property damage to others, such as a patient's slip and fall in the waiting room or water damage in rented premises caused by the dentist or an employee. Such insurance also covers personal injury in such matters as slander, false advertising or invasion of privacy. If a dentist's business liability policy has a low liability limit, perhaps because the same policy has been renewed for many years, the dentist should consider obtaining a commercial umbrella policy. This type of policy adds a layer of liability coverage on top of the "primary" business liability insurance and pays after the primary limit has been reached. Premiums for such coverage often compare favorably to trying to increase liability limits on the primary insurance.

Another type of insurance is workers' compensation insurance. When the dentist has employees, workers' compensation insurance provides payments to employees for injury or occupational disease suffered on the job. Many states require a business with employees to have workers' compensation coverage.

168. Can I Insure Against Damage to My Practice?

Business liability insurance protects your business in the event of a suit for personal injury or property damage. What about the replacement cost for damage to the dentist's practice? This type of damage is covered by property and casualty insurance. Property insurance provides for the replacement of lost or damaged property, such as operatory or office equipment. Important: be sure coverage limits reflect current value of office equipment and contents. This coverage protects against risks that can destroy a dentist's livelihood and should be considered essential costs of doing business, just like professional liability insurance.

169. What Insurance Helps Protect My Income?

All dentists are aware of the importance of life and disability insurance to handle family income needs in the event of death or disability. The ADA sponsors high-quality, attractively priced term and universal life insurance products as well as income disability protection and supplemental medical coverage plans. Details can be obtained from the ADA Council on Members Insurance and Retirement Programs. In addition, in the business context, the ADA sponsors an office overhead expense plan. This plan pays for operating expenses of a dentist's practice, such as rent, mortgage, and the cost of a replacement dentist and payroll while he or she is disabled, thus protecting the practice in the case of a dentist's temporary absence as a result of disability.

Related References and Resources

- ADA Members Insurance Plans
  insurance.ada.org

170. What Other Insurance Issues Are Important?

Every dentist should take steps to be informed of the business risks he or she is insured against, and those exposures that call for new or additional coverage. For example, a dentist and staff who travel to several locations will need to consider employer's non-owned automobile liability insurance and in-transit loss insurance, not otherwise covered by property and casualty insurance. A thriving practice might consider the cost of practice interruption insurance that provides compensation for lost or reduced income resulting from suspension of practice as a result of power outage or severe weather to be well worth the premium. In evaluating business risks, a dentist may wish to consider obtaining liability coverage for employment law claims. Our insurance advisor can help you assess what additional coverage might be important in your circumstances.

Finally, no discussion of insurance issues would be complete without addressing Personal Umbrella Liability Insurance. Some dentists may wish to consider the purchase of an umbrella (or excess) personal liability insurance policy. The purpose of this policy is to provide coverage that would supplement the dentist's liability coverage contained in his or her homeowners or automobile insurance policies. In the event of a liability claim covered by a homeowners or automobile policy which exceeds the coverage limits of that policy, a personal umbrella liability policy could provide additional protection.

It is important to understand that personal umbrella liability policies do not provide coverage against liability exposures such as professional liability (malpractice) or other liability arising out of other business aspects of a dental practice.

Related References and Resources

- Question 126: Will My Liability Insurance Cover the Financial Loss Caused by a Data Breach?

- Chapter 9: Introduction to Employment Law

Payment, Collections, and Reimbursement

Chapter 24.
Payment and Collections

For many dentists, payment and collection difficulties are among the most routine business problems they face in their practices. This chapter will discuss some of the common pitfalls and ways to protect against them.

171. Which NPI Do I Use to Submit a Claim? I Have a Type 1 NPI for Myself and a Type 2 NPI for My Corporation/Group/Partnership.

There are two types of National Provider Identifiers (NPIs). Type 1 is for individual dentists or hygienists who provide health care services. Like a Social Security number, your Type 1 NPI identifies you as an individual and is permanent in nature, even if you move from one group or practice to another.

A Type 2 NPI is for businesses entities such as corporations, LLCs, LLPs, group practices, and professional corporations, including those that are paid in their business or corporate name or under their federal employer tax identification number (EIN). Group practices have a Type 2 for the practice plus a Type 1 for each dentist who works in the office.

You should review each claim form carefully to determine which NPI is required. You may need to use both your Type 1 and Type 2 NPIs on a single form. For example, on the standard ADA Dental Claim Form, there is a space at field 54 for entering a "treating dentist's" (Type 1) NPI and a space at field 49 for entering the "billing entity's" (Type 2) NPI.

A dentist generally uses a Type 1 NPI to submit a claim as an individual provider or to sign a claim as the "treating dentist." A dentist will also use a Type 1 NPI when a pharmacist requires the NPI of the prescribing dentist, and when a specialist requires the NPI of the referring dentist. The Type 2 NPI, on the other hand, is for a business entity (other than a sole proprietor) that is entitled to payment for services.

It is important to be on your guard because NPI numbers have been stolen and used for illicit purposes.

To complete a claim where a group practice has multiple providers (for example, Dr. Jones, Dr. Smith and Dr. Gray), use the Type 2 NPI to designate the practice as the named payee on the claim form (that is, the entity entitled to payment, such as Jones Dental Group, Inc.) rather than the treating dentist's individual Type 1 NPI.

Related References and Resources

- Chapter 5: Practice Formats: Business/Legal Structure

- CMS, National Provider Identifier Standard (NPI) FAQ and Application Information
  www.cms.hhs.gov/Regulations-and-Guidance/HIPAA-Administrative-Simplification/ NationalProvidentStand/index.html?redirect+/NationalProvidentStand

- CDT: Current Dental Procedure Codes
  adacatalog.org or 1.800.947.4746

172. A Patient Refused to Pay for What His Insurance Refused to Cover — What Can I Do?

In this case, your basic options are (a) to sue or (b) to forgo your right to collect the payment due. However, there are things you can do to make your future collections efforts more successful.

Dentists often presume that patients will remit co-pays, pay for any portion of the bill that is not covered by insurance, and remit full payment even if their insurance refuses to pay the claim. But when a patient refuses to pay, the dentist has to make a judgment call weighing the risks and rewards of pursing a collection action. The collection process is not without cost, in both time and money. And it is not a sure bet. In a lawsuit, the patient will be given the opportunity to explain his or her position, which is likely to be that the dentist agreed to do the work in question without holding the patient financially accountable for the disputed amount (such as, "Dr. Smith told me not to worry about insurance, and that he would collect whatever he could from my insurance company."). In such a case, the court may wind up believing the patient, or at least have some doubt as to who owes what to whom. Knowing the risks in filing a collection suit, many dentists in such situations have decided to forgo their right to sue. In addition to the value of your time, and the expense involved in the collection process, there are also reputational risks, such as an aggrieved patient posting negative comments on social media, or yellow journalism (imagine: "Dentist Sues War Hero's Dad").

One way to bolster the dentist's legal position in future cases, and potentially make collections efforts more successful and less costly, is to have patients sign a clear agreement up front (before dental work is commenced), acknowledging their responsibility for the total amount due, regardless of what the insurance carrier ultimately pays. A signed document to this effect can be a stark reminder to a patient who later refuses to pay, and send a clear message to the patient early in the collection process that this agreement will be used against the patient in court, if payment is not forthcoming.

In addition, you may wish to follow the lead of the many dental offices that post and publish their financial policies. These policies can be displayed on a plaque at the receptionist's desk and can be published in the practice's brochure, website, or in a special mailing. While likely not as helpful to the dentist's collection case as having the patient's signature on an agreement accepting financial responsibility, evidence that the patient was on notice in this manner would likely be a positive in a legal action for collection purposes.

Finally, there are certain things that you should not do, such as withholding the records of non-paying patients, both for ethical and legal reasons.

Related References and Resources

- Question 173: When Should I Use a Collection Agency? Are There Limits to What Can Be Done In Collections? Is Small Claims Court Worth It? How Does It Work?

- Question 182: If a Patient Is Behind On Payments, Can I Withhold Records or Stop Treatment?

173. How can I Better Position My Practice to Minimize the Need to Send Non-Paying Patients to Collection and Improve My Practice's Chance of Prevailing in Collection Matters?

There is a way to bolster the dentist's legal position in future cases, and potentially make collections efforts more successful and less costly and that is to have patients sign an agreement up front before dental work is commenced, acknowledging their responsibility for the total amount due, regardless of what the insurance carrier ultimately pays. A signed document to this effect can be a stark reminder to a patient who later refuses to pay, and send a clear message to the patient early in the collections process that his or her agreement will be quickly used against the patient in a court of law if necessary.

Another possibility is to follow the lead of the many dental offices that post and publish their financial policies. These policies are frequently displayed on a plaque at the receptionist's desk and can be published in the practice's brochure, newsletter, website, or in a special mailing. While this may not be as effective as having the patient sign a written agreement accepting responsibility, it is a step in the right direction for collection purposes.

174. A Patient Is Refusing to Give Our Dental Office His or Her Social Security Number (SSN). Can I Refuse to Treat the Patient? Why Would a Patient Be Reluctant to Provide This Information? Can Collecting Social Security Numbers Pose a Legal Risk for a Dental Practice?

Patients who are reluctant to disclose their Social Security numbers may be concerned about the possibility of identity theft. In some cases, dental practices have legitimate reasons to ask patients for their Social Security numbers. For example, a dentist who requires a credit report before beginning an expensive course of treatment may require the patient's Social Security number because most credit bureaus require this information in order to run the report. A dentist may also require a patient's Social Security number to file a claim with a dental benefit plan, although many third-party payers have developed unique IDs for this purpose. Dental practices that use Social Security numbers to identify patients may wish to develop a system of unique patient IDs as well.

It is possible that you could legally refuse to treat a patient who refuses to provide a Social Security number, as long as you are not required to treat the patient under patient abandonment or ethical considerations, and provided you are not requesting the Social Security number for discriminatory reasons. But the laws do not require a patient to give a Social Security number to you either. Individuals are only required to provide their Social Security numbers to certain governmental agencies, banks and securities brokers, and their employers.

Without a legitimate reason to require a patient's Social Security number, refusing to treat without the Social Security number could be viewed as discrimination. There may be situations where it is not necessary for a dental practice to collect a Social Security number from a patient. For example, a dental practice can require a photo ID to verify identity, or an insurance number to verify coverage. Using alternatives to the Social Security number may ultimately benefit your practice because possessing patient Social Security numbers could lead to problems such as identity theft; for example, if your patient account records are lost or stolen.

Most states have laws requiring notification if there is a breach involving an individual's name and certain sensitive information such as Social Security number, credit or debit card number, or driver's license or state ID number. In some states the list is longer and may include data elements such as health plan numbers. Some states also have laws requiring specific safeguards to protect such sensitive information, such as secure disposal laws. Secure disposal laws generally require the use of secure methods when disposing of sensitive data. A qualified attorney could provide the details of the laws in your state.

In addition, the Federal Trade Commission may allege that failure to maintain reasonable and appropriate data security for consumers' sensitive personal information violates the Federal Trade Commission Act's prohibition of unfair and deceptive trade practices.

The Federal Trade Commission recommends taking stock of the personal information in files and on computers and keeping only what is needed for your business. Because of the risk of identity theft to the consumer, and the risk to the dental practice posed by federal and state data security laws, a dental practice may wish to restrict data collection to information that must be collected and retained for business and legal reasons.

Related References and Resources

- Question 107: What Effect Will the HITECH Provisions of the American Recovery And Reinvestment Act of 2009 (ARRA) Have Upon HIPAA? And How Will That Affect Dentists' Compliance with HIPAA Privacy and Security Rules

- FTC, Data Security
  www.business.ftc.gov/privacy-and-security/data-security

- The HIPAA/HITECH Breach Notification Rule
  ADA.org/en/member-center/member-benefits/legal-resources/publications-and-articles/ hipaa-and-data-security/the-hipaa-hitech-breach-notification-rule

- FTC, Protecting Personal Information: A Guide for Business
  www.business.ftc.gov/documents/bus69-protecting-personal-information-guide-business

175. Who Pays When Parents Are Divorced?

The divorce decree will usually establish which parent is primarily responsible financially for a child's dental expenses. However, especially if the parent who is not primarily responsible is the one who is bringing the child to the office for care, it may be prudent to get that parent to agree, in writing, that he or she will pay for care in the event her or his former spouse fails to honor the decree. Not unlike a patient with insurance, the person authorizing care can be held accountable for payment contractually, irrespective of whether the insurance company — or in this case, the former spouse — pays what is owed. Is it necessary to do this? No. But it is an option, recognizing that the divorce decree dictates rights and responsibilities between the divorced couple, not between them (or either of them) and the dentist.

176. Can I Check My Patient's Credit History Before Agreeing to Provide Care?

Yes. It is perfectly reasonable for a dentist to have an expectation that full payment will be made for services rendered, and a credit check may provide the dentist some measure of comfort in this regard. You will need to follow all the Fair Credit Reporting Act, including getting the patient's permission to run the check. And of course, be sure not to discriminate when requesting permission to run a credit check (for example, avoid making such requests based on race or disability status).

There are three major consumer reporting companies in the United States. All have varying charges for membership fees, access terminal fees, monthly minimums and report costs. If you wish to investigate this approach, again, thoroughly discuss it with your professional advisors.

The federal Fair and Accurate Credit Transactions Act (FACTA) imposes certain requirements on entities that obtain consumer reports for conducting business.

Related References and Resources

- Chapter 16: FACTA: Red Flags and Disposal Rules

- Equifax
  www.equifax.com

- Experian (formerly TRW)
  www.experian.com

- Trans Union
  www.transunion.com

177. What Are the Payment Card Industry Data Security Standards (PCI DSS)?

The Payment Card Industry Security Standards Council has mandated data security standards for "merchants" (businesses that are set up to accept credit or debit cards as payment for goods or services). Compliance with these standards, known as the Payment Card Industry Data Security Standards (PCI DSS), is generally required in the agreement between the dental practice and the credit card company or bank.

PCI DSS requires that merchants satisfy twelve different elements of a program aimed at maintaining the security of credit card information. The requirements include many technical elements such as maintaining data firewalls, encryption and anti-virus protections, as well as policy-type elements such as training staff and maintaining a list of service providers (e.g., companies who have access to the dental practice's payment card data). A dental practice may need an IT professional to help the dental practice comply with some of the standards, which means there may be a cost to achieving compliance.

Credit card companies treat merchants differently according to the volume of transactions the merchant handles. While a dental practice must comply to the extent required by the applicable agreement, certain aspects of the compliance program may depend on the volume of transactions.

A dental practice that does not comply may be subject to financial penalties or prevented from processing credit card transactions depending on the terms of their agreements. Dental offices that accept credit and debit cards should review their credit card service provider agreements or call their service provider to determine the requirements for their individual situations.

A PCI DSS compliance program may need to be updated from time to time (for example, if the PCI Council changes the standards). A new version of the standards, PCI DSS version 3.0, became effective on January 1st, 2014. After December 31st, 2014, all compliance validations must be to PCI DSS version 3.0.

Related References and Resources

- PCI Security Standards Council
  www.pcisecuritystandards.org/index.php

- PCI Security Standards Council FAQ
  www.pcisecuritystandards.org/faq

178. If the Patient Doesn't Accept My Work or Refuses to Come Back to Let Me Finish It, and I've Already Collected Insurance for It, Do I Have a Problem?

Perhaps. If you submitted a claim for work already completed, there should be no problem. On the other hand, if you billed before work was done, there may be a question of insurance fraud. An example might be where the dentist starts a multiple visit procedure, such as a root canal, and the patient refuses to return to allow the dentist to complete the procedure. In such a case, the dentist should return any advance dental plan payment for work not done. Another example might be where a patient needs a cast, post and core to support a crown. If the dentist does only the foundation work but submits a claim for the crown as well, and the patient does not return for the crown, there may be an obligation to repay the carrier for the entire amount of the crown reimbursement. You can avoid this concern, of course, by submitting claims only for completed work.

179. Are There Legal Problems Giving Discounts to Family, Staff or Colleagues?

Probably not, if done within reason. For the same reasons that dentists are free to set their own fee schedules (subject to anti-discrimination laws), dentists may generally make appropriate exceptions for discounts. However, you should be aware that such discounts could impact how the dentist's usual fee is calculated and potentially raise insurance fraud concerns. This is especially true if discounts are given to a significant number of patients, and those discounts were not agreed to as part of a provider contract with an insurance company. If the dentist is offering non-contractual discounts to a large number of patients, is the dentist committing insurance fraud when submitting his or her "full fee" for payment and representing it as the dentist's "usual fee"? Historically, this issue has not been a particular legal problem for dentists, although some commentators have questioned excessive use of discounts. The prudent course for a dentist who wants to offer courtesy discounts is to limit the number of people who will qualify for the discounts, and the frequency of their use, so that the "full fee" is essentially the usual one.

180. Can I Extend Dental Coverage Through My Office to Patients Who Do Not Have It by Establishing My Practice's Own In-Office Dental Plan?

These general type of plans are, in a general sense, sometimes referred to as dental membership savings plans, dental membership discount plans, or as in-office dental insurance plans. You may be able to do so, but you must first look into your state insurance regulatory scheme, and you will need to consider some legal concerns before you set up an in-office plan (e.g., a plan where patients would pay a fixed annual premium, in exchange for which the patient might be entitled to receive certain procedures at no charge, such as preventive services, and other services upon a discounted fee structure). It is strongly recommended that you retain a qualified attorney admitted in your jurisdiction to assure that regulatory hurdles are properly addressed, and in setting up the plan itself.

State Insurance Rules

Your state may have its own rules that affect establishment of an in-office insurance plan. Your state dental association may be able to help you address these, as well as your attorney.

Review Third-Party Payer Contracts

Your obligations under these contracts might present impediments to your establishing the plan, or to establishing it in the manner you wish. For example, if your contract with a third party payer guarantees that the payer will receive the lowest rate that you charge for any procedure, then establishing your plan may require that you lower your fee to the payer for each service where your in-office plan rate is less than the rate you have committed to with the payer!

It is important to understand any alternative means of calculating the fees, as you do not want to allow the payer a means to contest your in-house fee as lower than the contract fee. Note that the lowest rate you charge for a service may be calculated in more than one way. The payer could conceivably attempt to go back to the establishment of your plan to seek partial reimbursement of the previously paid fees, or merely attempt to set that amount off against future payments to you.

Clearly State the Plan

It is critical that you fully, accurately, and unambiguously describe the terms of the plan, both in the terms of your agreement with the patient as well as in advertisements or offers that you make to the general public (including to your patients). You should specifically describe the services that are covered by the plan (and state clearly those service that are not covered), what services will be provided at each visit, how frequently the patient may receive the covered services, any additional fees the patient might have to pay for certain services, any restrictions (e.g., limitations on refunds, the consequences of missed appointments, referral to specialists, eligibility for enrolling in the plan, etc.). A clear and unambiguous written statement in the contract of what services are and are not covered will help minimize the chance of any dispute down the road.

Related References and Resources

- Michigan Dental Association, Extending Insurance to Your Patients Through Your Dental Office *www.youtube.com/watch?v=r4eb1CmANWQ* (Note: While this video addresses certain issues specific to Michigan, the discussion provides further useful guidance on these issues.)

181. Are There Legal Problems in Offering and Awarding Social Coupons to New or Existing Patients?

Possibly, depending on factors such as (a) the type of fee arrangement used, (b) the state in which you practice, and (c) whether you provide services payable under a federal health care program such as Medicare or Medicaid.

A social coupon refers to all forms of Internet-based coupons or vouchers, including those that can be shared via social media. Many providers of goods and services use marketers such as Groupon and LivingSocial to reach new customers. Unfortunately, the payment structure that traditionally underlies social couponing programs may be problematic for dentists (and other health care providers) under both state and federal law.

A social coupon refers to all forms of Internet-based coupons or vouchers, including those that can be shared via social media. Many providers of goods and services use marketers such as Groupon and LivingSocial to reach new customers.

For example, many states have regulations that prohibit fee splitting between a dentist and a third party. If you agree to follow the traditional payment model and allow the social coupon company to keep a percentage of the revenue received from the coupon and remit the remainder to you, then your offer and award of the social coupon may violate these state fee splitting regulations.

Further, if you provide services payable under a federal health care program such as Medicare or Medicaid, you may be prohibited from offering and awarding social coupons under the federal anti-kickback statute. The federal anti-kickback statute makes it a criminal offense to knowingly and willfully offer, pay, solicit, or receive anything of value to induce or reward referrals for items or services reimbursable by a federal health care program. Again, if you agree to follow the traditional payment model and allow the social coupon company to keep a percentage of the revenue received from the coupon and remit the remainder to you, then your offer and award of the social coupon may violate this prohibition (and it may not fit any of the statute's safe harbors).

Social coupon companies have shown some willingness to revise their payment methodologies to help dentists avoid violating fee splitting laws. For example, in Oregon, certain social coupon companies proposed using a new fee arrangement with Oregon dentists, under which all fees paid by the patient would be passed through to the dentist and the dentist would then pay an advertising fee directly to the social coupon company. In response, the Oregon dental board issued a letter stating that the new fee arrangement would not violate the board's fee splitting rules.

However, even with a non-traditional fee arrangement, there are other legal and ethical issues that you must consider before using social coupons to promote your dental practice. For example, social couponing may have unintended consequences with respect to your contractual obligations. If you have a contract with a third party payor that contains a "most favored nation" clause (a clause guaranteeing an insurer the best price that you charge for a particular service), then the price charged pursuant to a social coupon arrangement may be argued to be the basis of a breach of this provision of the contract, as the payor may claim that you must offer the same discount with respect to the insured individuals, or perhaps even require you to rebate an equivalent per patient discount to the insurer.

For more on social couponing, consult your state dental association. For legal considerations related to social couponing, consult an attorney familiar with such issues in the state in which you are located. For ethical considerations related to social couponing, see Section 4.E.1. of ADA Principles of Ethics and Code of Professional Conduct.

Related References and Resources

- ADA Principles of Ethics and Code of Professional Conduct
  ADA.org/en/about-the-ada/principles-of-ethics-code-of-professional-conduct

182. If a Patient Is Behind on Payments, Can I Withhold Records or Stop Treatment?

Generally no. For dentists that are HIPAA covered entities, the answer to the first part of this question is easy: as a matter of federal law, payment problems are not a basis for withholding properly requested records. The same was probably true in most states before HIPAA; dentists who are not HIPAA covered entities need to follow state law in this regard.

In addition to the requirements of HIPAA and state law, Section 1.B (Patient Records) of the ADA Principles of Ethics and Code of Professional Conduct counsels that a dentist is obligated to provide any information in accordance with applicable law that will be beneficial to the patient's future treatment when requested by a patient or another dental practitioner. Advisory Opinion 1.B.1 of the ADA Code of Ethics specifically advises that the obligation to provide records exists "whether or not the patient's account is paid in full."

Whether and when treatment can be stopped raises questions of patient abandonment, which is a state law and an ethical issue. Accordingly, if these issues arise, it will be important for you to consult with your state society or a qualified attorney. As a general rule, most states and Section 2 of the ADA Principles of Ethics and Code of Professional Conduct require completion of treatment, and the patient's payment obligation is viewed as a separate issue. Stopping treatment over payment delays or disputes is thus problematic. If there is proper documentation in place establishing a patient's obligation, a prudent course of action might be to send the account to collection or initiate litigation to recover what is owed. At the same time, you should finalize whatever treatment must be completed to avoid any charge of abandonment.

Related References and Resources

- ADA Principles of Ethics and Code of Professional Conduct
  ADA.org/en/about-the-ada/principles-of-ethics-code-of-professional-conduct

183. Am I Required to Continue Treatment If the Patient Is in Bankruptcy?

It depends. The analysis is similar to that in the prior question. An important distinction, however, is that a bankruptcy court may issue an order that can affect the dentist's rights and obligations (for example, to continue ongoing treatment). It is a good idea to communicate with a bankruptcy attorney about the status of proceedings, both to help you know whether you may have an ongoing duty to treat, and when and how to file a claim to try to secure payment due for your services.

184. Can I Charge Interest on Overdue Amounts? What About Collection Costs?

There does not appear to be any general federal prohibition on charging interest on late payments, though individual state law may vary.

If your practice is considering doing so, you should consider maximizing the chances that a court will permit this charge. The best way to do so is to disclose the policy upfront, and to have the patient sign an agreement acknowledging that he/she is aware of and agrees that a specified (and reasonable) rate of interest will be charged on late payments (note that the rate of interest that can be charged on late payments might be limited by state law). If your practice already has a form agreement that is signed by the patient acknowledging responsibility for non-covered amounts, an additional provision regarding interest and collection costs is worth considering. With such a signed acknowledgement by the patient, we believe it likely that in many if not most jurisdictions a small claims court would entertain awarding such amounts.

We believe that a similar analysis can be made with respect to reasonable out of pocket collection costs and expenses that you have actually incurred due to the patient's failure to timely meet patient's payment obligations, if the patient has previously executed an agreement acknowledging patient's liability for such costs and expenses.

Note, however, that in many cases a small claims judge's sympathies may be swayed by the debtor's unfortunate circumstances, and thus may look for a way to avoid awarding interest or collection costs on top of the treatment fee. In addition, your state law may restrict amounts that can be collected above the actual fee. Thus, consider including a provision in your agreement allowing a court to revise the agreement to reflect any such limitations or equitable considerations (such provisions are sometimes referred to as "blue-pencil" or "severability" provisions, and enforceability of such provisions varies by state). Such a provision might, for example, allow the court to award the interest amount but not the collection costs. A qualified attorney can assist you in drafting language appropriate for your practice and your jurisdiction, as well as with respect to debt collection practices that may be prohibited under federal (in particular under the Fair Debt Collection Practices Act) and state law.

185. When Should I Use a Collection Agency?

If your office has tried to collect payment several times and is still unsuccessful, another option is to use a collection agency. The collection agency controls the collection process once the dental practice turns an account over to it. In addition to keeping the dental practice up to date with the status of accounts, the agency collects the payments directly, retains a percentage as its fee, and remits the remainder to the practice.

If the dentist is a covered entity under HIPAA, a compliant business associate agreement with the collection agency is likely required. In any event, disclosures of patient information to the collection agency should be limited to the information that is necessary for collection of the debt, and nothing more.

186. Are There Limits to What Can Be Done in Collections?

Yes, federal and state law regulate debt collection efforts. At the federal level, the key law for dental practices is the Fair Debt Collection Practices Act, enacted to prevent and prohibit abuses by debt collectors. The following summarizes information about the rights and obligations of debtors from the website of the Federal Trade Commission and provides a good outline of what a debt collector can and cannot do when attempting to collect a debt:

The FDCPA does not apply to creditors attempting to collect debts in-house. Debtors are responsible for their debts. If they fall behind in paying their creditors or an error is made on their account, they may be contacted by a "debt collector." A debt collector is any person, other than the creditor, who regularly collects debts owed to others. This includes lawyers who collect debts on a regular basis. You have the right to be treated fairly by debt collectors.

The Fair Debt Collection Practices Act (FDCPA) applies to personal, family, and household debts. This includes money owed for the purchase of a car, for medical care, or for charge accounts. The FDCPA prohibits debt collectors from engaging in unfair, deceptive, or abusive practices while collecting these debts.

A Debtor's Rights Under the Fair Debt Collection Practices Act:

   A. Debt collectors may contact you only between 8 a.m. and 9 p.m.

   B. Debt collectors may not contact you at work if they know your employer disapproves

   C. Debt collectors may not harass, oppress, or abuse you

   D. Debt collectors may not lie when collecting debts, such as falsely implying that you have committed a crime

   E. Debt collectors must identify themselves to you on the phone

   F. Debt collectors must stop contacting you if you ask them to in writing

Related References and Resources

   • FTC, Debt Collection
     www.consumer.ftc.gov/articles/0149-debt-collection

187. How Does Small Claims Court Work? Is It Worth It?

When your collections efforts have failed to motivate a patient to take care of an overdue account, another avenue is small claims court. Small claims courts provide an inexpensive and simplified process for the collection of relatively small debts. Access to small claims court depends on how your state defines "small" in terms of collections of outstanding patient accounts. You can obtain this information by calling the small claims division of your municipal or county court, or by accessing the appropriate website. In some states, small claims court services may be able to handle the process for you. They usually charge either a fee or a percentage of the recovered claim for representing you in court.

Keep in mind that going to small claims court will entail certain expenses as well as your time, and could potentially include a trial. Even if you win, you may be required "to go the extra mile" to engage in post-judgment collection. A situation such as this could result in the loss of that patient, future referrals, and damage your reputation in the community (consider, for example, the possibility of a highly negative online review). Another problem with pursuing a lawsuit is the potential that the patient may assert a malpractice claim as a defense to payment. In many instances, dentists simply decide to cut their losses and sever the relationship with the patient.

188. What Should I Do if the Patient Wants a Refund, or a Nominal Sum for Malpractice?

It depends. A dentist can certainly stand behind his or her work and deny a request for a refund. However, many dentists accommodate such requests, for patient relations reasons or to avoid lawsuits. If your decision is to honor the refund request, it is prudent to have the patient sign a release in which the patient agrees to release, indemnify and hold you harmless from any claim related to the dental care in question. The release may specify that there has been no claim or admission of malpractice. It may also contain the patient's promise not to sue. The precise form of release to use may vary by state law, and your state society, legal counsel or malpractice carrier may have an appropriate form for you to use that will satisfy your state law.

When settling such a claim, do not forget the National Practitioner Data Bank (NPDB). If there was a written demand claiming malpractice, and payment is being made through the practice's account (as opposed to the dentist's personal funds), there may be a duty to self-report the settlement to the NPDB. The NPDB does not consider a waiver of a debt to be a reportable payment, so if a patient accepts a waiver of fee as a settlement the waiver is not reportable to the NPDB. There are very specific rules for what must be reported to the NPDB, depending on the facts in any particular case. Chapter E of the NPDB Guidebook provides information about reporting requirements, including when a practitioner must report and the timing and contents of the report.

Related References and Resources

- Question 10: Must a Settlement of a Malpractice Claim Be Reported to The Data Bank?

- The National Practitioner Data Bank
  www.npdb.hrsa.gov or 1.800.767.6732

Chapter 25.

Insurers and Other Commercial Payers

Many dentists choose to deal with insurance companies, either by signing participating provider agreements or by simply submitting claims. On the one hand, this has led to stable or increased patient volume and significant payment for services rendered. On the other, it has led many dentists to voice complaints about perceived insurance company abuses. Some of the more common questions are discussed in this section.

189. The Plan's Explanation of Benefits Makes It Seem Like I'm Overcharging. Is That Legal?

The legality of the plan's actions will turn largely on the specifics of what it is saying in its Explanation of Benefits (EOBs). If the plan is providing accurate information, in an appropriate way, it may be permissible. If the plan's EOBs are relying on inaccurate data or disparaging the dentist, the plan arguably has legal exposure. In fact, the ADA's first two class action lawsuits against insurance companies Aetna and WellPoint on behalf of non-participating dentists alleged such practices constituted an unlawful interference in the dentist-patient relationship. The ADA continues to monitor EOB language and sometimes attempts to negotiate language modification. If you believe an EOB has cast you in a bad light, you may wish to contact the ADA to speak with Dental Benefits staff.

190. I Submitted a Claim to an Insurance Company Six Months Ago, and I Still Haven't Received My Reimbursement. What Can I Do?

This will depend on the terms of your insurance contract, whether your state has any prompt payment laws, and the facts of your particular case. Has the insurance company given you any explanation as to why they haven't paid your claim? Has the company asked you for any additional documentation to support the claim? If you have provided the documentation you believe is necessary to support your claim, and you don't think the company has any valid reason to delay your claim, ask your attorney whether your state has any prompt payment laws. More than 20 states require various entities processing dental claims to reimburse dentists within a specified period after receiving a "clean claim" from the dentist. Several other states have statutes that might be interpreted to mandate prompt reimbursement of dental claims. If your state has such a statute, you will want to find out what information must be included in a claim before it is considered "clean." Also, if you have a contract to provide dental treatment to the insurer's enrollees, check your contract to see if it contains a clause requiring the insurer to pay your claims within a certain time period.

191. An Insurance Company Is Withholding Payment for Part of the Claims I Submitted to Them Recently. They Say They're "Offsetting" an Amount They Overpaid Me Previously. Can They Do This?

Maybe. If you have a dental provider contract with the insurer, check to see whether it contains a clause permitting them to "offset," or hold back, part of your reimbursement if the insurer believes it previously overpaid you. If not, determine whether the contract contains a section that incorporates other documents, such as a policy manual, into the contract. If it does, review the policy manual or other document to see if it contains any provision permitting the insurer to offset alleged overpayments.

If the contract or other document does contain a section allowing offsets, check to see what recourse you have if you disagree with the company's conclusion that it previously overpaid you. If you want to contest the offset, follow that procedure. However, if you have no contractual relationship with the insurer, then the insurer has no contractual basis for withholding reimbursement for current claims on the ground that it overpaid prior claims.

192. Dental Benefit Plan XYZ Claims I'm a Participating Provider in Their Plan, and That I Have to Treat All of Their Enrollees Who Come to My Office and Accept Their Fees as Full Reimbursement. How Can This Be? I Never Signed a Contract With Plan XYZ.

Find out what basis Plan XYZ has for claiming you're one of its participating providers. It is possible that you could be one of its participating providers, even though you never signed a contract with the plan. This generally could happen one of two ways. First, you may have signed a dental provider contract with an insurer or other plan that requires you to participate with all of the insurer's or plan's affiliates. If Plan XYZ is an affiliate of the entity with which you contracted, you might be bound to be a participating provider for Plan XYZ. Ask your attorney or state society whether this type of "all products" clause is allowed in your state.

Second, you may have signed a dental provider contract with an insurer or another plan that allows the entity with which you contracted to assign its rights and obligations to another party. If the insurer or plan transferred the agreement to Plan XYZ, then, once again, you may be a participating provider for Plan XYZ. If you are faced with either of the two situations described above, the terms of your agreement with Plan XYZ should be governed by the provisions of the contract you originally signed with the first insurer or plan.

What if you don't want to participate in Plan XYZ? Then you probably will have to terminate the original contract, following the termination procedures set out in that agreement. Keep in mind that if you are participating in a number of plans under one agreement, you may have to terminate your participation in all of the plans.

193. Can an Insurance Plan Force Me to Allow It to Audit Out-of-Network Charts, or Does HIPAA Prevent This?

A dentist who is a HIPAA "covered entity" (which means the dentist is required to comply with the HIPAA regulations) may not be permitted to disclose to a health plan information about patients who are not covered by that plan. However, if you have a contract with a health plan, the contract may state that the plan has the right to audit charts of all patients, including out-of-network patients. Under HIPAA privacy regulations, the in-network chart component of an audit should not be a problem unless the patient has requested restricted disclosure to the plan (See " Restricted Disclosure to a Plan" below). Among other things, in-network patients are probably on notice through their health plan and through the dentist's HIPAA Notice of Privacy Practices that their benefits are subject to their plan's audit rights, and an audit is part of the plan's health care operations.

A covered entity dentist may under certain conditions share patient records with other covered entities (such as the patient's own health plan) for purposes of the other covered entity's health care operations (as defined by HIPAA). A dentist may be permitted to disclose patient information to a health plan for an audit if both the dentist and the health plan have a current or prior relationship with the patient, and if the information that is disclosed pertains to those relationships. This means that HIPAA may allow a covered entity dentist to permit Health Plan ABC to review records of the dentist's patients who are covered, or were previously covered, through ABC.

A dentist may be permitted to disclose patient information to a health plan for an audit if both the dentist and the health plan have a current or prior relationship with the patient, and if the information that is disclosed pertains to those relationships.

However, what if Health Plan ABC required a dentist to disclose records of non-ABC patients (such as patients who always have been covered by Insurer XYZ)? In that case, HIPAA would prevent a covered entity dentist from disclosing those records to ABC unless the patients authorized the dentist to do so. Obtaining the necessary HIPAA authorizations could be extremely burdensome, if not impossible. Furthermore, even if the dentist is a HIPAA covered entity, he or she also will have to meet the requirements of any state laws which give greater protection to patient privacy than the HIPAA regulations, and dentists who are not HIPAA covered entities must comply with state privacy laws. Therefore, dentists also need to comply with any applicable laws in their states that require them to obtain consent from a patient before disclosing the patient's records to another party, such as a health plan. Accordingly, a dentist should carefully weigh this issue before signing a participating provider agreement, and may wish to modify any such audit provision.

Restricted Disclosure to a Plan

A HIPAA covered dental practice may not disclose a patient's information to the patient's own plan if the patient has asked the dental practice not to give the information to the plan, as long as:

- The disclosure is for the purpose of carrying out payment or health care operations and is not otherwise required by law, and

- The information pertains solely to a health care item or service for which the patient or someone else (including a different plan) has paid the dental practice in full.

Related References and Resources

- Question 98: Do I Have to Comply With HIPAA?

- OCR, Uses and Disclosures for Treatment, Payment, and Health Care Operations
  www.hhs.gov/ocr/privacy/hipaa/understanding/coveredentities/usesanddisclosuresfortpo. html

- Restricted Disclosures to Health Plans
  ADA.org/en/member-center/member-benefits/legal-resources/publications-and-articles/ hipaa-and-data-security/restricted-disclosures-to-health-plans

- *The ADA Practical Guide to HIPAA Compliance: Privacy and Security Manual*
  adacatalog.org or 1.800.947.4746

The Patient

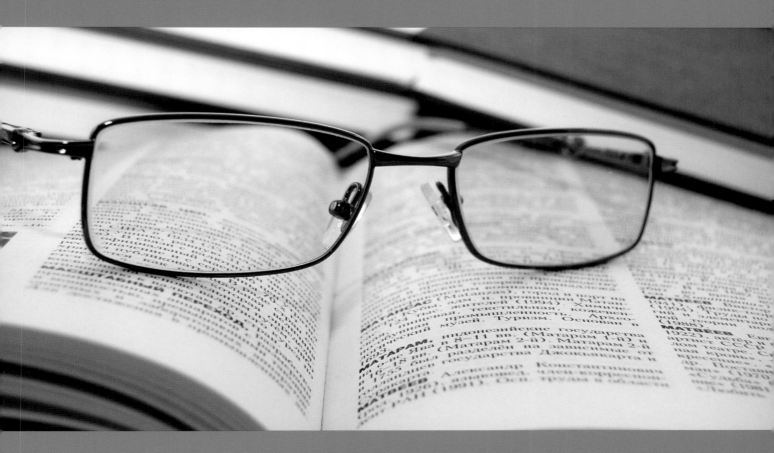

Chapter 26.
The Dentist-Patient Relationship

The dentist-patient relationship is grounded in trust and confidence. Underlying the relationship are the expectation of confidentiality and privacy, the notion that what is shared for treatment purposes will not leave the dental office, and a feeling of safety, tied to a belief that competent care will be provided with quality results at an appropriate price. Legally, the relationship can be thought of as a contract that binds the dentist to provide appropriate care for the agreed-upon fee.

Keeping patient information confidential frees patients to talk openly about their health care needs. Behind this protection is the principle that open and relaxed communication between professionals and patients is essential to appropriate treatment. This means that a patient may safely communicate information about an illness, or information that could possibly be embarrassing, such as a communicable disease, to the dentist or dental team member. This helps the dentist fulfill his or her treatment obligations.

Let's take a look at some key issues in the dentist-patient relationship.

194. What Rights Does a Patient Have to Privacy and Confidentiality?

Patients have many rights concerning their health information. Key among them are rights with respect to privacy and confidentiality. These issues have become increasingly important in health care in recent years. Concerns about privacy and confidentiality have spurred legislation such as HIPAA, which among other things gives patients certain rights with respect to their health information.

In HIPAA covered entity dental offices, HIPAA establishes certain patient rights that pertain to issues such as:

- Accessing, copying, and inspecting their health information

- Requesting an amendment to their health information

- Obtaining an accounting of certain disclosures of their health information

- Requesting restrictions on disclosures

- Requesting reasonable alternative means of receiving communications

- Submitting complaints about alleged violations of HIPAA and the dentist's own policies and procedures

A covered entity must comply with HIPAA and with any state law that is more stringent than HIPAA. Dental practices that are not HIPAA covered entities must comply with applicable state privacy laws. For example, some states require a health care provider to obtain a patient's consent before releasing patient information can be released — even to another health care provider. In other states, consent to share information with the patient's physician may be implied, or the law may provide that coordinating care with the physician is authorized without patient permission. Some states may have heightened confidentiality provisions for sensitive information, such as HIV status.

A covered entity must comply with HIPAA and with any state law that is more stringent than HIPAA. Dental practices that are not HIPAA covered entities must comply with applicable state privacy laws.

Breaching privacy or confidentiality can open the door to HIPAA complaints, substantial penalties, and potentially even private lawsuits. Perhaps more significantly it can also lead to sanctions under the state practice act, including loss of licensure. It is very important that the dentist and all dental team members comply with applicable law and maintain the privacy and confidentiality of patient information except in cases where disclosing it is allowed or required by law (for example, when it is obligatory for the dentist to report certain health hazards to the appropriate authorities).

The privacy and confidentiality of patient records is also addressed in the ADA Principles of Ethics and Code of Professional Conduct. Section 1.B. of the ADA Code of Ethics states that a dentist is obligated to maintain the confidentiality of patient records. Advisory Opinion 1.B.2. contains additional information concerning the confidentiality of patient records in the face of a request for patient information from another practitioner and advises that it may be necessary to seek the patient's consent prior to divulging records that contain information of a sensitive nature.

Related References and Resources

- Chapter 15: HIPAA, State Law and PCI DSS: Patient Information

- HIPAA 20 Questions
  ADA.org/DentistGuidetoLaw

- ADA Principles of Ethics and Code of Professional Conduct
  ADA.org/en/about-the-ada/principles-of-ethics-code-of-professional-conduct

195. What Should I Do to Protect Patient Information?

In addition to complying with applicable federal and state statutory and regulatory requirements, dental offices should take meaningful, reasonable steps to help protect privacy and confidentiality. There is no one-size-fits-all list of what must be done. However, your efforts should take into consideration factors such as the nature of the practice, the design of the office, and any specific legal requirements, including those in applicable state law.

It often comes down to exercising common sense and taking practical steps such as the following:

- Avoid leaving patient information where others can read the content. This includes patient charts and also electronic information. Be careful with charts — keep them filed, out of plain sight, or turned over. Keep computers displaying patient information out of view, or use screen savers or other innovations to keep the information inaccessible to unauthorized individuals.

- Avoid asking patients sensitive questions where other patients can hear the conversation, or even crucial segments of it, including during telephone conversations with patients.

- Avoid discussing confidential patient information with your dental team members where other people can hear the conversation.

Think about the situation if the roles were reversed and you were the patient. Or reflect on how your physician handles the privacy and confidentiality of your health information. Would you want your physician calling out your name and diagnosis so others might hear? Or leaving your opened chart on a billing counter that everyone stands around or walks by?

Moreover, the healthcare sector is increasingly moving toward electronic health records. Dentists should protect their data files with security measures for their computers and computer systems and with data encryption techniques. Dentists who are HIPAA covered entities must comply with HIPAA Privacy Security and Breach Notification requirements, which contain specific provisions for electronic health records.

Related References and Resources

- Chapter 15: HIPAA, State Law and PCI DSS: Patient Information

- HIPAA 20 Questions
  ADA.org/DentistGuidetoLaw

196. My Patient Is in a Lawsuit. Do I Have to Testify? Doesn't the Dentist-Patient Privilege Help Me Avoid This?

It depends on your state laws. While the concept of the doctor-patient privilege is engrained in U.S. culture, it is important to keep in mind that the privilege does not protect the doctor; rather, it belongs to the patient.

The extent and scope of such a privilege in dentistry varies by state. In some states, there is a dentist-patient privilege, often as a subset of a law focusing on physician-patient relationships. In others, a dentist-patient privilege is not specified or covered by a physician law; in such states, a dentist would have no privilege to invoke if subpoenaed to testify, and might have to disclose private or sensitive information. It is critical that you know your state law — both to ensure you know what privilege you and your patients can rely upon, and so you do not inadvertently breach whatever privilege may exist.

This variance of state dentist-patient privilege law is all the more reason for dentists to know and abide by applicable privacy and confidentiality laws, and put procedures in place to protect patient information.

197. What If I See Signs of Abuse or Neglect Upon Examination?

Notwithstanding privacy and confidentiality concerns, dentists are obliged to report certain sensitive information to the authorities. Dentists are mandated reporters of suspected child or elder abuse and neglect in all 50 states (most states also make hygienists mandatory reporters as well). Several states also require reporting of Intimate Partner Violence (IPV). Formerly referred to as domestic violence, this term includes abuse within and outside of marriage, including date rape and violence within a gay or lesbian relationship.

Like other mandatory reporters, dentists are required to report suspected cases of child or elder abuse or neglect to the appropriate authorities or social service agency and in some cases to the police. All 50 states grant statutory immunity from civil or criminal liability to mandatory reporters for reports of child abuse and neglect that they make in good faith to the designated authority. The definitions of abuse and neglect vary by state. It is important to know the specific reporting requirements in your state and follow them carefully to avoid potential liability and to obtain any available immunity for good faith reporting. Not following the law may create legal exposure for the reporting professional. Dentists who are legally obligated to report are also exempted from state laws that protect the confidentiality of patient information. Under HIPAA, a covered entity may under specified circumstances report signs of abuse or neglect without obtaining authorization to disclose patient information.

Penalties may be assessed against a mandated reporter who fails to report a reasonable suspicion of abuse or neglect. Criminal penalties and professional discipline are possible, and failure to report may expose the dentist to liability for professional negligence as well.

Related References and Resources

- ADA Principles of Ethics and Code of Professional Conduct
  ADA.org/en/about-the-ada/principles-of-ethics-code-of-professional-conduct

- Child Welfare Information Gateway
  www.childwelfare.gov/index.cfm

Chapter 27.
Diagnosis and Treatment

How do dentists reach the goal of providing quality care? The starting point is a good health history, together with a thorough examination, leading to a sound diagnosis and the development of an appropriate treatment plan, followed by the patient's acceptance and informed consent to be treated. The dentist provides proper technique, thorough documentation, and any necessary instructions. These elements of quality care also help satisfy the legal requirements of practicing dentistry.

198. Are There Specific Legal Concerns to Watch for When Taking a Health History?

Yes. The key is to obtain the information you need to properly diagnose and provide treatment, with thorough documentation along the way. A good health history will help reveal information a dentist needs to know about a patient's condition in order to develop an appropriate treatment plan.

Some dentists handle the history orally, asking a series of questions (including many open-ended ones) designed to generate the needed information and simultaneously documenting the answers. Others ask the patients to complete health history forms with very specific questions, followed by any necessary discussion.

Unless your state has specific requirements regarding health histories, or you have contracted with another party (such as an insurance plan) to take health histories a certain way, use the approach that helps you obtain and document the most complete and accurate health history. The key is to get the information you need to properly diagnose and treat, and have a good, contemporaneous written record to substantiate your diagnosis, clinical decisions, and treatment recommendations so you can respond to any allegations that may be later made against you regarding your services. Your state society, attorney, or malpractice carrier can guide you as to state law requirements as well as the risk management aspects of health histories.

A small number of member dentists have reported being sued for malpractice in part because they did not use the ADA health history form, or because their office's health history form did not include all of the same questions as the ADA form. The defenses in such cases have properly pointed out that the ADA form is not mandatory, and that the form itself reflects the importance of dialogue between doctor and patient. Still, use of the ADA form helps minimize the risk of defending such suits.

199. How Often Should Patients Be Asked to Update Their Health History Forms?

As a matter of good patient care, as well as risk management, dentists have new patients complete health history forms. For the same reasons, patient health history information should be updated regularly.

A returning patient, at each and every visit (and before any treatment or procedure is commenced), should be asked whether there have been any changes to his or her medical history since the last visit, including any changes in medications and dietary supplements. The patient's record should contain a dated notation that the patient was asked about health and medication changes. If a patient indicates there have been changes, they should be noted, in writing, in the patient's chart.

Patients should be asked on a regular basis to review their most recent medical history form and either to complete a new form (if a number of changes need to be made) or to note the changes directly on the original form and initial and date the changes. If changes are made directly to the original form, it may make sense to have both the patient and dentist re-sign and date the form in acknowledgment of the changes.

A patient's health history form should be updated at intervals appropriate to his or her age and medical history. The decision as to the frequency is primarily professional, rather than legal. Your professional liability insurance company and your attorney may be consulted for more information.

Patient health history forms should be treated as confidential patient health records.

Maintaining accurate and updated patient health history records is important, not only to properly treat your patients, but also to help provide the basis for you and your carrier to establish a proper defense should a claim later arise.

Related References and Resources

- Chapter 15: HIPAA, State Law and PCI DSS: Patient Information

- HIPAA 20 Questions
  ADA.org/DentistGuidetoLaw

200. Are There Legal Issues Regarding Treatment Planning?

Yes. A key to legally sound treatment planning is to focus on the patient's dental needs. Take care not to discriminate based on federally protected factors including race, religion, gender, disability and so forth, or applicable state or local categories such as sexual orientation. What you deem to be the proper treatment plan for dental reasons should be put before each patient. Once you do so, keep in mind that while discussing the treatment plan may be an invaluable part of securing informed consent, you must still secure patient consent to treatment.

201. Who Must Give Informed Consent?

Informed consent is something a dentist must obtain from each patient (or from the patient's legal decision-maker, such as a parent, guardian, or personal representative).

The need for informed consent is based on the "assault and battery" principal of the old common law: an individual is technically not allowed to lay hands on another without permission — indeed, threatening to touch another person without consent is considered an "assault," and an unwanted touching technically constitutes a "battery. By extension, you need to get permission before you touch and treat patients. In health care, that permission must be based on adequate information. The doctrine of informed consent is based on the concept that an individual can only consent if he or she is adequately informed. Once informed, the individual can give consent.

202. So How Do I Go About Getting Informed Consent?

What you need to do varies according to the situation. Let's start with some good news. Not all situations require written informed consent. Indeed, sometimes the need for express patient permission to treat is waived or implied. At one extreme, this would include the case of an emergency in which treatment of an unconscious patient is medically necessary and no surrogate is available to give consent. The other extreme would be a simple, common procedure for which there is no meaningful risk, and which the patient has agreed to undergo by sitting in the chair (for example, an oral examination and — for most patients, but not those with certain heart conditions — a prophy). Your state society attorney and malpractice carrier may have helpful local information for you about waived or implied consent.

For everything else, the important thing to remember is that securing informed consent is a process. While the specific requirements may vary by state, the essence of this process is that the dentist explains the patient's dental problem, the nature of the proposed treatment, the potential risks and benefits of the treatment, any alternatives to the treatment, and the risks and benefits of the alternative treatments (including no treatment). The patient is given ample opportunity to ask questions about these and related issues, and adequate time to make a decision without being "pressured" to make a hasty decision.

The important thing to remember is that securing informed consent is a process. While the specific requirements may vary by state, the essence of this process is that the dentist explains the patient's dental problem, the nature of the proposed treatment, the potential risks and benefits of the treatment, any alternatives to the treatment, and the risks and benefits of the alternative treatments (including no treatment).

Keep in mind that in the case of patients without decision-making capacity, care should be taken to ensure that you get consent from the patient's lawful decision-maker (such as the patient's parent, guardian, or personal representative). State law determines who may consent to treatment on behalf of another. State law also determines the age at which a person can consent to treatment, and the circumstances under which a minor may consent to treatment (for example, states may give the right to consent to treatment to minors who support themselves and live apart from their parents, or to minors who are pregnant or parents of children). If a parent will not be present in the dental office during a minor's treatment (for example, if a parent drops a child off for treatment, or if a minor patient drives herself to an appointment), obtain the parent's informed consent before treatment and be sure you will be able to contact the parent before proceeding further if complications develop. State laws generally provide that in an emergency situation a dentist may proceed without parental consent if delaying treatment could endanger the child's life or health.

203. Should I Use an Informed Consent Form?

An informed consent form can be an effective risk management tool for your practice. Such a form documents in writing that the patient understands, agrees with, and authorizes the treatment plan, and gives the dentist permission to proceed with treatment.

Using an informed consent form as a culmination of the informed consent process discussed in the prior questions can be a very effective risk management tool, particularly for dental procedures with established or foreseeable risks, or those for which a reasonable patient would expect to receive a formal explanation of the risks. In addition, a written informed consent form can be used as, or in combination with, a financial authorization form to obtain the patient's written agreement to be responsible for payment.

It is important to remember that having a patient sign a written consent form does not excuse you from the responsibility of having an adequate discussion with the patient about the proposed treatment. Be careful to avoid falling into the habit of routinely obtaining signed consent forms with no discussion other than "sign here so I can take care of you." Doing so would raise questions about whether you actually secured informed consent and could significantly impair the defense of a malpractice lawsuit.

Related References and Resources

- Chapter 24: Payment and Collections

An informed consent form can be an effective risk management tool for your practice. Such a form documents in writing that the patient understands, agrees with, and authorizes the treatment plan, and gives the dentist permission to proceed with treatment.

204. What If The Patient Refuses to Consent?

The key here is to document the refusal. Should a patient not agree to a recommended procedure, or refuse the treatment, you should inform the patient of the risks that may arise from such a refusal and document that the patient understands those risks. This can be done in the chart or — better yet — on an informed refusal form, signed by the patient and kept in the patient's record. Obtaining informed refusal does not release the dentist from the responsibility of providing the standard of care. For example, if a patient refuses to have radiographs taken and the dentist believes that radiographs are a necessary prerequisite to proper care in that case, the dentist may wish to refer the patient to another dentist.

Informed consent and refusal are complex issues. Dentists may wish to take continuing education courses on these subjects.

Related References and Resources

- Chapter 28: Referrals

- General Guidelines for Referring Dental Patients
  ADA.org/en/home-cps/practice/operations/efficient-systems/general-guidelines-for-referring-dental-patients

205. Can I Proceed with Treatment Even If the Patient Will Not Consent to Recommended Diagnostic Procedures?

It's not a good idea to proceed with treatment if the patient will not consent to the diagnostic procedures you recommend. However, sometimes patients refuse recommended diagnostic procedures (especially x-rays) and demand treatment anyway. As a general rule, this demand can be refused. Indeed, if you have recommended diagnostics in order to be able to develop a treatment plan, you may open the door to a malpractice claim if you proceed with treatment against your own recommendations. Your notes in the patient's chart might be the first exhibit used against you at trial!

206. Can I Provide Care That the Patient Wants But I Do Not Think Is Indicated?

It's not a good idea to go against your own professional judgment. If the patient wants treatment that in your professional opinion is unwarranted, be careful about providing the requested care. This can be especially risky when you believe that providing the care has the potential to harm the patient's health. You are the licensed professional and must use your clinical judgment, even if that means telling patients you cannot do what they ask. And imagine how your testimony at trial would sound if you go against your own professional judgment.

207. Did I Commit Malpractice? What Is the Standard of Care?

Let's first describe what is meant by the phrase "standard of care." The typical malpractice case alleges that the dentist, through acts or omissions, failed to provide appropriate quality care, or take reasonable precautions when doing so, thereby causing harm to the patient, usually during dental treatment. Implicit in this formulation is a failure to treat in accordance with the standard of care.

The typical malpractice case alleges that the dentist, through acts or omissions, failed to provide appropriate quality care, or take reasonable precautions when doing so, thereby causing harm to the patient, usually during dental treatment.

Since a malpractice case goes to the heart of the question of whether a defendant-dentist followed the standard of care, it is perfectly reasonable for a dentist to want to know what the standard is. Unfortunately, there is no simple, one-size-fits-all answer. Determining the standard of care in a given case is fact-specific: it depends on particulars such as the procedures involved and the norm in the community. In fact, in a lawsuit each side has the opportunity to present expert testimony regarding what it believes to be the standard of care. It is then up to the judge or jury hearing the facts of the case to decide what the standard is and whether it has been violated.

While ADA positions and recommendations may be cited as evidence of the standard of care, the ADA does not actually set the standard. Indeed, ADA's patient care information, including our dental parameters, always make it clear that treatment recommendations are always and ultimately left to the professional judgment of the dentist.

Related References and Resources

- CNA, Determining the Standard of Care
  www.dental-risk.com/RiskManagement/CNARiskManagementArticlesForms.aspx

208. I'm a Volunteer Dentist, Donating Dental Services. Do the Same Rules Apply?

Dentists who volunteer their services may have some liability protection under federal and state laws. The federal Volunteer Protection Act (VPA) protects a volunteer clinician acting within the scope of his or her duties in a nonprofit organization or governmental entity from liability for simple negligence (subject to exceptions for misconduct related to crimes of violence, sexual offenses, civil rights violations and other offenses). A volunteer can still be held liable for gross negligence, although the VPA limits the award of punitive damages to those cases in which there is clear and convincing evidence of willful or criminal misconduct, or conscious, flagrant indifference to the rights or safety of the individual harmed. The VPA also limits awards for non-economic damages (pain and suffering) to the proportion of harm caused by the volunteer.

The VPA allows states to enact statutes declaring that the VPA shall not apply in that state if all parties to a lawsuit are citizens of the state, and states may impose certain additional requirements or conditions. States may also enact legislation that affords additional protection to "clinical volunteers" who provide routine care, and a number of states have enacted such legislation. In some cases, the state legislation specifically refers to "dentists," and in others the state law may apply to dentists, depending on the wording.

States with such legislation tend to choose one of two routes to provide protection for care. Some states change the negligence standard of care for volunteers — that is, they raise the standard for liability from simple negligence to gross negligence. Often called a "willful or wanton" or "reckless" standard, this approach makes it more difficult for plaintiffs to prove liability. This is the approach used in the federal VPA statute. Other states indemnify the volunteer clinician as if he or she were a government employee. Under this model, the state establishes a legal defense fund to cover monetary damages as well as legal defense costs. Often these statutes cap the total compensation that can be paid for claims. Certain conditions may be specified, such as the setting in which the care is delivered or the existence of a formal agreement between the clinician and the state. Consult your state dental society, counsel, or volunteer program sponsor for information on whether and how these laws apply to you.

Before agreeing to provide dental services on a volunteer basis, you may wish to inquire whether your professional liability insurance policy would apply to any claim that may arise from your volunteer work. It would also be prudent to ask whether the volunteer organization provides liability coverage to professionals who serve as volunteers.

Be aware that volunteer protection laws apply to negligence claims and do not exempt health care providers from the other legal requirements that they encounter in private practice. However, certain administrative burdens may be lessened for dentists doing volunteer work. What may be a reasonable precaution in a private office setting may not be possible at an outdoor community health fair.

Related References and Resources

- Chapter 23: Insuring Your Practice

- CNA, Voluntary Dentistry Is Not Risk-Free
  www.dental-risk.com/RiskManagement/CNARiskManagementArticlesForms.aspx

Chapter 28.
Referrals

209. Are There Legal Issues to Consider When I Make a Referral?

In addition to a dentist's professional and ethical obligations concerning patient referrals, legal issues should be considered as well, such as the following:

Disabilities law. A dentist who refers patients with disabilities such as HIV/AIDS may violate the Americans with Disabilities Act if the referral is based on the dentist's personal comfort level rather than on a scientific basis.

Privacy law. When communicating with another health care provider regarding a referral, keep in mind confidentiality and privacy laws including HIPAA (if you are a HIPAA covered entity) and any applicable state laws. HIPAA does not require patient authorization for disclosures for treatment purposes. However, state law may require you to obtain the patient's consent to disclose his or her health information to another treatment provider.

Negligent referral. To minimize the risk of a tort claim for negligent referral, a dentist should consider the qualifications of professionals to whom he or she refers patients. A referral could be considered negligent if the dentist knew or should have known that the dentist to whom the patient was referred was likely to perform in a negligent manner.

Fraud and abuse. A dentist risks violating federal and state anti-kickback and self-referral laws if he or she might receive a direct or indirect benefit from referring a patient. For example, a dentist who receives remuneration from the professional to whom the dentist refers a patient who is a medicare or medicated beneficiary may be in violation of the federal anti-kickback statute. A dentist who refers a beneficiary for certain "designated health services" to a professional or entity with which the dentist (or a family member) has a financial relationship risks violating the federal self-referral law (also known as the "Stark Law"). States may enact anti-kickback and self-referral laws that are similar to, or even more stringent than, the federal statutes.

Certain transactions and business practices are protected by "exceptions" to the federal Stark law and "safe harbors" to the federal Anti-Kickback Statute. For example, there is a Stark exception and an AKS safe harbor that relate to office space leases. Complying with the requirements of the office lease exception and safe harbor can help protect a dental practice that, for example, leases office space from a hospital with which the dental practice has a referral relationship. A qualified attorney can provide information about fraud and abuse risks and any applicable exceptions and safe harbors that might help reduce those risks.

Contracts. Dentists who participate (or whose patients participate) in a contractual arrangement related to dental services may have restrictions with regard to referrals. Such arrangements should be carefully reviewed. Contractual obligations do not alter the standard of care owed to a patient.

Related References and Resources

- Question 210: How Does the Federal Law Regulating Self-Referral (Stark Law) Affect My Dental Practice?

- Question 211: When Might the Stark Law Apply?

- Question 212: How Could the Federal Anti-Kickback Statute Affect My Practice?

- Question 219: Must I Treat Patients with HIV, HCV or Other Infectious Diseases?

- Chapter 15: HIPAA, State Law and PCI DSS: Patient Information

- HIPAA 20 Questions
  ADA.org/DentistGuidetoLaw

- OIG, A Roadmap for New Physicians: Avoiding Medicare and Medicaid Fraud and Abuse
  http://oig.hhs.gov/compliance/physician-education/index.asp

- CMS, Physician Self Referral
  www.cms.gov/Medicare/Fraud-and-Abuse/PhysicianSelfReferral/index.html?redirect=/ physicianselfreferral/

210. How Does the Federal Law Regulating Self-Referral (Stark Law) Affect My Dental Practice?

Under the federal Physician Self-Referral Law ("Stark law") a dentist may not refer a patient to receive "designated health services" payable by Medicare or Medicaid from entities with which the dentist or an immediate family member has a financial relationship, unless an exception applies. Financial relationships include both ownership/investment interests and compensation arrangements.

No payment may be made for designated health services rendered as a result of a prohibited referral, and an entity must timely refund any amounts collected for designated health services performed under a prohibited referral. Civil money penalties and other remedies may also apply under some circumstances.

A dentist can violate the Stark law even without knowing or intending to. It is important to understand this law and to check with a qualified attorney if you have any concerns about your referrals or about your financial relationships (or those of your family members) with designated health services providers to whom you refer patients.

The Stark law is a federal law, and some states have also adopted self-referral laws. State self-referral laws may be more stringent than the federal law. A dentist must comply with both the federal Stark law and any applicable state self-referral law.

Related References and Resources

- CMS, Physician Self Referral: List of Designate Health Services
  www.cms.gov/Medicare/Fraud-and-Abuse/PhysicianSelfReferral/index.html?redirect=/ physicianselfreferral

211. When Might the Stark Law Apply?

Under Stark, a dentist may not refer a patient for certain "designated health services" payable by Medicare or Medicaid to an entity with which the dentist or an immediate family member of the dentist has a direct or indirect "financial relationship," unless an exception applies. "Entity" also includes an individual or sole practitioner.

A "financial relationship" includes an ownership or investment interest (including a debt interest) or a compensation arrangement (such as an employment or independent contractor arrangement, or a lease of space or equipment). A qualified attorney can help you evaluate any financial relationships that you are aware of (or should reasonably be aware of) to determine whether they present a problem under Stark.

"Immediate family member" includes the dentist's spouse, parent, child, sibling, mother-in-law, father-in-law, son-in-law, daughter-in-law, brother-in-law, sister-in-law, stepparent, stepchild, stepbrother, stepsister, grandparent, grandchild, or the spouse of a grandparent or grandchild.

Special rules apply to group practices. The practice's financial relationships may be imputed to certain individual dentists in the practice. Also, if a dentist in a group practice controls or directs other dentists' referrals, those referrals may be imputed to that dentist. Group practices may wish to review their compensation formulas to make sure they comply with Stark. If you are in a group practice, a qualified attorney can check for Stark problems that could arise out of dentist compensation or referrals.

Under Stark, a dentist may not refer a patient for certain "designated health services" payable by Medicare or Medicaid to an entity with which the dentist or an immediate family member of the dentist has a direct or indirect "financial relationship," unless an exception applies.

The Stark law and regulations, including the list of designated health services, are amended from time to time, so it is important to keep up to date. Designated health services currently includes radiology and certain other imaging services, prosthetics and prosthetic devices and supplies, outpatient prescription drugs, inpatient and outpatient hospital services, and certain other health services.

In some cases, a dentist or dental practice may be a designated health services entity (for example, if a dental practice provides certain imaging services for a medical practice). In that case, the dentist or practice should consider any financial relationships when it receives referrals.

Stark also imposes reporting requirements on certain health care entities. A qualified attorney can help you determine whether you must report information to the federal government concerning your financial relationships under Stark.

Penalties for violating Stark can be severe. A designated health services entity cannot bill (and must refund any payment made) for a service that violates Stark. The federal government can impose civil monetary penalties on dentists who make referrals that violate Stark and on those who fail to comply with reporting requirements.

Although Stark prohibits certain referrals only with respect to patients who qualify for Medicare and Medicaid, it is prudent for a dental practice that refers patients for designated health services (or that provides designated health services) to have a compliance policy in place that applies to all patients and not just to patients who are Medicare or Medicaid beneficiaries. A simple oversight could lead to Stark liability, because it can be difficult to keep track of which patients qualify for Medicare or Medicaid at any given time.

The Stark law and regulations provide a number of exceptions that may allow referrals for designated health services even though a financial relationship exists. Each exception has specific requirements that must be met in order for the exception to apply. A qualified attorney can determine whether an exception applies and what must be done to comply with the exception.

Example: A dentist is part-owner of an imaging facility, and wishes to refer patients to that entity for designated health services. A qualified attorney can determine whether a Stark exception applies and, if so, how to comply with the exception.

Related References and Resources

- CMS, Physician Self Referral: List of Designate Health Services
  www.cms.gov/Medicare/Fraud-and-Abuse/PhysicianSelfReferral/index.html?redirect=/physicianselfreferral

212. How Could the Federal Anti-Kickback Statute Affect My Practice?

Federal law makes it a crime to pay or receive (or even to offer or solicit) any kind of remuneration for a referral for which a federal health care program (such as Medicare) will pay in whole or in part. Such a kickback, bribe, or rebate can be a felony, even if the remuneration is not in cash. A criminal violation of the Anti-Kickback Statute can result in a fine of up to $25,000 per claim submitted, imprisonment for up to five years, and exclusion from participation in federal healthcare programs. Civil monetary penalties are provided in cases of "reckless disregard," or "deliberate ignorance."

A criminal violation of the Anti-Kickback Statute can result in a fine of up to $25,000 per claim submitted, imprisonment for up to five years, and exclusion from participation in federal healthcare programs.

A number of "safe harbors" have been established to protect certain kinds of transactions. For example, space and equipment rentals between parties to a referral can be permissible as long as the transaction meets the requirements of the applicable safe harbor. If you have a concern about a transaction or referral, check with a qualified attorney to make sure it does not violate the Anti-Kickback Statute and to determine whether a safe harbor might apply.

Example: A physician offers to pay a dentist $50 for every patient the dentist refers to the physician. The dentist seldom bills Medicare, but some of his patients are covered by Medicare for other health care services. The physician may violate the Anti-Kickback Statute if he or she offers remuneration for a referral. If the dentist accepts the offer, the dentist may violate the Anti-Kickback Statute, too.

Example: A physician rents office space from a dentist and the dentist sometimes refers patients to that physician. The dentist rarely bills Medicare, but some of her patients are covered by Medicare for other medical services. The dentist and the physician may help minimize the risk of an Anti-Kickback Statute violation by making sure the lease fits into the "space rental" safe harbor to help minimize the risk that the rental payments may be construed as kickbacks for referrals. Among other things, the space rental safe harbor requires that the lease be documented in a signed writing, that the term be at least one year, that the rent is specified in advance and is consistent with fair market value and that the rent does not take into account the volume or value of referrals.

Related References and Resources

- The Federal Anti-Kickback Statute, Promotional Discount Programs, Discounts and Rebates FAQ *ADA.org/en/member-center/member-benefits/legal-resources/publications-and-articles/ fraud-and-abuse/the-federal-anti-kickback-statute-promotional-discount-programs- discounts-and-rebates-faq.*

- OIG, A Roadmap for New Physicians: Avoiding Medicare and Medicaid Fraud and Abuse *http://oig.hhs.gov/compliance/physician-education/index.asp*

Chapter 29.
Thorny Patient Treatment Issues

Over the years ADA lawyers have responded to thousands of calls from dentists and their dental teams about patient treatment issues. This section will discuss some of the thorniest questions that have been asked.

213. Do I Have to Hire Sign Language Interpreters for Hearing Impaired Patients?

In some cases, yes. Under the Americans with Disabilities Act (AwDA), a dental office is a place of public accommodation and is prohibited from unlawful discrimination by reason of disability. A place of public accommodation may not discriminate against people with disabilities such as hearing impairments and must supply "auxiliary aids and services" when necessary to ensure effective communication, unless doing so would cause an undue burden. State laws may impose even more stringent requirements regarding interpreter services. In addition, dental practices that are Medicaid or Medicare providers are required under Section 504 of the Rehabilitation Act of 1973 to provide auxiliary aids to individuals with disabilities, at no additional cost, where necessary to ensure effective communication with individuals with hearing, vision, or speech impairments.

Sometimes dentists must retain the services of sign language interpreters and in other cases this is not required. The AwDA requires you to make the services of an interpreter available if one is needed to achieve equally "effective communication" with the hearing impaired individual (the patient or prospective patient or their legal surrogates, if any). The need for auxiliary aids and services may vary from individual to individual (some deaf patients prefer reading lips and others do well exchanging notes) and even treatment-by-treatment (an interpreter may be needed for a complex procedure, but perhaps not for a simple one such as a prophy). The dentist should assess the need on a case-by-case basis.

When deciding whether an interpreter is necessary, consider the needs and preferences of the individual and the complexity and length of the communications that will be involved. Consider whether you will need an interpreter to secure an informed consent, or whether you will need an interpreter if foreseeable complications arise. A dentist will often know in advance if a patient has a hearing impairment, and practices often ask all new patients if they need accommodations of any kind when scheduling appointments. If so, the dental practice can discuss appropriate accommodations in advance of the office visit. The National Association of the Deaf (NAD) advises patients: "Requests for accommodations should be made in advance, when possible, so the health care provider has enough time to obtain the necessary accommodations."

The requirement to provide auxiliary aids and services can extend others besides patients. For example, if the patient is a child who can hear but the child's parent is hearing impaired, you may need to hire an interpreter to communicate with the parent to achieve effective communication. Of course, this effective communication is a good idea for risk management purposes as well and can help you make sure that the parent has given informed consent for treatment of the child.

Barrier-Free Health Care Initiative

In 2012, the U.S. Department of Justice (DOJ) announced the Barrier-Free Health Care Initiative to help people with disabilities, especially those who are deaf or hard of hearing, have medical information provided to them in a manner that is understandable to them. U.S. Attorneys' offices and the DOJ's Civil Rights Division have targeted enforcement efforts on access to medical services and facilities. The DOJ has announced settlements with a number of health care providers to ensure that they provide effective communication to people who are deaf or have hearing difficulties. The Barrier-Free Health Care Initiative is a multi-phase initiative that will include effective communication for people who are deaf or have hearing loss, physical access to medical care for people with mobility disabilities, and equal access to treatment for people who have HIV/AIDS.

HIPAA

A HIPAA covered dental practice that hires a sign language interpreter may need to have a compliant business associate agreement in place with the interpreter.

Related References and Resources

- NAD, Health Care Providers
  http://nad.org/issueshe or health-care/providers

- DOJ, Barrier-Free Health Care Initiative
  www.ada.gov/usao-agreements.htm

- OCR, Health Information Privacy: Business Associates
  www.hhs.gov/ocr/privacy/hipaa/understanding/coveredentities/businessassociates.html

- Health Information Privacy: Sample Business Associate Agreement Provisions
  www.hhs.gov/ocr/privacy/hipaa/understanding/coveredentities/contractprov.html

- FAQ on HIPAA Business Associates
  ADA.org/en/home-cps/practice/operations/regulatory/faqs-on-hipaa-business-associates

- HIPAA Business Associates: Am I One?
  ADA.org/en/home-cps/practice/operations/regulatory/hipaa-business-associates-am-i-one

- The ADA Practical Guide to HIPAA Compliance: Privacy and Security Manual
  adacatalog.org or 1.800.947.4746

214. Who Pays for the Interpreter? I'd Lose Money If I Had to Pay.

If an interpreter is used because sign language skills are needed to achieve equally effective communication, the dentist must pay for the services and cannot pass the charge along to the hearing impaired individual. However, this does not mean that the dentist must pay any time a patient brings an interpreter to an appointment.

If an interpreter is necessary to achieve effective communication, the simplest approach may be to pay the interpreter's charges for the initial visit, and if they are high, explore other interpreter options for future visits. A well-prepared dentist can have on hand a list of readily available resources, perhaps including lower cost interpreters (such as interpreters provided through local social service, religious, or government funded agencies). The best resources will vary locally, and sometimes they can be found through disability support groups such as the local hearing society or Easter Seals branch. Dentists cannot insist that patients use friends or family to interpret.

A dentist may wish to claim that providing an interpreter is an undue burden, but the interpreter's fee is measured against the practice's overall financial picture, not the treatment in question. Dental offices that provide interpreter services may qualify for a tax credit. Consult a qualified tax advisor for professional advice.

Don't forget, the key is achieving effective communication.

Related References and Resources

- Chapter 22: Tax Issues (Provides information about the AwDA tax credit)

- DOJ, Excerpt from the Americans with Disabilities Act Title III Technical Assistance Manual
  www.ada.gov/reachingout/title3l2.html

- DOJ, Technical Assistance Manual in its entirety
  www.ada.gov/taman3.html

215. Must I Provide Foreign Language Interpreters?

Although the Americans with Disabilities Act requires health care providers to provide sign language interpreters, there is no "across the board" federal requirement that dentists provide foreign language interpreters for individuals who are "LEP" (Limited English Proficient). However, you may have to provide foreign language interpreters if you participate in Medicaid. State law may also require you to provide a foreign language interpreter in certain cases. Even if it is not required by law, finding effective ways to work through foreign language barriers makes good risk management sense. For example, an interpreter can help you make sure that you have truly secured informed consent before beginning treatment.

Dentists who receive federal financial assistance through the U.S. Department of Health and Human Services (HHS) (for example, by participating in Medicaid) may be required to provide foreign language interpreters for their LEP patients (not just those on Medicaid) under the civil rights laws that HHS enforces through the Office of Civil Rights.

The federal Office for Civil Rights (OCR) has stated:

> Small practitioners and providers will have considerable flexibility in determining precisely how to fulfill their obligations to take reasonable steps to ensure meaningful access for persons with limited English proficiency. OCR will assess compliance on a case by case basis and will take into account the following factors: (1) the number or proportion of LEP persons eligible to be served or likely to be encountered by the recipient's program, activity or service; (2) the frequency with which LEP individuals come in contact with the program, activity or service; (3) the nature and importance of the program, activity, or service provided by the recipient; and (4) the resources available to the recipient and costs. There is no "one size fits all" solution for Title VI compliance with respect to LEP persons, and what constitutes "reasonable steps" for large providers may not be reasonable where small providers are concerned. Thus, smaller recipients with smaller budgets will not be expected to provide the same level of language services as larger recipients with larger budgets.[15]

OCR has stated that it is available to provide technical assistance to HHS recipients, including sole practitioners and other small recipients, seeking to operate an effective language assistance program and to comply with Title VI.

This is a complex area. The ADA has objected to OCR's assertion that dentists are covered by these rules, and has questioned the clarity and scope of OCR's stated enforcement plans. Nevertheless, dentists participating in Medicaid programs have been asked to provide and pay for foreign language interpreters. Check to see if your state's Medicaid program reimburses dentists for the cost of providing an interpreter to LEP patients.

HIPAA

For HIPAA covered dental practices, a foreign language interpreter who is not a member of the practice's workforce may be a business associate who is required to sign a HIPAA-compliant business associate agreement before accessing patient information.

HIPAA does not require a covered dental practice to obtain a patient's authorization to disclose patient information to an interpreter who is a bilingual workforce member of the dental practice. If your practice is covered by HIPAA and a patient's friend or family member will serve as interpreter, you may request the patient's authorization to disclose patient health information to the interpreter, although you may, based on your professional judgment, reasonably infer that the patient does not object to disclosure to the interpreter.

Related References and Resources

- Dugoni School of Dentistry, Free Downloadable Dental Health History Form Translated into 40 Languages
  http://dental.pacific.edu/Professional_Services_and_Resources/Dental_Practice_Documents.html

- FAQ on HIPAA Business Associates
  ADA.org/en/home-cps/practice/operations/regulatory/faqs-on-hipaa-business-associates

- HIPAA Business Associates: Am I One?
  ADA.org/en/home-cps/practice/operations/regulatory/hipaa-business-associates-am-i-one

---

[15] Source: Office for Civil Rights, Questions and Answers Regarding The Department of Health And Human Services Guidance To Federal Financial Assistance Recipients Regarding the Title Vi Prohibition Against National Origin Discrimination Affecting Limited English Proficient Persons, *www.hhs.gov/ocr/civilrights/resources/specialtopics/lep/finalproposed.html*

- OCR, Health Information Privacy: Business Associates
  www.hhs.gov/ocr/privacy/hipaa/understanding/coveredentities/businessassociates.html

- OCR, Sample Business Associate Agreement Provisions
  www.hhs.gov/ocr/privacy/hipaa/understanding/coveredentities/contractprov.html

- OCR, Communicating with a Patient's Family, Friends, or Others Involved in the Patient's Care
  www.hhs.gov/ocr/privacy/hipaa/understanding/coveredentities/provider_ffg.pdf

- *The ADA Practical Guide to HIPAA Compliance: Privacy and Security Manual*
  adacatalog.org or 1.800.947.4746

- *ADA Health History Form (English and Spanish versions)*
  adacatalog.org or 1.800.947.4746

216. Do I Have to Allow Service Animals (Such as Seeing Eye Dogs) in the Operatory?

Under the Americans with Disabilities Act (AwDA), a dental office must allow people with service animals into all areas of the facility where patients are normally allowed to go. A dental office may have a "no pets" policy, but a service animal is not a pet. If a person with an animal enters your office, you or your staff may ask whether the animal is a service animal and what it is trained to do. If the person responds that the animal is not a service animal, is not trained to provide service, or is a pet, the animal may be excluded from the office. However, you and your staff must not ask about the individual's disability or require an ID card or certification for the animal. You many not charge extra fees for a service animal or treat the individual with a service animal less favorably than other patients.

You may not isolate the individual and service animal from other patients or ask a person with a service animal to remove it from the premises unless it is out of control and its owner does not take effective action to control it, or it poses a direct threat to the health or safety of others. If the service animal poses a significant risk to the health or safety of others, and you are unable to eliminate the risk by modifying your procedures, you must give the disabled individual an option to obtain services without having the animal on the premises. To determine whether the service animal poses a direct threat to the health or safety of others, you must make an individualized assessment based on reasonable judgment that relies on current medical knowledge or the best available objective evidence. In general, allergies and fear of animals are not valid reasons for denying access or refusing dental care to people with service animals.

Violations of the ADwA can result in money damages and penalties.

Under Title III of the AwDA, only dogs and miniature horses can qualify as service animals, but state law may permit other types of animals. A dental practice covered by Title III of the ADwA must also comply with applicable state law.

Related References and Resources

- Appendix 10: Service Animals in the Dental Office

217. Do I Have to Allow Motorized Wheelchairs in My Dental Practice? What About Segways?

Title III of the Americans with Disabilities Act (AwDA), which applies to dental practices as "public accommodations," requires facilities to allow people with disabilities who use wheelchairs (including manual wheelchairs, power wheelchairs, and electric scooters) and manually-powered mobility aids such as walkers, crutches, canes, braces, and other similar devices into all areas of a facility where members of the public are allowed to go.

> According to the U.S. Department of Justice:
>
> In addition, facilities must allow people with disabilities who use any OPDMD (other power-driven mobility devices, including Segways) to enter the premises unless a particular type of device cannot be accommodated because of legitimate safety requirements. Such safety requirements must be based on actual risks, not on speculation or stereotypes about a particular type of device or how it might be operated by people with disabilities using them.
>
> In deciding whether a facility must accommodate a particular type of OPDMD, the following factors must be considered:
>
> - The type, size, weight, dimensions, and speed of the device
> - The facility's volume of pedestrian traffic (which may vary at different times of the day, week, month, or year)
> - The facility's design and operational characteristics (e.g., whether its business is conducted indoors or outdoors, its square footage, the density and placement of furniture and other stationary devices, and the availability of storage for the OPDMD if needed and requested by the user)
> - Whether legitimate safety requirements (such as limiting speed to the pace of pedestrian traffic or prohibiting use on escalators) can be established to permit the safe operation of the OPDMD in the specific facility; and
> - Whether the use of the OPDMD creates a substantial risk of serious harm to the immediate environment or natural or cultural resources, or poses a conflict with Federal land management laws and regulations.
>
> It is important to understand that these assessment factors relate to an entire class of device type, **not** to how a person with a disability might operate the device...[16]

A dental practice may wish to make the above determination in advance in order to avoid concern or confusion before a patient's appointment.

---

[16] Source: Wheelchairs, Mobility Aids, and Other Power-Driven Mobility Devices, available at *www.ada.gov/opdmd.htm*

If a dental practice determines it can accommodate one or more types of OPDMDs in its facility, the dental practice is allowed to ask the person using the device to provide credible assurance that the device is used because of a disability. With respect to what a dental practice may, and may not ask, and what constitutes "credible assurance," the Department of Justice has stated:

> An entity that determines it can accommodate one or more types of OPDMDs in its facility is allowed to ask the person using the device to provide credible assurance that the device is used because of a disability. If the person presents a valid, State-issued disability parking placard or card or a State-issued proof of disability, that must be accepted as credible assurance on its face. If the person does not have this documentation, but states verbally that the OPDMD is being used because of a mobility disability, that also must be accepted as credible assurance, unless the person is observed doing something that contradicts the assurance. For example, if a person is observed running and jumping, that may be evidence that contradicts the person's assertion of a mobility disability. However, it is very important for covered entities and their staff to understand that the fact that a person with a disability is able to walk for a short distance does not necessarily contradict a verbal assurance — many people with mobility disabilities can walk, but need their mobility device for longer distances or uneven terrain. This is particularly true for people who lack stamina, have poor balance, or use mobility devices because of respiratory, cardiac, or neurological disabilities. *A covered entity cannot ask people about their disabilities" [italics supplied]*[17]

Related References and Resources

- DOJ, Wheelchairs, Mobility Aids, and Other Power-Driven Mobility Devices
  www.ada.gov/opdmd.htm

218. Are There Laws Prohibiting Discrimination Against Patients Who Are Part of a Protected Class?

Under Section 1557 of the Affordable Care Act, an individual cannot be excluded from participation in, be denied the benefits of, or be discriminated under any health program or activity which is receiving federal financial assistance, on the grounds of race, color, national origin, sex, sex stereotypes, gender identity, age, or disability. Sex discrimination includes sex stereotyping and gender identity, referring to discrimination based on the way an individual is "supposed" to behave based on perceived gender or sexual orientation.

Section 1557 gives the Department of Health and Human Services' Office for Civil Rights authority to investigate any potential violations.

An example illustrating Section 1557 was a complaint involving a medical center which had a policy of automatically assigning a male spouse as the guarantor when their female spouse received medical services. However, when a male spouse received medical services, the female spouse was not automatically assigned as the guarantor.

As a result of a U.S. Department of Health and Human Service (HHS) investigation, the medical center's policy was changed to ensure equal treatment regardless of the sex of the patient.

---

[17] Source: Wheelchairs, Mobility Aids, and Other Power-Driven Mobility Devices, available at *www.ada.gov/opdmd.htm*

Consequently, a dental practice that participates in a health program that receives federal financial assistance cannot engage in discriminatory practices against members of a protected class listed above.

Related References and Resources

- OCR, Corrective Actions Taken in Sex Discrimination Cases: Enforcement of "Section 1557" of the Affordable Care Act
  www.hhs.gov/ocr/office/1557_bulletin.pdf

- OCR Section 1557 of the Patient Protection and Affordable Care Act
  www.hhs.gov/ocr/civilrights/understanding/section1557

219. Must I Treat Patients With HIV, HCV or Other Infectious Diseases?

Persons with infectious diseases may have disabilities as defined by applicable federal, state or local disabilities laws, and may thus be entitled to protections afforded by laws such as the Americans with Disabilities Act (AwDA) and similar state or local laws. For example, the AwDA defines a "disability" as a physical or mental impairment that substantially limits a major life activity; a person also has a disability if he or she has a record of such an impairment in the past, or is regarded as having such an impairment. According to the U.S. Department of Justice (DOJ) Civil Rights Division, "[p]ersons with HIV, both symptomatic and asymptomatic, have physical impairments that substantially limit one or more major life activities or major bodily functions and are, therefore, protected by the law."[18]

Moreover, the DOJ Civil Rights Division states that the AwDA also protects people who are discriminated against because they are regarded as having HIV/AIDS even if they do not actually have the disease, and persons who are discriminated against because they have a relationship or association with an individual with HIV/AIDS (for example, an HIV-negative woman whose roommate has AIDS).

Under the AwDA, a place of public accommodation, such as a dental office, must give people with disabilities an equal opportunity to use the facilities and obtain services. Unlike the *employment provisions* of the AwDA, which apply to employers with 15 or more employees, the *public accommodation provisions* of the AwDA apply to all professional offices of health care providers, regardless of size. A dental office would risk violating the AwDA if it categorically refused to treat patients with HIV/AIDS, or if it provided patients unequal or separate services based on their disabilities.

A dentist may refer an individual with HIV/AIDS to another provider if the individual is seeking treatment that the dentist does not provide; the test for discrimination is whether the dentist would also refer an HIV-negative individual to another provider for the same treatment. A dentist would risk violating the AwDA by referring all patients with HIV/AIDS on the basis that the dental office is not equipped to treat patients with HIV/AIDS, because providing routine dental care to people with HIV/AIDS does not require special equipment.

---

[18] Source: Questions and Answers: The Americans with Disabilities Act and Persons with HIV/AIDS, *www.ada.gov/aids/ada_q&a_aids.htm*

A public accommodation such as a dental office may exclude an individual with a disability if the individual poses a "direct threat" to the health and safety of others. The AwDA defines "direct threat" as "a significant risk to the health or safety of others that cannot be eliminated by a modification of policies, practices, or procedures or by the provision of auxiliary aids or services." A determination of a direct threat must be based on current medical evidence and reasonable judgment, taking into consideration the individual's abilities and disabilities and the particular activity involved. It cannot be based on generalizations or stereotypes.

A dental patient with active tuberculosis is more likely to pose a direct threat than a patient with HIV/AIDS or HCV, because TB is airborne and is not stopped by universal precautions. CDC guidelines recommend postponing nonurgent dental treatment and keeping a patient with tuberculosis in the dental office no longer than the time necessary to arrange a referral to an appropriate medical setting to evaluate infectiousness. The CDC guidelines provide that urgent dental care for a patient with tuberculosis should be provided in a setting with specific environmental controls.

Your state's dental practice act, department of professional regulation, or public health department may require dentists and dental hygienists to report any contagious, infectious, and communicable diseases of which they become aware if the disease is a danger to public health. Consult your attorney or state dental society for the requirements in your state.

Related References and Resources

- Some Laws that Can Affect Dentistry
  ADA.org/DentistGuidetoLaw

- CDC Guidelines for Infection Control in Dental Health-Care Settings
  www.cdc.gov/mmwr/preview/mmwrhtml/rr5217a1.htm

- CDC Guidelines for Preventing the Transmission of Mycobacterium tuberculosis in Health-Care Settings, 2005
  www.cdc.gov/mmwr/pdf/rr/rr5417.pdf

A dentist may refer an individual with HIV/AIDS to another provider if the individual is seeking treatment that the dentist does not provide; the test for discrimination is whether the dentist would also refer an HIV-negative individual to another provider for the same treatment.

220. Can I Ask a Patient If He or She Has Any Infectious Diseases — HIV in Particular?

Yes, if you are asking for the right reasons. Merely inquiring about disease status is not discriminatory, particularly if the question is asked in order to provide the best possible patient care. Failing to ask this question of every patient could open the door to a charge of malpractice. However, targeting the question only to certain people, or using a "yes" answer to deny or inappropriately alter or restrict care may lead to a discrimination claim. The ADA Health History Form asks about HIV, and clearly states that none of the information secured via the form will be used to discriminate.

Information about HIV is particularly sensitive and some states impose special safeguards for information about a patient's HIV status. For example, a state may require such information to be segregated from the patient's general health record. Check the rules in your state for managing patient information regarding HIV.

HIPAA governs the privacy and confidentiality practices of covered dental practices. HIPAA covered dental practices must also comply with applicable state laws that are more stringent than HIPAA.

Your state's dental practice act, department of professional regulation, or public health department may require dentists and dental hygienists to report any contagious, infectious, and communicable diseases of which they become aware if the disease is a danger to public health. Consult your state attorney or dental society for the requirements in your state.

Related References and Resources

- Chapter 15: HIPAA, State Law and PCI DSS: Patient Information

- HIPAA 20 Questions
  ADA.org/DentistGuidetoLaw

- HIV
  ADA.org/en/member-center/oral-health-topics/hiv

221. What Are the Rules About Managing an Obese Patient?

Dentists and their staffs are sometimes concerned that an obese patient may need to be lifted into or out of the chair or that the patient may break the chair, risking harm to both the patient and the dental team.

In certain cases, obesity may meet the definition of a "disability" under federal, state, or local discrimination laws. While someone who is a bit overweight may not satisfy the legal definition of a "disability" and thus may not be afforded legal protection, a morbidly obese person, whose weight substantially limits one or more major life activities, may qualify for protection.

The federal Americans with Disabilities Act (AwDA) defines a "disability" as a physical or mental impairment that substantially limits one or more major life activities; a person is also deemed to have a disability if he or she has a record of such an impairment in the past, or is regarded as having such an impairment.

Under the AwDA, a dental practice may not exclude a disabled individual unless the patient poses a "direct threat" to the health and safety of others. In determining whether an individual poses a direct threat to the health or safety of others, a dental practice must make an individualized assessment, based on reasonable judgment that relies on current medical knowledge or on the best available objective evidence to ascertain:

- The nature, duration and severity of the risk

- The probability that the potential injury will actually occur

- Whether reasonable modifications of policies, practices or procedures, or the provision of auxiliary aids or services will mitigate the risk

A dental office may establish objective safety criteria based on objective requirements (not based on stereotypes or generalizations about persons with disabilities). The AwDA does not require modifications that would fundamentally alter the nature of the service (for example, it does not require a dentist to provide services outside his or her dental specialty) or auxiliary aids that would be an undue burden. Modifications in policies only must be made if they are reasonable and do not fundamentally alter the nature of the service provided. The duty to mitigate probably does not extend to lifting heavy people in and out of the dental chair, especially if doing so has a real likelihood of causing you or your staff harm.

Do not simply assume your chair will break and potentially harm the patient, you, or your team. Find out about your equipment. What is its load capacity (based on its specifications, not speculation)? If the capacity is less than the patient weighs, can the capacity be inexpensively enhanced, or might it be time for a new chair? Again, keep in mind the AwDA requires reasonable modifications and auxiliary aids, not cost-prohibitive ones. Financial considerations such as the cost of purchasing a new chair should be evaluated in determining whether an auxiliary aid would be an undue burden.

State and local disabilities laws may be more stringent than the federal Americans with Disabilities Act. A dental practice must comply with both the federal statute and any applicable state and local laws.

Related References and Resources

- Some Laws That Can Affect Dentistry (Americans with Disabilities Act Section)
  ADA.org/DentistGuidetoLaw

- DOJ, Myths and Facts About the Americans with Disabilities Act
  www.ada.gov/pubs/mythfct.txt

- NIH, Medical Care for Obese Patients
  http://win.niddk.nih.gov/publications/medical.htm

222. How Do I Handle a Drug-Seeking Patient — One I Suspect May Be Calling Around for Prescriptions?

Dentists are often the target of patients who seek to obtain prescription drugs to abuse or to sell. A dental practice can take certain measures to help identify potential drug-seeking behavior and help safeguard the practice. These measures should be implemented subject to applicable laws, including those privacy laws.

Characteristics of Drug-Seeking Patients

In its publication, "Don't Be Scammed by a Drug Abuser," the U.S. Department of Justice Drug Enforcement Administration (DEA) outlines common characteristics of drug abusers and modus operandi often used by drug-seeking patients. For example, dentists should be alert to a patient who is extremely slovenly or over-dressed, exhibits unusual behavior in the waiting room, shows unusual knowledge of controlled substances, requests a specific controlled drug and is reluctant to try a different drug, exaggerates medical problems or simulates symptoms, or has cutaneous signs of drug abuse. Drug-seeking patients sometimes insist on being seen right away, try to make an appointment toward the end of office hours, claim to be traveling through town, claim to be allergic to non-narcotic analgesics, claim a prescription has been lost or stolen, request refills more often than originally prescribed, or say that they are a patient of a practitioner who is unavailable (or refuses to give the name of their regular practitioner).

Examples of Safeguards

If you are suspicious that a patient or prospective patient may be drug-seeking, the DEA recommends that you not "take their word for it" or dispense drugs just to get rid of them. Instead, you should:

- Request a photo I.D. (or other I.D. and Social Security number) and place photocopies of the documents in the patient's record

- Confirm the patient's telephone number, and confirm his or her current address at each visit

- Perform a thorough exam

- Document the exam result and the questions you asked the patient

- Write any prescriptions for limited quantities

You may also wish to:

- Confirm suspicious stories, such as treatment begun by another dentist in another community, by calling the other dentist, if allowed under state and federal law

- Depending on applicable state and federal laws (including HIPAA, if your practice is a covered entity), contact local pharmacies regarding suspected prescription abuse

- Consult a qualified attorney about responding to requests for patient information from law enforcement authorities, and about contacting law enforcement to report suspected criminal activity

Prescription Drug Monitoring Programs (PDMP)

Many states have implemented prescription drug monitoring programs. A PDMP is a statewide electronic database that collects data on substances dispensed in the state. The state agency that administers the PDMP makes data from the database accessible to authorized individuals. State law determines who is authorized to access data and for what purpose. In most states, prescribers and dispensers of drugs may access the PDMP database, and some states require prescribers and dispensers to access the PDMP in certain circumstances.

DEA and State Law Requirements

Know your DEA and state requirements and fulfill any DEA or state reporting obligations that may be triggered by the facts. For example, do not prescribe or dispense controlled substances outside of a formal dentist-patient relationship or outside the scope of your practice. The DEA Practitioner's Manual summarizes and explains the basic requirements for prescribing, administering, and dispensing controlled substances under the Controlled Substances Act and the DEA regulations.

Disabilities Law

Under Title III of the Americans with Disabilities Act (AwDA), which applies to dental practices as "public accommodations," the term "disability" does not include psychoactive substance use disorders resulting from current illegal use of drugs. "Current illegal use of drugs" means illegal use of drugs that occurred recently enough to justify a reasonable belief that a person´s drug use is current or that continuing use is a real and ongoing problem. "Drug" is defined as a Schedule I — V controlled substance. An individual who is currently engaging in the illegal use of drugs is not considered an "individual with a disability" under the AwDA, when a dental practice acts on the basis of such use.

However, the AwDA does not permit a dental practice to discriminate on the basis of illegal use of drugs against an individual who is not engaging in current illegal use of drugs and who:

1. Has successfully completed a supervised drug rehabilitation program or has otherwise been rehabilitated successfully

2. Is participating in a supervised rehabilitation program

3. Is erroneously regarded as engaging in such use

Thus, a person who no longer engages in the illegal use of drugs could meet the definition of disability.

Patient Privacy Law

Another issue to keep in mind is patient privacy. The laws in some states require safeguards to protect certain categories of sensitive patient information, such as a mental health diagnosis or information about a substance abuse disorder. HIPAA requires covered dental practices to have in place appropriate safeguards to protect the privacy of patient information, and covered dental practices must also comply with state law that is more stringent than HIPAA. Dental practices that are not covered by HIPAA must comply with applicable state law.

Dentists are often privileged to know their patients over a long period of time, and to treat many members of the same family. This may make a dentist want to take additional steps when he or she is concerned about a patient's alcohol or drug use, such as expressing concern to a family member and offering to be of support in urging the patient to seek help. The importance of keeping confidentiality and privacy laws in mind before traveling this path cannot be understated.

Libel and Slander

Finally, a quick note about voicing your suspicions: remember, they are only suspicions. Cast them as such, rather than as fact. Anything more can open you up to charges of libel and slander if your suspicions turn out to be inaccurate.

Related References and Resources

- Question 70: What if I Suspect an Employee or Co-Worker Is Abusing or Taking Drugs from the Dental Office?

- Chapter 15: HIPAA, State Law and PCI DSS: Patient Information

- HIPAA 20 Questions
  ADA.org/DentistGuidetoLaw

- DEA, Don't Be Scammed by a Drug Abuser
  www.deadiversion.usdoj.gov/pubs/brochures/drugabuser.htm

- NAMSDL, National Alliance for Model State Drug Laws
  www.namsdl.org/prescription-monitoring-programs.cfm

- NASCSA, The National Association of State Controlled Substance Authorities (list of state PDMP contacts)
  www.nascsa.org

- Prescription Drug Monitoring Programs
  www.deadiversion.usdoj.gov/faq/rx_monitor.htm

- DEA Regulations
  www.deadiversion.usdoj.gov/index.html

- DEA Practitioner's Manual
  www.deadiversion.usdoj.gov/pubs/manuals/pract/section1.htm

- DEA, Drug Addiction in Health Care Professionals
  www.deadiversion.usdoj.gov/pubs/brochures/drug_hc.htm

- OCR, Communicating with a Patient's Family, Friends, or Others Involved in the Patient's Care
  www.hhs.gov/ocr/privacy/hipaa/understanding/coveredentities/provider_ffg.pdf

- Drug Use: Talking With Your Patients
  ADA.org/en/member-center/oral-health-topics/drug-use

- Laws That Can Affect Dentistry
  ADA.org/DentistGuidetoLaw

223. How Can I Learn More About My Responsibilities in Regard to Infection Control?

The CDC issued Guidelines for Infection Control in Dental Health-Care Settings in December of 2003. The CDC guidelines do not by themselves have the force of law. However, many states incorporate CDC recommendations by reference in state law. Other states look to CDC guidance in interpreting state law. Accordingly, in some states, compliance with the CDC guidelines is, at least as a practical matter, mandatory. The guidelines may also be looked to as evidence of a standard of care that a dentist is expected to meet.

CDC Guidelines may also affect compliance with the OSHA "general duty" clause. In addition, several OSHA standards and directives apply to protecting workers against transmission of infectious agents, such as OSHA's Bloodborne Pathogens standard.

The CDC infection control guidelines include dental unit water quality, using sterile water irrigation and sterile gloves for surgical procedures, and separately disposing of extracted teeth containing amalgam.

An important switch in the 2003 CDC Guidelines was from universal to standard precautions. Universal precautions focused on preventing unprotected contact with blood or other fluids containing blood from all individuals regardless of their serostatus for bloodborne pathogens. Standard precautions expand upon this principle by adding unprotected contact with all bodily fluids (except sweat) regardless of whether or not blood is present. Standard precautions also include prevention of unprotected contact with mucous membranes and non-intact skin.

Related References and Resources

- OSHA Bloodborne Pathogens Standard
  www.osha.gov/pls/oshaWeb/owadisp.show_document?p_table=STANDARDS&p_id=10051

- CDC Guidelines for Infection Control in Dental Health Care Settings — 2003 PowerPoint Presentation
  www.cdc.gov/oralhealth/infectioncontrol/guidelines/slides/001.htm

- CDC Guidelines for Infection Control in Dental Health-Care Settings — 2003
  www.cdc.gov/mmwr/preview/mmwrhtml/rr5217a1.htm

- The ADA Practical Guide to OSHA Compliance: Regulatory Compliance Manual
  adacatalog.org or 1.800.947.4746

224. Is It True That I Can Apologize to a Patient for an Unexpected Outcome and That My Apology Can't Be Used Against Me in Court If the Patient Sues?

Before making any statements to patients regarding an unexpected outcome or adverse event it is important to understand the particular details of the situation, the laws of your state, and the likely effect of such statements. A qualified attorney can provide information about applicable law and the possible legal implications of statements made to patients and others. Information may also be available from your professional liability carrier.

Some states have passed legislation providing that statements of apology or grief made by medical professionals cannot, under certain circumstances, be used against them in court. The legislation varies widely from state to state. Before relying on such a law to make a statement, it is important to know the details of the applicable law, such as whose statements are protected, what kinds of communications the law protects, to whom protected statements may be made, and if the law covers any statement of fault or if the law protects only apologies.

Apology laws are based on the theory that disclosure following adverse events, and apologies when appropriate, may enhance communication between health care providers and patients, improve provider–patient relations, and facilitate resolution of any claims or settlements. However, it is unclear what effect these laws will have on malpractice litigation or on communications between health care practitioners and their patients.

225. What Should I Do If a Patient Leaves My Practice in the Middle of Treatment Against My Advice?

A dentist is obligated to discuss with a patient the treatment being recommended and any reasonable alternatives that exist. That disclosure allows the patient to make an informed decision concerning the treatment that he or she will receive. That same philosophy should be followed if a patient decides to abandon a course of treatment that has already begun (or refuses to accept any treatment). In such cases, the dentist should provide the patient with a description of the potential consequences of failing to undertake or continue a course of treatment. Generally speaking, once armed with that information, a patient has the freedom to reject or discontinue treatment.

There may be reasons unknown to the dentist that are contributing to the patient's decisions, such as a job demotion, loss of employment or a change in benefits received. You may wish to privately discuss with the patient whether any events or conditions unknown to you are contributing to the decision to discontinue or refuse treatment and whether any accommodations are possible between the dental practice and the patient that might allow the treatment to continue.

In cases where treatment is refused or discontinued, the dentist should make sure that the patient's records reflect the advice given and the patient's decision to refuse that advice and discontinue or forego treatment.

When such an event occurs, the dentist may also wish to consider whether it is in the patient's best interests to continue under the doctor's care. The dentist should assess whether he or she will be able to offer the quality of care the patient deserves given that the patient has discontinued or refused a treatment previously recommended by the dental professional. This, too, may involve a candid conversation with the patient.

If it is ultimately determined that you can no longer provide the care that is deserved by the patient and, after consulting with your personal attorney, state dental society or state dental board, have determined that dismissal of the patient is proper, you should inform the patient of that fact. It is important not to abandon the patient during the transition process. Legally and ethically you may have a duty to provide access to care for a reasonable time during the transition process.

You should consider notifying the patient in writing of the dismissal and also providing an explanation of the reason for dismissal. With that notice, you should state the reasonable period of time within which you will provide, or make arrangements for, emergency care while the patient seeks another dentist. Bear in mind, this period or other aspects of the dismissal process may be dictated by law in some states.

To facilitate the continuity of care, you should consider offering referrals to other providers and providing specifics and timetables for continuing care — especially for a patient in whose case you believe continuity of care might be at risk. Providing information about referrals may lessen the risk that the patient will not seek further care. Finally, document the dismissal in the patient's records and make sure that copies of any records needed by a new dentist are made available in a timely manner.

226. What Are My Obligations Concerning a Colleague Who I Believe to Be Impaired or to Lack Essential Clinical Skills?

This is one of the most challenging issues that a dentist may face in dealing with his or her professional colleagues. And it is an issue that may present serious ramifications for a dentist who is believed to be treating patients while impaired through the misuse of, for example, prescription pain medications or alcohol, or is believed not to possess the necessary skill levels needed to perform treatments that the dentist is undertaking. The situation may also result in unintended consequences for the reporting dentist if care is not taken.

With regard to the dentist who is believed to be treating patients while impaired, it is important that anyone thinking of reporting this situation have first-hand knowledge of the impairment. It should be kept in mind that there may be a fine line between use and abuse, and taking correctly prescribed therapeutic doses of a medication may not signify impairment or inability to practice. Although possibly embarrassing or awkward, the best approach in this situation may be to address the potential impairment issue with the dentist directly. If it is the case that alcohol or medication is being consumed that impairs the dentist's judgment or clinical skills and thereby endangers the welfare of patients, you should urge the dentist to seek professional help and to curtail those aspects of the practice that are adversely affected by the impairment.

It is critically important when addressing these sensitive issues to do so in private, outside of the hearing of staff or patients. You may also wish to consider the best manner to address the situation. An electronic communication such as an email or a text message is probably not advisable because of privacy concerns as well as other issues. Privacy is critical because of the personal nature of the issue and the possible reputational damage that an overheard conversation might cause. An overheard conversation or inadvertently seen email on the subject might also subject the inquiring dentist to a claim of defamation.

If, after a conversation about the issue, the problem continues, you may wish to consult with your state society concerning the availability of professional assistance for the impaired dentist and discuss the matter in confidence with such a professional.

With respect to a dentist whom you believe lacks the clinical skills needed to adequately perform treatments being undertaken, you should carefully examine the situation to ensure that the skill level of the dentist in question is indeed inadequate. This may mean that more than one instance of alleged inadequate treatment needs to be presented. You should also consider the necessity of speaking with the dentist in question about the treatment to determine under what circumstances and conditions the treatment was performed. In that conversation, if warranted, you may wish to suggest to the dentist that he or she forgo undertaking further treatment like that presented until steps are taken to bolster skills in the area.

If, after a thorough and impartial examination of all the facts and circumstances surrounding the treatment in question, you firmly believe that a dentist is deficient in certain clinical skills and personal discussions with the dentist do not curtail the problem, you should consider whether to report the issue to the appropriate reviewing agency of the local or state dental association.

When speaking with patients concerning the treatment performed by a prior dentist, care should be taken not to disparage the treatment of the previous dentist. When statements are made concerning treatment by a prior dentist that are unsupportable and, therefore, unjustified, such comments may form the basis of a disciplinary action against the dentist making the statements, as explained in Section 4.C. and Advisory Opinion 4.C.1.of the ADA *Principles of Ethics and Code of Professional Conduct.*

Related References and Resources

- The ADA Ethics Hotline
  ADA.org/en/about-the-ada/principles-of-ethics-code-of-professional-conduct/ada-ethics-resources/ada-ethics-hotline

Chapter 29.
Terminating the Relationship

There are times when a dentist may have to, or want to, stop seeing his or her patient. Questions then arise about how to do so. At the federal level, various anti-discrimination laws may come into play, as may HIPAA (with respect to the patient's records), but the key in terminating a dentist-patient relationship is usually state law, particularly on abandonment. Be sure to consult with your state dental society, state board of dentistry, or your attorney regarding this issue.

227. I'm Closing My Practice. What Must I Tell My Patients? How and When Do I Tell Them?

It depends on what your state law requires. Generally, the key is to inform your patients, with reasonable time for them to secure the services of another dentist, while not interrupting dental care. Contract considerations may also come into play (for example, if you are bound by an associateship or insurance company agreement).

Perhaps you are relocating, retiring, or can no longer practice due to illness. Regardless of the reason, patients should be informed that you are closing your practice and terminating their treatment. Moreover, ending the relationship generally requires that the termination not jeopardize the patient's oral health, and that the patient be given reasonable opportunity to secure the services of another dentist.

The notice of termination should specify the date the dentist-patient relationship will end. In addition, it can be helpful, when appropriate, to include the following information in the notice:

- Reason for termination

- Emergency care will be provided in the interim

- Information on referrals

- Statement that copies of patient records will be available to the patient or the new dentist at the patient's request

- Specifics and timeframes for continuing care

State law may address how patients must be notified (e.g., by letter, or through publication of a notice in a local newspaper). State law may also require that ongoing dental care be continued for a specified period of time until other arrangements can be made.

If these steps aren't taken, the termination may be viewed as abandonment — wrongful cessation of the dentist-patient relationship, particularly where the patient's treatment is incomplete.

Related References and Resources

- Closing a Dental Practice
  success.ada.org/en/practice/ownership-life-cycle/closing/closing-a-dental-practice

228. How Do I Handle a Threatening or Abusive Patient? How Do I Dismiss an Unruly Patient From My Practice?

A violent, threatening or abusive patient presents special challenges. In addition to your own physical safety, you also need to consider your responsibility for the safety of your staff. In the most serious situations (where violence has occurred, or where a threat of physical harm is specific and immanent), you should consider reporting the situation to the police. When memorializing the danger by reporting it to the police, recognize HIPAA and state privacy law concerns and avoid going beyond the necessary report details into extraneous protected health information (for example, if you are aware that the patient is on specific medications, this may not be information necessary to disclose in reporting the violent or threatening behavior).

If a patient becomes uncooperative or non-compliant and you do not want to continue treatment, determine if state law will allow termination, and if so, how to properly terminate care in accordance with that law. For example, there may be requirements as to notification and continuity of care. Also consider your contractual obligations. While many insurance contracts do not state dismissal terms, some may require specific procedures for dismissing a covered patient (these may be in their manual). Follow these rules where possible. (e.g., an HMO may require 1) a notice period to patient, or 2) pre-dismissal notice of some period of time to the carrier).

It is important to remember that dismissing a patient could cause problems if the termination is a pretext for doing something you would otherwise like to, but could not, legally do. For example, if the patient is uncooperative because of a disability, have you evaluated your legal obligation under the AwDA and explored and extended possible accommodations? Would you be terminating someone similar who did not have a disability? The AwDA Amendments Act, enacted September 25, 2008 and effective as of January 1, 2009, significantly broadened the definition of "disability" under the AwDA. The definition of "disability" may be even broader under the law of your state.

Finally, remember one common pitfall: termination of care for non-payment or for late payment will likely violate the laws of abandonment, since most states require completion of treatment before termination as a general rule, and view a patient's payment obligation as a separate issue.

Related References and Resources

- Chapter 24: Payment and Collections

- Some Laws That Can Affect Dentistry
  ADA.org/DentistGuidetoLaw

- OMIC, When Patients Become Difficult, Hostile, or Violent
  www.omic.com/when-patients-become-difficult-hostile-or-violent-2

Appendices

Appendices

Appendix 1:

Checklist of Questions to Ask When Forming a Group Practice

Note: When two or more dentists begin discussions to form a group practice, each dentist should be represented by separate counsel to advise them as to their individual interests and responsibilities, and to facilitate negotiations.

The following checklist outlines issues that are likely to arise when dentists form a group practice. The questions are common to many different practice formats. For a discussion of practice format options, see Chapter 5: Practice Formats: The Business/Legal Structure.

- **Antitrust:** Antitrust issues should be considered at the outset of any discussions, before information is shared and negotiations begin. For further discussion of antitrust law, see Chapter 21: Antitrust.

- **Confidentiality:** The parties should have any necessary agreements and protections in place before exchanging any confidential information. Exchange of any patient information must comply with applicable federal and state confidentiality and privacy laws (e.g., HIPAA covered entities must comply with HIPAA, and may be required to have recipients of information sign appropriate business associate agreements). For more information about patient privacy and confidentiality see Chapter 15: HIPAA, State Law and PCI DSS: Patient Information and, HIPAA 20 Questions at *ADA.org/DentistGuidetoLaw*.

- **Due diligence:** The parties should conduct a thorough background investigation that includes:

  o Prospective group members' background

    - Curriculum Vitae
      - Education
      - Licensure
      - Membership and standing in professional organizations

    - History of disciplinary or liability experience (should include a search of the Office of Inspector General's (OIG) list of excluded individuals and entities (found at *https://oig.hhs.gov/exclusions*)

    - Compatibility of practice style and philosophy

    - Short term goals for the group practice

    - Long-term goals and vision for personal career and group practice
      - Strategic
      - Financial

    - Ability to contribute capital to the group practice

    - Dentists may wish to consent to allowing the others to conduct background and credit checks (for information about issues that arise in connection with background and credit checks, see Question 65: What Information Should Be Included in a Background Check for a Potential Employee? Can a Credit Check Be Run Before Hiring a New Employee?)

- Prospective location
  - Market analysis for general area, for example:
    - Demand for dental services
    - Population and demographic trends
    - The ADA Survey Center can provide State and County Demographic Reports, which include number and demographics of dentists and the population of a geographic area
  - Choice of office space
    - Use existing space, or seek new space
    - Review existing lease for any restrictions
    - Purchase or rent space
    - Square footage requirements
    - Utilities required
    - Accessibility issues
    - Necessary remodeling
    - Transportation, convenience, parking
    - Review local zoning restrictions/requirements

- **Business name**
  - Can be dentists' names (alphabetically or in a different order)
  - Assumed business name (e.g., "Any Town Family Dental Center")
    - must be searched and cleared for use and registered with the state/county (the registration processes differ by state and by type of entity)
    - consider federal or state protection of the trademark or other rights to the name
    - understand state laws and regulations regarding the use of fictitious or assumed names in dental advertising
  - Check state licensure laws for requirements regarding name of practice
  - Register domain name for website

- **Form of business entity** (for a discussion of business format options see Chapter 5: Practice Formats: The Business/Legal Structure)
    - For example, corporation, limited liability partnership (LLP) or limited liability company (LLC)
    - Tax, financial, and liability considerations
    - Check any restrictions on choice of business entity (found in state licensing and business organization statutes)
  - Types of agreements that must be drafted (operating agreements, partnership agreements, bylaws, shareholder agreements, employment and associateship agreements, etc.)
  - Permitted activities of the entity (broad or narrow)

- **Capitalization and financing**
  - o Ownership proportions
  - o Initial contributions of owners (for example, cash, loans, real estate, equipment, or intellectual property contributions such as business name, website design, trademark, logos, practice forms, brochures or other publications)
  - o Infusions of capital
    - How parties will decide whether additional capital is required
    - Under which circumstances will parties be required to provide additional capital
    - The consequences of failing to provide additional capital
  - o Financing
    - Borrowing
    - Security
    - Guaranties
- **Decision-making process and parties' rights and responsibilities**
  - o Strategic decisions versus day-to-day business decisions
  - o Rights with regard to selecting management (officers, board of directors, manager or managing partner(s), office manager, etc.)
  - o Adding a new owner — how to decide, select, determine share and rights
  - o Which decisions require unanimity or a supermajority, for example:
    - Large capital expenditures
    - Approving operating budget
    - Financial guarantees
    - Additional capital contributions
    - Borrowing money or otherwise incurring debt
    - Disposing of a substantial portion of the practice's assets
    - Contracts not in the ordinary course of business
    - Contracts between the practice and one or more owners
    - Selecting or changing an auditor, attorney, accountant, or business manager
    - Opening new location or adding a new line of business (such as a new service, product line, or dental specialty)
    - Purchasing major pieces of equipment
    - Adding a new dentist owner, employee, or independent contractor
    - A dentist's request for an elective extended leave of absence (for example, taking off one or more months to practice charity dentistry abroad)

- Significant changes to fee schedule (e.g., greater than a percentage benchmark amount per year)

- Distributions or dividends to owners

- Hiring and firing employees, or certain key employees

- Certain contracts (such as leases, independent contractor agreements, third party payer, long-term supply contracts, utilities or communications, electronic medical records, website, and other technology)

- Dissolution or liquidation

- **Fiduciary duties of each dentist owner**

  o Restrictions on competition of owner dentists with the group practice

  o Business opportunities

  o Transactions between an owner dentist (or family member) and the practice (conflict of interest)

- **Duties of each owner dentist:**

  o Hours

  o Scope of practice

  o Management responsibilities

- **Compensation and benefits, such as:**

  o Distribution of profits

  o Salaries, draws

    - Restrictions based on value of capitalization

    - Restrictions based on revenue

  o Health insurance, profit sharing, bonus, pension or retirement contributions and other benefits

  o Vacation, sick and personal days, leave of absence

  o Any licensing fees or royalties for intellectual property

  o Cost of maintaining license

  o Continuing education, seminars and conferences (travel and accommodations?)

  o Distribution of profits from selling products in the dental office

- **Bank**

  o Number and kinds of accounts

  o Signatory and depository rights to various accounts

  o Authority to enter into credit arrangements on behalf of the group practice

- **Ownership of, access to, and right to copy documents, including dental records and business records**

- **Dispute resolution procedures**
    - Mechanisms for negotiating/resolving disputes
    - Confidentiality during dispute resolution
- **Provisions for an owner dentist who wishes to exit the group practice**
    - Circumstances under which an owner dentist may exit, for example:
        - Failure of the practice to reach financial goals
        - Breach of an obligation or ethical duty by an owner dentist
        - Death, disability, retirement, withdrawal from practice or bankruptcy of an owner dentist
        - Economic collapse or downturn in the local market
        - Stalemate over practice strategy
    - Mechanism for exiting the practice, including buyout provisions
    - Rights of owner dentists to sell their interests to third parties
        - Option of other owner dentists to purchase on same terms
        - Right of first refusal
        - Procedure if an owner dentist with right to acquire interest is financially unable to do so
        - Covenants not to compete and non-solicitation agreements (state law determines reasonableness and enforceability — see Question 150: Are Restrictive Covenants Enforceable?)
- **Unwinding the group practice**
    - Dissolution (planned, unplanned, death, disability, disagreement)
    - Time frame for dissolution benchmarks
    - Dispute resolution process to prevent deadlocks, such as:
        - Arbitration
        - Swing director
        - Instituting termination procedures
    - Distribution of and rights to assets upon dissolution (including business name and other intellectual property)
    - Notices to patients upon dissolution, rights to (and obligations with respect to) patients lists, dental records, business records
    - Voluntary or involuntary (forced) dissolutions
    - Bankruptcy
    - Post-dissolution contractual arrangements
    - Antitrust laws upon dissolution (and covenants not to compete)
    - Confidentiality upon dissolution

Appendix 2:
Buy-Sell Agreements (Background)

Contract for the Sale of a Dental Practice

The sale of a dental practice requires the buyer and seller to consider and negotiate a wide variety of issues. Each dental practice is unique, and so is every transaction.

To provide a general idea of some of the issues involved when a dental practice is sold, the following outline lists topic headings that may be found in a contract for the sale of a practice.

These provisions are most typically found in contracts for transactions that are structured as "asset sales." In an asset sale, the buyer purchases certain assets (and, in some cases, accepts assignment of certain contracts, such as a lease) that the practice owns. An asset sale may include real estate, equipment and supplies, as well as the dental practice name, telephone number, patient records, and so forth. When a sale is structured as a sale of shares of stock (or of membership interest in an LLC) certain other provisions may apply.

Each transaction is different, but most purchase and sale contracts contain certain basic provisions.

Certain basic provisions found in a Contract for the Purchase and Sale of a Dental Practice may include the following:

- Parties to the Contract
- Date of the contract; closing date for the sale/purchase
- Purchase price
- List/Schedule of assets being transferred (sold, assigned), e.g:
    - Furniture
    - Fixtures
    - Owned equipment
    - Leased equipment (e.g., leased copiers)
    - Supplies
    - Goodwill
    - Books and records
    - Employment or independent contractor agreements with staff
    - Plate glass insurance
    - Receivables, if transferred

- Real estate (title or lease)
  - Telephone numbers
  - Telephone listings in directories
  - Right to use name of business or of the selling dentist for a period of time
  - Licenses for computer software
- List of assets (if any) being retained by seller (e.g., certain artwork, exercise equipment that may be located in the office)
- Allocation of purchase price for tax purposes (i.e., the dollar amount that goes toward):
  - Goodwill
  - Hard assets
  - Restrictive covenant
- Liabilities (if any) being assumed by the buyer
- Manner of payment of purchase price
  - How and when payment will be made
  - Amount of any down payment
  - Financing: whether the purchase price will be financed by the seller (in which case, there may be a promissory note) or by a financial institution (and whether there are any contingencies)
  - Security for payment of purchase price (if purchase price is seller-financed). Security can include the assets (including real estate, if any, subject to any restrictions of the mortgage lender) of the business being purchased.
- Consulting or employment agreement with former owner
- Non-solicitation agreement
- Non-competition/restrictive covenant
- Notices under bulk sales laws (e.g., to state department of revenue)
- Preservation of supplies, business, etc. pending closing
- Right of inspection
- Corporate status
- Risk of loss provisions pending closing
- Treatment of accounts receivable
- Custodian of records, access to records for selling dentist after closing
- Transition provisions — notices to patients
- Transfer of records
- Use of seller's name
- Insurance, utilities, taxes, laboratories

- Rework

- Indemnity provisions

- Seller's warranties and representations

- Buyer's warranties and representations

- Insurance policies, e.g:

    o Life insurance

    o Disability insurance

    o Professional liability insurance, tail coverage

    o Business liability insurance

- Warranties on equipment

- Contingencies

- Prorations — costs and expenses

- Miscellaneous provisions (such as entire agreement, binding on heirs, etc.)

Other Documents

In addition to the contract of sale, the transaction may include one or more of the following documents:

Confidentiality/Nondisclosure Agreement

This agreement, signed prior to the purchase of the practice, typically requires parties to refrain from disclosing confidential information about the potential sale, the business, or patient records. A potential purchaser may be asked to sign such an agreement in the initial stages of considering the purchase of a practice, prior to reviewing the practice's books and records. HIPAA or state law may come into play in connection with a confidentiality/nondisclosure agreement.

Business Associate Agreement

One or more of the parties may need to sign a business associate agreement (BAA) for HIPAA compliance. A potential purchaser may be required to sign a BAA before having access to patient records. The selling dentist may be required to sign a BAA in order to have access to patient records after closing for inspection or liability purposes. For more information about HIPAA, Business Associates see Chapter 15: HIPAA, State Law and PCIDSS: Patient Information, and HIPAA 20 Questions at *ADA.org/DentistGuidetoLaw*.

Bill of Sale

An instrument that lists and transfers title to the personal property being sold.

Assignment of Contracts

A provision either in the sale agreement or a separate document assigning any pertinent agreements. For example, copier service agreements, equipment leases, plate glass insurance, telephone numbers, or business listing agreements with directory services.

Assignment of Lease

To transfer rights under an existing lease, the parties will typically sign a separate instrument that serves to assign the lease to the new tenant (Note: Landlord consent to the assignment is often required).

Promissory Note

A written promise to repay an amount borrowed or financed.

Security Agreement

If personal property is pledged as collateral for payment of a promissory note, a security agreement may be used to secure the collateral against the claim of other creditors. An additional document, such as a financing statement, may be filed with the applicable state or local authority to "perfect" the creditor's security interest in the collateral.

Employment or Independent Contractor Agreement

If the selling dentist will be hired back after the sale of the practice (or if another dentist will be active in the practice as an employee or independent contractor) an agreement may be used to set forth the appropriate terms. See Question 61: When Hiring an Associate Dentist, Do I Need a Written Contract And, If So, What Should Be in It? and Appendices 3 and 4 (Sample Employee Associateship Agreement and Sample Independent Contractor Associateship Agreement).

Real Property Sales Contract

If one of the assets being sold is real estate (for example, the building that houses the dental practice), then a separate contract covering the real property will be required, and a deed may need to be prepared and filed.

Personal Guaranties

A document requiring a buying dentist to personally assume liability. Third party financiers, such as landlords or banks, may require this document, even if the purchasing dentist is incorporated or has formed an LLC.

Appendix 3:

Sample Employee Associateship Agreement

This sample agreement is reproduced only as an example. It is intended only to familiarize parties considering entering into such an arrangement with certain matters that may become part of their agreement; neither inclusion of provisions such as those below, nor the below language itself, are advocated nor recommended. This sample does not constitute legal advice and should in no circumstances be used, in whole or in part, without review by and consultation with your personal attorney. The law varies from jurisdiction to jurisdiction and parts of this sample agreement may be invalid, incomplete or unenforceable depending upon the jurisdiction in question.

Sample Employment Agreement

This Agreement is entered into as of _____, 20__ (the "Effective Date"), by and between Thomas Owner, D.M.D., a Sole Proprietor ("Employer") practicing dentistry at _____ (the "Initial Practice Location"), and April Associate, D.D.S., an individual ("Employee"), reflecting an employment arrangement between Employer and Employee.

1. Employment. Employer hereby employs Employee and Employee hereby accepts such employment as a general dentist upon the following terms and conditions.

2. Professional Services. Employee shall render professional general dental services at the Practice Location, and at any reasonably proximate geographic location (within XX miles of the Initial Practice Location) that Employer may open an office while Employee is employed by Employer (such additional office(s), together with the Initial Practice Location, are hereinafter individually and collectively a "Practice Location"), on a full time basis on behalf of and at the direction of Employer, to existing and to new patients of Employer whom Employer assigns from time to time to Employee. Employee shall be committed to the enhancement of Employer's general dental practice and shall use his or her reasonable efforts to further the goals of and to promote such practice. A "new patient" shall mean a patient who makes his or her first appointment or obtains dental care for the first time at a Practice Location.

3. Equipment and Supplies. Subject to Paragraph 11 of this Agreement regarding Compensation, Employer shall furnish each Practice Location with such equipment, dental instrumentation, and supplies as Employer reasonably considers necessary and appropriate for Employee's use in rendering professional services pursuant to this Agreement.

4. Standards of Practice. Employer and Employee shall at all times conduct themselves in accordance with the ethical standards of the dental profession, and shall abide by all protocols of treatment and quality of care policies as may be reasonably established from time to time by Employer or to which Employer or Employee is subject. Employer covenants that at all times during the term of this Agreement, Employer covenants that all standards and protocols established by Employer shall comply with (1) all applicable federal, state, and local laws, regulations and ordinances, (2) the professional standards then prevailing in the community, and (3) currently accepted methods, practices and code of ethics of the American Dental Association. Employee covenants that at all times during the term of this Agreement, Employee's services so rendered shall comply with (1) all applicable federal, state, and local laws, regulations and ordinances, (2) the professional standards then prevailing in the community, and (3) currently accepted methods, practices and code of ethics of the American Dental Association. At _____'s expense, Employee shall remain fully licensed to practice dentistry in [state], maintain membership(s) in professional societies as appropriate, and attend such professional meetings and continuing dental education programs as may be necessary to maintain his or her professional knowledge and skills as reasonably determined by Employer.

5. Hours. Employee shall be available to render professional services on behalf of Employer for five (5) days per week on a monthly basis during Employer's regular business hours including, at the election of Employer, after-hours emergency appointments and extended morning and evening hours in accordance with a schedule to be developed by Employer reasonably prior to the day(s) Employee is scheduled to work.

6. Billing and Collections. Employee agrees and acknowledges that Employer alone has the right to bill and receive payment from patients and third-party payers for services rendered by Employee hereunder, and Employee shall not bill any patient or third-party payer for such services. Employee shall assist, upon Employer's reasonable request, with preparation, submission or certification of any bills related to the services provided hereunder. Any payment received by Employee from any source whatsoever, and whether in cash, or by check, or in any other form, for services performed by Employee hereunder shall be held in trust for the benefit of Employer and shall be immediately remitted to Employer by Employee. Employee acknowledges that the amount of fees charged to patients of Employer and the use of such funds shall be determined in the sole discretion of Employer.

7. Patient Records. Employee shall prepare and maintain records for patients he/she treats at any Practice Location, in accordance with accepted standards of practice in the community, applicable laws, including laws regarding confidentiality, privacy, and security of dental records, the reasonable policies and procedures established by Employer, and the terms of applicable third-party payer agreements. Such patient records shall be the property of Employer. Employee shall not have general access to the patient records of Employer, but access only to those records of patients Employee treats. All patient records, histories, charts, and other information regarding patients treated or matters handled by Employee under this Agreement, regardless of whether any of the foregoing are in Employee's possession, shall be the property of Employer, subject to all applicable federal, state and local laws, regulations and ordinances and any applicable code of ethics. If, however, on termination or expiration of this Agreement for any reason, a patient shall so request, Employee reasonably requires access to such records for the purpose of defending a malpractice or disciplinary claim, or the Employer otherwise considers it appropriate, Employee shall have access to or be furnished copies of applicable documents requested by patient, expenses of duplication to be borne by the Employee.

8. Patient Flow. Employer shall assign patients to Employee from existing patients and may from time to time assign new patients to Employee. Employee shall have the duty to assist in building the referral base of the Practice and in seeking to secure new patients.

9. Business Records. Employee shall not have general access to the business records of Employer. Employee shall have access to the business records only to the extent reasonably necessary to verify compensation due Employee.

10. Restrictive Covenant/ Non-Solicitation. Employee acknowledges and agrees that during the course of Employee's association, Employee shall become privy to confidential business information, trade secrets and proprietary information of Employer. Therefore, and in consideration of Employee's association, working on patients of record and being introduced to referral sources and prospective patients, and the time and expenses incurred in training and promoting Employee, during the term of this agreement and for a period of XX months following the expiration, or earlier termination (for whatever reason) of this agreement (whether at the end of the initial term of this agreement or any renewal or any successive term or terms, or periods of employment), Employee shall not:

    a. Engage directly or indirectly in the practice of general dentistry whether as a partner, employee, independent contractor, associate or otherwise, within _____ ( ) [e.g., miles, city blocks] of the Initial Practice Location [, nor at any Practice Location at which Employee had worked for more than (XX) days in the previous (XX) months];

    b. Solicit patients or employees of the practice through notices, announcements, telephone calls, or other forms communication, including written, oral, or electronic communication;

    c. Hire any employee of Employer; or

    d. Use or disclose Employer's patient lists or the identities of individual patients, referral sources, practice forms, or business development plans.

If Employee violates the terms of this restrictive covenant, in addition to all other remedies Employer shall have will be the right to obtain injunctive relief to prohibit Employee from such practices; additionally, due to the irreparable damage Employee's violation will cause the Employer, and because the parties cannot ascertain with any certainty the damage that Employee will cause to Employer, Employee agrees that she shall immediately pay to the Employer, during any period for which injunctive relief has not been secured or if injunctive relief is not granted, not as a penalty but as liquidated damages, $ _____ together with any costs and attorneys' fees incurred in seeking enforcement of the provisions of this restrictive covenant.

11. Compensation. As compensation for all services rendered by Employee hereunder, Employer shall pay to Employee ____(percent) of Employee's adjusted gross monthly collections, that is, gross fees received by Employer for services which Employee performs and completes during such period, (a) net of any discounts, credits, and refunds authorized by the Employer, and (b) less ____percent (percent) of Employee's laboratory expenses incurred. Employee shall be paid semimonthly in arrears on the fifteenth and last day of each month, subject to all applicable withholding taxes.

12. Employment Policies. Employer's employment policies, as may be amended from time to time at Employer's sole discretion, including those set forth in Employer's Employee Handbook, are incorporated herein by reference and shall apply to Employee with the following exception(s):

    a. Employment-at-will. The Term and termination of Employee's employment shall be governed by the provisions of this Agreement;

    b. [Specify any other policies that do not apply to this employee: e.g., vacation, etc.]

13. Professional Liability Insurance. Employee, at his or her expense, shall obtain and shall maintain during the term of this Agreement a policy of professional liability insurance coverage for errors and omissions resulting, in whole or in part, from the acts of Employee in connection with Employee's duties hereunder on a claims made basis, in amounts of not less than (X) Million Dollars ($X,000,000) per claim and (X) Million Dollars ($X,000,000) annual aggregate, and shall at least annually provide a copy of the binder of insurance evidencing the coverage. Employee must require that any insurance carrier provide Employer at least 15 days' prior written notice of any cancellation, termination, modification or amendment. By entering into this Agreement, Employee agrees to indemnify and hold Employer harmless and defend against any claims or liabilities arising out of, or relating to, any acts or omissions of Employee in connection with treatment provided by Employee, including but not limited to attorneys' fees and litigation costs.

14. Term and Termination. This Agreement shall commence as of the Effective Date and shall continue in effect for _____ (__) years (the "Term"), automatically renewable for successive periods of _____ (__) months each (each a "successive term"), unless sooner terminated by either party providing 60 days' prior written notice to the other of intent to terminate. If Employer terminates this Agreement by providing 60 days' prior written notice, Employer may at his option permit Employee to continue to render professional services to patients of the practice during the 60 day period following delivery of the notice to terminate, or pay to Employee the amount of _____ dollars ($__) upon delivery of the notice to terminate, provided however

that in the event of Employee's death this agreement shall automatically terminate. If Employer breaches any of his promises to Employee under this Agreement, Employee shall have the right to terminate this Agreement without prior notice. Notwithstanding any other provision of this Agreement, Employer may terminate this Agreement without notice or payment if:

    a. Employee fails to perform her duties or promises under this Agreement;

    b. Employee engages in any criminal activity other than minor traffic violations, or commits any act involving fraud or dishonesty; or

    c. Employee breaches any warranty or representation in this Agreement.

15. Option to Acquire an Interest in the Practice. Beginning on the "Option Commencement Date," which shall mean the last day of the Term or any successive term, provided Employee has been continuously employed by Employer pursuant to this Agreement from the Effective Date until the end of the Term or such successive term or terms, the Employee will have the option to acquire an interest in the Practice on the terms set forth in the document entitled "_____," which is attached hereto as Exhibit A and incorporated herein by reference.* To exercise this option, Employee shall send notice (pursuant to Paragraph 21 of this Agreement) of Employee's intent to exercise the option, with such notice to be sent to Employer within the "Option Period;" the Option Period shall commence as of the Option Commencement Date and shall expire at 11:59 PM on seventh (7th) day following the Option Commencement Date. Closing for exercise of the option shall be scheduled at a mutually convenient date for Employer and Employee within XX (xx) days following notice by Employee of Employee's intent to exercise the option.

    * Note: see Appendix 1: Checklist of Questions to Ask When Forming A Group Practice for an overview of issues to be considered when dentists form or acquire an interest in a group practice.

16. Option to Purchase. If prior to the Effective Date Employer dies, becomes disabled (as defined in Employer's disability insurance policy), retires or withdraws from the practice, Employee shall have the option to purchase the practice, exercisable by a writing to Employer or Employer's representative, at its appraised value, excluding good will, as determined by each party selecting an independent appraiser with experience in valuing dental practices in the area or region, which appraisers shall agree upon a third independent appraiser with such experience who shall alone make the appraisal for this purpose and whose selection and determination shall be final. If subsequent to the Effective Date, but prior to the termination of this Agreement, Employer shall attempt to sell the practice to a party other than Employee, Employer shall notify the Employee of such intent, and Employee shall have the right of first refusal to purchase the practice from Employer on identical terms and conditions. Employee's option to purchase or right of first refusal, as the case may be, shall be exercisable by a written notice specifying Employee's intent and delivered to Employer or Employer's representative within 60 days of the event prompting such option or right. If, for any reason, Employer shall not complete the sale to such third party within (xx) days of dispatch of notice of intent to sell to a third party, any attempt by Employee to sell the practice to any third party shall remain (or again be) subject to Employee's option to purchase or right of first refusal.

17. Representations and Warranties. Employee represents and warrants that:

    a. He/She is licensed to practice dentistry under the laws of the state of _____;

b. He/She is not bound by any agreement as a current or former employee, independent contractor, partner, or in any other capacity under which he/she formerly practiced or currently practices dentistry, including any agreement that prohibits competition, that would prevent Employee from performing Employee's duties hereunder;

c. He/She is not and has never been named in any action or claim for professional negligence or liability or in any disciplinary action brought by or on behalf of any licensing authority or professional society; and

d. He/She is not currently, and is not aware of any grounds under which he/she might be, included on the Office of the Inspector General's list of excluded individuals/entities.

18. Entire Agreement. This Agreement constitutes the entire agreement between Employee and Employer with respect to the subject matter hereof and supersedes all prior communications, offers and negotiations, oral and written. This Agreement may not be amended or modified in any respect whatsoever, except by an instrument in writing signed by the parties.

19. Nonassignment. Employee shall not assign her duties or responsibilities under this Agreement to another party or parties. Employer reserves the right to assign his duties or responsibilities under this Agreement, subject to Paragraphs 15 and 16 of this Agreement.

20. Choice of law. This Agreement and any dispute hereunder shall be governed by the laws of

_____.

21. Notices. Any notice required or permitted to be given pursuant to this Agreement shall be given in writing and shall be delivered in person or by first class mail postage prepaid return receipt requested and addressed as follows:

To the Employer: [name]: _____

[address]: _____

_____

_____

To the Employee: [name]: _____

[address]: _____

_____

_____

This Agreement is signed by the parties and effective as of the Effective Date.

Thomas Owner, D.M.D.,
A Proprietorship

April Associate, D.D.S.

_____

Thomas Owner

_____

April Associate, individually

Appendix 4:
Sample Independent Contractor Associateship Agreement

This sample agreement is reproduced only as an example. It is intended only to familiarize parties considering entering into such an arrangement with certain matters that may become part of their agreement; neither inclusion of provisions such as those below, nor the below language itself, are advocated nor recommended. This sample does not constitute legal advice and should in no circumstances be used, in whole or in part, without review by and consultation with your personal attorney. The law varies from jurisdiction to jurisdiction and parts of this sample agreement may be invalid, incomplete or unenforceable depending upon the jurisdiction in question.

Independent Contractor Status. An associate's status as an independent contractor depends on the application of Internal Revenue Service rules to the details of the relationship between the dentist and the associate and determines whether payroll taxes are required to be withheld from his or her compensation. Consult your attorney to determine whether an associate will be deemed an employee or an independent contractor under the IRS rules. For information about the distinction between an employee and an independent contractor, see Question 149: Should the Associate Be an Independent Contractor or Employee?

Restrictive Covenant. State laws may limit the enforceability of restrictive covenants applied to independent contractors (as opposed to employees). Consult your attorney regarding the enforceability of restrictive covenants in your area. Restrictive covenants are discussed in Question 150: Are Restrictive Covenants Enforceable?

Antitrust. As competitors or potential competitors, the independent contractor and each dentist who owns or is employed by the practice should be aware of antitrust laws (see Chapter 21: Antitrust). Agreements (or even discussions) among competitors with regard to subjects such as fees or market division can result in civil liability or criminal prosecution. Consult an attorney with experience in antitrust law to ensure that the relationship with the independent contractor does not expose the parties to antitrust liability.

Stark (Self-Referral) Law. The relationship contemplated in this agreement may constitute a "financial relationship" under self-referral (Stark) law (see Chapter 28: Referrals for a discussion of about Stark law). A qualified attorney can provide information concerning the Stark law and its exceptions.

HIPAA. If the practice or the Independent Contractor is a HIPAA Covered Entity, it may be necessary for one or both parties to sign a Business Associate Agreement. Each party will wish to consult with a qualified attorney who can provide information concerning whether either will be considered a "workforce member" or "Business Associate" under HIPAA, and about the recently expanded responsibilities of a HIPAA Business Associate.

Sample Independent Contractor Agreement

This Agreement is entered into as of _____, 20__ (the "Effective Date"), by and between Colleen Contractor, D.D.S., an individual ("you" or "your" or "the Independent Contractor") and Smith and Johnson, Inc., a professional corporation ("we" or "our" or "the Practice,") with offices at 100 Main Street, Anywhere, U.S.A, (the "Practice Location") reflecting an independent contractor association between you and the Practice.

1. Association. You will be associated as an independent contractor with the Practice as a general dentist on a part-time basis commencing on _____. The term of your association shall be for _____ months, starting on the Effective Date (the "term"), the association automatically renewable for successive periods equal to the term in length (each a "successive term"), but either you or the Practice shall have the right to terminate your association, for any reason and without liability, upon thirty (30) days' prior written notice to the other. Upon termination, you will vacate the premises and promptly remove all of your patient records and personal supplies and belongings. In the event that the Practice terminates this Agreement by providing 30 days' prior written notice, the Practice may at its option permit you to continue to render professional services at the Practice during the 30 day period following delivery of the notice to terminate, or pay you the amount of _____ dollars ($__) upon delivery of the notice to terminate, provided however that in the event of your death the Practice may terminate this Agreement immediately without notice or payment. If the Practice breaches any of its promises to you under this Agreement, you shall have the right to terminate this Agreement without prior notice. Notwithstanding any other provision of this Agreement, the Practice may terminate this Agreement effective immediately without notice or payment if:

    a. You fail to perform your duties or promises under this Agreement;

    b. You engage in any criminal activity other than minor traffic violations or commit any act involving fraud or dishonesty; or

    c. You breach any warranty or representation in this Agreement.

2. General Duties. As an independent contractor, you will be responsible for scheduling and maintaining office hours to treat your patients, as you deem appropriate. The Practice shall not exercise any control or direction over the professional aspects of your providing services, which control and direction shall be your sole responsibility, provided, however, that such services are to be rendered in accordance with the provisions of this Agreement and the bylaws, rules and regulations, standards and policies of the Practice and any regulatory agency with jurisdiction over matters subject to this Agreement. At all times, your services so rendered shall comply with (1) all applicable federal, state, and local laws, regulations and ordinances, (2) the professional standards then prevailing in the community, and (3) currently accepted methods, practices and code of ethics of the American Dental Association. You will at your own expense maintain memberships in professional societies as appropriate, and attend such professional meetings and continuing dental education programs as may be necessary to maintain your professional knowledge and skills.

3. Compensation. You will pay the Practice the greater of $____ or $____ per hour for your use of the operatory, monthly in arrears by the [date] of each month for prior month's use of one operatory, equipment, and office personnel (with the exception of your chairside dental assistant, whom you will compensate under Paragraphs 5 and 7 of this Agreement). [Alternate approach:

You will pay the Practice _____ percent (____ percent) of your gross collections, that is, gross fees billed and collected attributable to services which you perform and complete at the Practice, less (a) any professional or other discounts which you grant, and (b) _____ percent (____ percent) of the laboratory charges for your production.] As an independent contractor, you will be solely responsible for your own fee schedule, for all billing for services you render, and for all contractual allowances, free care, discounts, bad debts, collections, and costs related to the foregoing.

4. Responsibility for taxes. As an independent contractor of the Practice, and not an employee, you will be solely responsible for payment of all federal income and self-employment taxes related to your income related to your professional dental services at the Practice. By agreeing to become associated with the Practice, you agree to indemnify and hold harmless Drs. Susan L. Smith and James S. Johnson personally and the Practice from any personal, state or federal tax liabilities related to your income taxation or withholding.

5. Business expenses. The Practice will be responsible for paying rent, utilities, business liability insurance, and for providing dental equipment and office staff support (with the exception of your chairside dental assistant) and one operatory available by schedule. You shall be responsible for dental supplies, your own dental instrumentation, your own professional malpractice insurance coverage, your own laboratory billings, and hiring and compensating your chairside dental assistant.

6. Indemnification. By entering into this agreement, you hereby agree to indemnify and hold Drs. Susan L. Smith and James S. Johnson individually and the Practice harmless for any malpractice liability resulting from treatment provided by you and any of your acts or omissions in connection with treatment you provide under this Agreement, including but not limited to attorneys' fees and litigation costs. It is your responsibility to obtain malpractice insurance in the minimum amount of _____ Dollars ($_____) per claim and Three Million Dollars ($3,000,000) annual aggregate, and to provide a copy of this policy to the Practice prior to your commencement and at least annually provide a copy of the binder of insurance evidencing such coverage. You must require that any insurance carrier provide the Practice at least 15 days' prior written notice of any cancellation, termination, modification or amendment.

7. Patient flow and management responsibilities. It is your responsibility to develop and secure your patient base. You will attend general practice meetings at the request of the Practice. You will be specifically responsible for the direction, hiring or termination of the chairside dental assistant assigned or hired by you and in either event compensated by you.

8. Patient records. Your association as an independent contractor with the Practice does not entitle you to general access to the patient records of the Practice. You shall complete, in a timely manner, all patient records of each patient whom you treat and shall maintain the security, privacy, and confidentiality of such records as required by applicable federal, state, and local laws, regulations and ordinances. All patient records, histories, charts, and other information regarding patients treated or matters handled by you under this Agreement, regardless of whether any of the foregoing are in your possession, shall be your property subject to all applicable federal, state and local laws, regulations and ordinances and any applicable code of ethics. On termination or expiration of this Agreement for any reason, you shall be responsible for maintaining and moving your records. We each agree to sign and abide by a HIPAA Business Associates Agreement if required by law.

9. Business records. Your association as an independent contractor with the Practice requires you to maintain business records, but does not entitle you to general access to the business records of the Practice. You shall have access to the business records of the Practice only to the extent necessary to verify compensation due from you to the Practice should a dispute arise.

10. Option to Enter Practice. The parties contemplate that you shall enter the Practice as an equity owner at the end of the term or any successive term of this Agreement. You and the Practice covenant and agree that at the end of such term or successive term you shall have the option to acquire capital stock in the Practice on the terms provided in the _____ document attached hereto as Exhibit A.* Termination of this Agreement by either party pursuant to any of the termination provisions in Paragraph 1 of this Agreement shall operate to extinguish such option to acquire capital stock in the Practice.

    If prior to the end of the term, the end of any successive term, or the termination of this Agreement pursuant to Paragraph 1 of this Agreement, Dr. Smith or Dr. Johnson dies, becomes disabled (as defined in the applicable disability insurance policy), retires or withdraws from the practice, you shall have the option to purchase that dentist's interest in the Practice, exercisable by a writing to the Practice, on the terms set forth in the document entitled "_____" that is attached hereto as Exhibit B. If prior to the end of the term, the end of any successive term, or the termination of this Agreement pursuant to Paragraph 1 of this Agreement, Dr. Smith or Dr. Jones shall attempt to sell his or her interest in the Practice to a party other than you, you shall have the right of first refusal to purchase said interest in the Practice on identical terms and conditions. Your option to purchase or right of first refusal, as the case may be, shall be exercisable by a written notice specifying your intent and delivered to the Practice within 60 days of the event prompting such option or right.

    * Note: see Appendix 1: Checklist of Questions to Ask When Forming A Group Practice for an overview of issues to be considered when dentists form or acquire an interest in a practice

11. Representations and Warranties. You represent and warrant that:

    a. You are licensed to practice dentistry under the laws of the state of _____;

    b. You are not bound by any agreement as a current or former employee, independent contractor, or partner, or in any other capacity under which you formerly practiced or currently practice dentistry, including any agreement that prohibits competition, that would prevent you from performing services hereunder; and

    c. You are not and have never been named in any action or claim for professional negligence or liability or in any disciplinary action brought by or on behalf of any licensing authority or professional society.

12. Restrictive Covenant. You acknowledge and agree that during the course of your association with the Practice, you shall become privy to confidential business information, trade secrets and proprietary information of the Practice. Therefore, and in consideration of your association with the Practice, for a period of ___ after the expiration of this Agreement (whether at the end of the term of this Agreement or any successive term or terms, or if you or the Practice terminates this Agreement), you shall not:

    a. Engage directly or indirectly in the practice of general dentistry whether as a partner, employee, independent contractor, associate or otherwise, within ____ ( ) [miles, city blocks, or feet] of the Practice Location,

b. Solicit patients or employees of the Practice through notices, announcements, telephone calls, or other forms communication, including written, oral, or electronic communication;

c. Hire any employee of the Practice; or

d. Use or disclose the Practice's patient lists or the identities of individual patients, referral sources, practice forms, or business development plans.

13. Entire Agreement. This Agreement contains the entire agreement with respect to your status as an independent contractor at the Practice and supersedes all prior communications, offers and negotiations, oral and written, and any oral discussions which you may have had with Drs. Smith or Jones or their representatives. This Agreement may be amended by you and the Practice only by an instrument in writing signed by you, Dr. Smith, Dr. Jones, and the Practice.

14. Nonassignment. You may only assign your duties or responsibilities under this Agreement to another party or parties with the prior written consent of the Practice. The Practice reserves the right to assign its duties or responsibilities under this Agreement, subject to Paragraph 10 of this Agreement.

15. Choice of law. This Agreement and any dispute hereunder shall be governed by the laws of _____.

16. Notices. Any notice required or permitted to be given pursuant to this Agreement shall be given in writing and shall be delivered in person or by first class mail postage prepaid return receipt requested and addressed as follows:

To the Independent Contractor: [name]:_____

[address]: _____

_____

_____

To the Practice: Smith & Johnson, Inc.
                                100 Main St.
                                Anywhere, USA

17. Severability. If any term or provision of this Agreement is deemed to be invalid, unenforceable, or illegal for any reason, such term or provision shall be stricken from the Agreement and shall not affect the validity, enforceability, or legality of the remainder of the Agreement.

This agreement is signed by the parties and effective on the date first written above.

Smith and Johnson, Inc.   Colleen Contractor, D.D.S.

By:_____   By:_____

Susan L. Smith, D.D.S., President   Colleen Contractor, individually

Appendix 5:
New Employee Checklist

Employee Name: _____

Date of Hire:_____

Home Telephone Number: _____

Action List

1. Prior to New Employee's Arrival:

- Notify staff of new employee, including name, position, and start date.

- Prepare new employee's work area, if applicable, and any necessary equipment or supplies.

- Order name badge, if applicable.

2. Complete New Employee Documentation:

- Complete employee documents including state and federal forms such as W-4 and I-9 (see Question 165: What Are My Requirements Regarding Payroll Taxes?). Make sure these documents are signed and dated.

- Make sure Social Security number is on file.

- Comply with U.S. Citizenship and Immigration Services regulations.

- Obtain copies of any applicable licenses and certifications. Contact the authority that issued the licenses or certificates to verify that they are accurate and that the individual's status is active and in good standing.

- Make sure employment application (signed and dated) and resumé are on file.

- Obtain the name and phone number of an individual to contact in the event of an emergency.

- Create a personnel file for the employee.

- Complete any necessary OSHA documentation or requirements for the new employee, such as the following:

  o As appropriate, create a confidential, separate "Employee Medical Record" for the employee to comply with OSHA recordkeeping requirements.

  o Determine whether the employee has "occupational exposure" to bloodborne pathogens and, if necessary, update your OSHA exposure determination document (for the OSHA definition of "exposure determination," visit the U.S. Department of Labor, Occupational Safety & Health Information (OSHA) website at *www.osha.gov/pls/oshaWeb/owadisp. show_document?p_table=STANDARDS&p_id=10051*).

o Discuss any immunizations, such as hepatitis vaccine, that are required or recommended for the new employee's job (for example, under OSHA or state health department regulations). Verify and document immunization status as appropriate.

- Decide whether an office key should be given to the employee. Document all of the items that you give to an employee when you hire him or her. Ask each new employee to review and sign the list, and make sure the employee understands that he or she must return the items and equipment when employment ends.

- Provide the employee with a copy of your employee office manual and ask the employee to sign a receipt indicating that he or she has read and understands the contents of the manual. When the employee returns the signed form, place it in the personnel file.

- Provide the new employee with a copy of the job description and retain a signed copy acknowledging receipt of the job description in the employee's personnel file.

- Schedule and provide any required training depending on the specific hazards in your office to which the employee will be exposed (e.g., bloodborne pathogens, hazardous chemicals, fire, etc.), as well as any other necessary training (clinical, office software systems, HIPAA, etc.). Some states require training in dental radiography procedures for certain staff members. Contact your state dental society for more information. Memorialize all training when it has taken place.

3. Office Tour:

- Tour the office and introduce the new employee to coworkers. Review parking area, time cards, storage for personal belongings, employee lounge, etc.

- Show the new employee where supplies are stored, and if appropriate explain how supplies are accessed, rotated, inventoried, and replaced.

- Explain office security policies. Go over alarm system and instructions on opening and closing the office.

- Review emergency procedures and equipment for situations such as fire, tornado, or power outage.

4. Office Policies and Procedures:

- Review Office Policies and Procedures.

- Go over the philosophy and mission statement of your dental practice. Discuss the standards of performance that are required in your dental practice.

- Review and document your review of the practice's patient confidentiality policies and any applicable state confidentiality and privacy laws. If your practice is required to comply with HIPAA, this review should include HIPAA privacy and security policies. Have the new employee sign any necessary confidentiality agreement and place the agreement in the personnel file. Schedule any necessary training and document the training as it is completed.

- Discuss any employee benefits (such as medical and dental benefits, insurance, or pension plans) for which the individual is or may become eligible.

- Review infection control procedures and bloodborne diseases policy, as well as personal protective attire.

- Discuss anti-harassment policies and provide your new employee with a copy of the policy if it is not included in the employee office manual (see "Sample Anti-Harassment Policy," *ADA.org/DentistGuidetoLaw*).

- Discuss pay rates, overtime, pay days, and incentive plans.

- Discuss your communications policy, such as personal use of telephone, email, etc., and your electronic communications policy (see Sample Electronic Communications Policy, *ADA.org/DentistGuidetoLaw*). Provide the employee with a copy of the policies if they are not included in the employee office manual.

- Distribute a copy of your dental office organizational chart and job descriptions of your dental practice, if one exists.

- Discuss performance evaluation process and schedule. Set a date for the employee's first performance appraisal (e.g., 90 days from start date).

- Discuss work schedule.

- Discuss attendance policy, and whom to contact in cases of absences and tardiness.

- Discuss dress, appearance, and uniform policies.

- Review patient contact procedures.

- Discuss any other office policies, procedures, or patient services you'd like to highlight.

- Let the employee know that you are available to meet with him or her to thoroughly answer any questions as they arise.

Appendix 6:
Termination Checklist

Employee Name: _____

Action List

1. Before the Termination:

- Consulting an employment attorney prior to terminating the employee can minimize the possibility that the terminated employee will bring a lawsuit for "wrongful termination," defamation, discrimination, or other civil action. Even at-will employers (see Question 60: What Office Policies Do I Need?) can be liable for terminating an employee for unlawful reasons such as discrimination or retaliation for filing a workers' compensation claim.

- If the termination will be voluntary, collect from the employee a hard copy of a signed resignation letter.

- If the termination will be involuntary, consider the following issues before taking any action to terminate the employee:

  - Are you an at-will employer or do you have an employment contract with the employee? If there is a contract, what are its provisions for termination?

  - How will you characterize the termination?

  - If you are terminating for performance problems, are the problems documented in performance reviews and other personnel file documents (such as warnings and disciplinary action)? Even if you are an at-will employer, it is important that the personnel file contain such documentation to substantiate a valid, nondiscriminatory reason for the termination. Review files to determine whether other employees with similar performance problems were treated equally.

  - If you are terminating because the employee's services are no longer required (for example, due to an economic slowdown), can you substantiate the reason with statistics or other documentation?

  - If you suspect criminal misconduct such as embezzlement or drug diversion, you will likely wish to consult an employment attorney before taking action to determine your legal rights and responsibilities, and to help minimize your legal risk and the risk of harm to your practice.

  - If you plan to prepare a termination letter or written memorandum setting forth your reasons for termination, you may wish to ask your attorney to prepare it or review the document before you deliver it to the employee.

- Review your office policies and manuals, and any relevant contracts, to make sure you are following the termination policies and procedures that they establish.

2. To Do:

- Set up exit interview date.

- Provide employee with information about benefits, including COBRA information if applicable.

- Obtain office key from the employee and cancel key-card access. Staff member should turn in keys, tokens, or cards that allow access to a property, building, or equipment, preferably at the time of termination.

- Locks or combinations of locking mechanisms should be changed upon a termination. You should change the password for any office security (alarm) system as well as any other access codes.

- Review list signed by employee (when employment began) and verify that all equipment and office-related items have been returned.

- Cancel voicemail and email account, if applicable.

- If the employee had check writing or any banking responsibilities, cancel these authorizations with the institution.

- As necessary, explain to other employees what has taken place (without providing any detail as to the reason the individual is no longer employed) and how to handle phone calls or patient inquiries about the terminated employee.

- Dentists who are required to comply with the HIPAA security regulations will have to implement certain termination procedures. The following procedures are advisable for HIPAA compliance and useful for all dentists:

  - If the practice has a Security official (dentists covered by HIPAA will need to appoint someone to this role), document and provide communication of each termination in a timely manner to the Security Official.

  - Removed terminated employee from access list.

  - Terminate, suspend, or delete the employee's user accounts and access privileges.

  - Document termination procedures as required by HIPAA.

- Prepare and deliver the employee's final paycheck. Check your employee office manual and state laws to determine whether the check should include an amount for unused vacation time or sick leave.

3. Going Forward:

- Determine how to handle inquiries from prospective employers about the terminated employee. To minimize legal risk of a lawsuit for defamation or other civil actions, some employers adopt a policy of simply confirming (not volunteering) job title, salary, and dates of employment. Ask your attorney for the best approach under the laws of your state.

- Review all suspended accounts for activity or attempted activity and report any such activity for investigation as a potential breach.

- Audit termination procedures periodically to ensure effectiveness.

Appendix 7:

Sample Website Development Agreement

This sample agreement is reproduced only as an example. It is intended only to familiarize parties considering entering into such an arrangement with certain matters that may become part of their agreement; neither inclusion of provisions such as those below, nor the below language itself, are advocated or recommended. This sample does not constitute legal advice and should in no circumstances be used, in whole or in part, without review by and consultation with your personal attorney. The law varies from jurisdiction to jurisdiction and parts of this sample agreement may be invalid, incomplete or unenforceable depending upon the jurisdiction in question.

IMPORTANT: If the website developer will have access to, store, or transmit any protected health information (PHI) or electronic patient health information (ePHI), as defined by HIPAA, from the dentist, a Business Associate of the dentist, or the dentist's patients, then the dentist should require a Business Associate Agreement with the Developer that meets HIPAA requirements (see Appendix 11: Sample HIPAA Business Associate Agreement and Appendix 8: HIPAA Business Associate Checklist). For more information about HIPAA, see Chapter 15: HIPAA, State Law and PCI DSS: Patient Information, and HIPAA 20 Questions at *ADA.org/DentistGuidetoLaw*.

Finally, regardless what a contract's provisions may say about indemnification, payment of damages, and the like, it is important to remember that the dentist may find it impossible to be made whole in the event the contract is breached or in the event a third party makes a claim if the website developer has few resources. Dentists have been left holding the bag when the web developers the hired are college students working out of their rooms.

Sample Website Development Agreement

THIS AGREEMENT is made this [Date] by and between [Name of Developer], a [Type of Organization] with offices at [Address] (the "Developer"), and [Name of Company], a [Type of Organization] with offices at [Address] (the "Company").

WITNESSETH:

WHEREAS, Company desires to engage Developer to develop, create, test, and deliver a Website to be known as ["Name of Site"] as a work made for hire and to house the Website on Developer's Web Server and make the Website available on the Internet;

and

WHEREAS, Developer is interested in undertaking such work; and

WHEREAS, Company and Developer mutually desire to set forth the terms applicable to such work;

NOW, THEREFORE, for the mutual consideration set forth herein, the adequacy of which is hereby acknowledged, Company and Developer, intending to be legally bound, hereby agree as follows:

1. TERM AND TERMINATION

A. Term of Agreement. This Agreement shall be effective as of the Effective Date and shall remain in force for a period of _____ (xx) years, unless otherwise terminated as provided herein.

B. Termination of Work. Company may, at its sole option, require Developer to terminate any or all work outstanding, or any portion thereof, immediately upon written notice. Upon receipt of notice of such termination, Developer shall inform Company of the extent to which performance has been completed through such date and collect and deliver to Company whatever work product and deliverables then exist in a manner prescribed by Company. Developer shall be paid for all work performed through the date of receipt of notice of termination as specified herein, and Company obligations toward Developer hereunder shall cease. Developer may not terminate any work under this Agreement without the prior written consent of Company.

C. Survival. In the event of any termination or expiration of this Agreement, any obligations and responsibilities of Developer that given its purpose, interpretation or context, logically should survive the expiration or termination of this Agreement (e.g., any warranties that are not expressly time limited), should survive, shall so survive, and shall continue in effect and inure to the benefit of and be binding upon the parties and their legal representatives, heirs, successors, and assigns. The termination of any provision of this Agreement shall not excuse a prior breach of that provision.

2. DEVELOPER'S RESPONSIBILITIES

A. Scope of Work. Company hereby retains the services of Developer to design, develop, and host a Website (the "Website") for Company in accordance with the proposal submitted by Developer to Company dated [Date] (the "Proposal"), a copy of which is attached hereto as Exhibit A and the terms of which are expressly incorporated herein by reference.

B. Schedule. The "Schedule" for the development of the Website is attached hereto as Exhibit B, the terms of which are expressly incorporated by reference. Time is of the essence with respect to the performance of the work to be provided hereunder. The parties agree that the Schedule has been represented and warranted by the Developer based upon the work in this Agreement proceeding from start to finish without any substantial interruptions, delays or changes in the work which are caused by or attributable to Company.

C. Changes. Changes to this Agreement or to any of the specifications of the Website as noted in the Proposal shall become effective only when a written change request is executed by the President/Manager/Owner of Company and Developer. Developer agrees to notify Company promptly of any factor, occurrence, or event coming to its attention that may affect Developer's ability to meet the requirements of this Agreement, or that is likely to occasion any material delay in the Schedule.

3. WEBSITE DESIGN

A. Design. The design of the Website shall be in substantial conformity with the Proposal and other material provided to Developer by Company or by the Company to the Developer which is attached hereto as Exhibits [insert Exhibit numbers] and expressly incorporated herein by reference. Developer shall develop the Website to project the highest professional image. Developer shall not include any of the following in the Website or in Company's directory on Developer's Web Server: text, graphics, sound, or animations that might be viewed as offensive or related in any way to sex or any illegal activities; links to other Websites that might be viewed as offensive or related in any way to sex or any illegal activities; impressionistic or cartoon-like graphics (unless provided or approved in advance by Company); destructive invisible text, or any other type of hidden text, metatags, hidden information, hidden graphics, or other hidden materials when intended for unauthorized uses or not compatible with search engine optimization; or destructive elements or destructive programming of any type.

B. Materials Provided by Company. All materials to be supplied by Company may be provided via transportable or removable media (e.g., flashdrive) or via File Transfer Protocol (FTP). Files will be provided in HTML format, standard word processing text format or, if images, as TIFFs, GIFs, JPEGs or Photoshop files.

C. Specifications for Home Page. Company's Website will consist of a Home Page (the "first" page for the Website) that can be reached by typing one of the following Uniform Resource Locators (URLs) into a Web browser: [insert URLs]. Developer will use its best efforts to register the "Company.COM" domain name for the benefit of Company (or such other name as may be registrable and acceptable to Company) and will assign all rights thereto to Company. Company agrees to pay all registration fees associated with such registration. If Company already has a domain name, Developer will coordinate redirecting the address to the new host. Should Company desire a specific domain name, which is already owned by another party, negotiations for said domain name may only be undertaken by Company.

D. Accessibility of Website During Construction. Throughout the construction of the prototype and the final Website, the Developer shall make the Website available to Company on a password protected server for Company's review and acceptance. Until Company has approved the final Website, none of the Web Pages for Company's Website will be released to the public.

E. Project Planning Meetings. After both parties have signed this Agreement, the parties shall meet at Company or a mutually convenient location and at a mutually convenient date and time to discuss project planning. The parties shall endeavor to hold this meeting within one week after both parties have signed this Agreement.

F. Search Engine Optimization. Developer will utilize search optimization techniques to maximize viewing of the Website according to commonly accepted practices and in accordance with the Webmaster guidelines of standard search engines, including but not limited to Google, Bing, Yahoo and MSN.

G. Delivery of Deliverables. Upon Company's approval of its final Website, or upon termination of this Agreement, whichever occurs earlier, Developer shall deliver to Company all code, documentation, reports, and other materials developed by Developer in the course of its performance under this Agreement and any other items reasonably necessary for the operation of Company's Website (other than third party operating system software, third party networking software, Web browsers, and hardware) and all changes and enhancements thereto (the "Deliverables").

Documentation shall be delivered in printed format and in electronic format. Code shall be delivered in electronic format. The transfer of electronic materials shall be accomplished by copying them to removable storage (such as flash drives) or via FTP. Files will be provided in HTML format, standard word processing text format or, if images, as TIFFs, GIFs, JPEGs or Photoshop files. Developer shall maintain its back-ups and one set of the final materials provided to Company for a period of six months after Company's approval of its final Website. If this Agreement is terminated prior to final approval, or at the expiration of this six month period, Developer will destroy all of its copies of the Website (including all back-ups thereof) and "wipe" all files constituting final or working copies of the Website (other than the final copy hosted on Developer's Web Server and one back-up copy thereof) from Developer's computers and back-up materials unless otherwise directed in writing by Company.

H. Advertising/Transaction Fees. Developer agrees to assist Company in the sale of any advertising or database searches or other programs to generate revenues from the use of the Website by third parties. In this regard, Developer will provide assistance in developing such programs for Company. In such event, the parties agree to enter into good faith negotiations to reasonably compensate Developer for such services.

4. WEBSITE HOSTING

A. Server Hosting. Developer agrees, at Company's option, to maintain the website on Developer's Web Server on a month-to-month basis, and to make maintenance modifications to the website from time to time in accordance with Company's directions. Such modifications shall be implemented within five (5) business days of Developer's receipt of Company's changes if the changes are easily implemented, and within ten (10) business days of Developer's receipt of Company's changes if the changes are not easily implemented. As part of this service, Developer agrees to make Company's website available to Internet users approximately 24 hours per day, to back-up the website at least once every two weeks, and to store said back-up materials in a safe and secure environment, fit for the back-up media, and not located at the same location as

Developer's Web Server. Also as part of this service, Developer agrees to use its best efforts to ensure reasonable response times for users accessing the Website. Developer agrees to maintain the Website on a secure server with firewall protection in accordance with industry standards.

B. Back-Up Copies. Upon notice from Company not more often than once each month, and also in the event of Company's termination of its use of Developer's Web Server as the host for the Website, Developer agrees to transfer a complete copy of Company's then-current Website, including all Code therefore, to Company, said transfer to occur by either copying them to removable storage (such as flash drives) or via FTP. Files will be provided in HTML format, standard word processing Text format or, if images, as TIFFs, GIFs, JPEGs or Photoshop files. The transfer method will be selected by Company in its discretion no later than 24 hours before the time the transfer is to take place. In the event such transfer results from Company's termination of its use of Developer's Web Server as the host for the Website, Developer shall maintain one complete electronic version of the Website, including all Code therefore (and shall "wipe" all other versions thereof off of its computers and media, including back-up copies), until Company informs Developer in writing that the transferred files appear to be complete, at which time Developer shall "wipe" its final copy of the Website off of its computers and media.

C. Transaction Logging. During the time that the Website is located on Developer's Web Server, Developer will make available on a monthly basis and free of charge an analysis of Website traffic, including source IP address, most commonly viewed pages and any other such data reasonably requested by Company. Developer shall set aside a portion of its server, such portion only accessible by designated Company staff or members, in which such analysis resides. The analysis may be viewed or printed out by Company at its option.

5. COMPENSATION

A. Price for Website Creation. The total price for all of the work set forth in the Agreement (excluding the Server Hosting and excluding post-approval modifications not part of the work to be supplied pursuant to the Proposal, or to this agreement as originally agreed by Company) shall be [_____] Dollars ($[_____]) (the "Development Fee"). This price covers all work of whatever nature on the Website contemplated in this Agreement (excluding Server Hosting, maintenance and post-approval modifications not implemented by Company). When both parties have signed this Agreement, Company will forward to Developer an initial deposit in the amount of [_____] Dollars ($[_____]) (the "Initial Deposit"). Company will pay the balance due to Developer in the amount of [_____] Dollars ($[_____]) (the "Balance Due") when the Website has been tested by the Company and is operational in a form reasonably acceptable to Company.

B. Price for Website Hosting. The price for the Server Hosting shall be [_____] Dollars ($[_____]) per month (the "Hosting Fee"). Charges for post-approval modifications to the Website or changes or additions to the material on the Website (including the database) shall be free if submitted to Developer by Company as "ready to implement" HTML pages. The cost of Server Hosting shall not increase for a period of one year from the date of Company's acceptance of its final Website. The Hosting Fee shall commence on the date the final Website is fully operational and accepted by Company and future Hosting Fees shall be due and payable on subsequent monthly anniversary dates of such operational date.

C. Invoicing. Subject to A. and B. of this subsection 5., Developer shall invoice Company on a monthly basis for the amount of work done during the applicable month. All payments are due thirty (30) days after receipt of an undisputed properly payable invoice. If there is a dispute with regard to whether work was actually completed or whether an invoice is properly payable, the amount of the invoice in dispute shall not be due until the dispute is resolved.

D. Expenses. The prices set forth above are inclusive of expenses. Except as expressly agreed otherwise in writing by Company, Developer shall bear all of its own expenses arising from its performance of its obligations under this Agreement, including without limitation expenses for facilities, work spaces, utilities, management, clerical and reproduction services, supplies, and the like. Company shall have no obligation to provide office space, work facilities, equipment, clerical services, programming services, or the like.

E. Links. Developer may, with the prior express written approval of Company, provide a link on the Website to a Marketplace area designated by Developer and acceptable to Company. The purpose of the Marketplace area is to sell products or generate other online transactions.

6. CONFIDENTIALITY

A. Confidential Information. "Confidential Information" means any confidential technical data, trade secret, know-how or other confidential information disclosed by either party hereunder in writing, orally, or by drawing or other form and which shall be marked by the disclosing party as "Confidential" or "Proprietary." If such information is disclosed orally, or through demonstration, in order to be deemed Confidential Information, it must be specifically designated as being of a confidential nature at the time of disclosure and reduced in writing and delivered to the receiving party within [_____] ([__]) days of such disclosure.

B. Exclusions. Notwithstanding the foregoing, Confidential Information shall not include information which: (i) is known to the receiving party at the time of disclosure or becomes known to the receiving party without breach of this Agreement; (ii) is or becomes publicly known through no wrongful act of the receiving party or any subsidiary of the receiving party; (iii) is rightfully received from a third party without restriction on disclosure; (iv) is independently developed by the receiving party or any of its subsidiaries; (v) is furnished to any third party by the disclosing party without restriction on its disclosure; (vi) is approved for release upon a prior written consent of the disclosing party; (vii) is disclosed pursuant to judicial order, requirement of a governmental agency or by operation of law.

C. Nondisclosure. Developer agrees that it will not disclose any Confidential Information to any third party and will not use the Company's Confidential Information for any purpose other than for the performance of the rights and obligations hereunder without the prior written consent of the Company, which may be withheld for any reason or for no reason. Developer further agrees that Confidential Information shall remain the sole property of the Company and that it will take all reasonable precautions to prevent any unauthorized disclosure of Confidential Information by its employees. No license shall be granted by the Company to Developer with respect to Confidential Information disclosed hereunder unless otherwise expressly provided herein.

D. No Confidential Information of Developer. It is understood and agreed that Company does not wish to receive from Developer any confidential information of Developer or of any third party. Developer represents and warrants that any information provided to Company in the course of entering into this Agreement or performing any work hereunder shall not be confidential or proprietary to Developer.

E. Sanctioned Public Disclosure. After Company has approved its final Website, Developer may list Company as a client of Developer and may include a link to the Website on Developer's Website. Developer may not issue any press release that refers to Developer's work for Company without Company's prior written approval, which may be withheld for any reason or for no reason at all.

F. Return of Confidential Information. Upon the request of the Company, Developer will promptly return all Confidential information furnished hereunder and all copies thereof.

G. Remedy for Breach of Confidentiality. If Developer breaches any of its obligations with respect to confidentiality and unauthorized use of Confidential information hereunder, the Company shall be entitled to equitable relief to protect its interest therein, including but not limited to, injunctive relief, as well as money damages notwithstanding anything to the contrary contained herein.

7. OWNERSHIP AND RIGHTS

A. Ownership of Work Product by Company. Except as set forth below, all elements of all Deliverables shall be exclusively owned by Company and shall be considered as "Works Made for Hire," (as such are defined under the U.S. copyright laws) by Developer for Company. Except as set forth below, Company shall exclusively own all United States and international copyrights and all other intellectual property rights in the Deliverables. It is understood and agreed that additional materials added to the Website in the future by Developer will belong exclusively to Company unless the parties otherwise mutually agree in writing.

B. Vesting of Rights. With the sole exception of any Preexisting Works identified in Section 7(C) below, Developer agrees to assign, and upon creation of each element of each Deliverable automatically assigns, to Company, its successors and assigns, for good and valuable consideration, the receipt and sufficiency of which is hereby acknowledged, ownership of all United States and international copyrights and all other intellectual property rights in each element of each Deliverable. This assignment is undertaken in part as a contingency against the possibility that any such element, by operation of law, may not be considered a work made for hire by Developer for Company. From time to time, upon Company's request, Developer or its personnel shall confirm such assignments by execution and delivery of such assignments, confirmations of assignments, or other written instruments as Company may request. Company and its successors and assigns shall have the right to obtain and hold in its own name all copyright registrations and other evidence of rights that may be available for the Deliverables and any portion(s) thereof.

C. Preexisting Works. In the event that any portion of any Deliverable (including the entirety thereof) constitutes a preexisting work for which Developer cannot grant to Company the rights set forth in paragraphs 7(A) and 7(B) above, Developer shall specify below: (1) the nature of such preexisting work; (2) its owner; (3) any restrictions or royalty terms applicable to Developer's or Company's use of such preexisting work or Company's exploitation of the Deliverable as a Derivative Work thereof; and (4) the source of Developer's authority to employ the preexisting work in the preparation of the Deliverable:

[Insert listing of Preexisting works here]

The works set forth above will be referred to as "Preexisting Works." The only preexisting works that may be used in the construction of any Deliverable are the Preexisting Works specified above and any Preexisting Works that may be approved in writing by Company prior to their use.

D. Indemnification/No Infringement. In performing services under this Agreement, Developer agrees not to design, develop, or provide to Company any items that infringe one or more patents, copyrights, trademarks or other intellectual property rights (including trade secrets), privacy, or other rights of any person or entity. If Developer becomes aware of any such possible infringement in the course of performing any work hereunder, Developer shall immediately so notify Company in writing. Developer agrees to indemnify, defend, and hold Company, its officers, directors, members, employees, representatives, agents, and the like harmless for any such alleged or actual infringement and for any liability, debt, or other obligation arising out of or as a result of or relating to (a) the Agreement, (b) the performance of the Agreement, or (c) the Deliverables. This indemnification shall include reasonable attorney fees and expenses.

8. AGREEMENTS WITH EMPLOYEES

No individuals or entities other than Developer and Developer's employees and independent contractors shall undertake any work in connection with this Agreement. Developer shall obtain and maintain in effect written agreements with each of its employees who participate in any of Developer's work hereunder. Such agreements shall contain terms sufficient for Developer to comply with all provisions of the Agreement and to support all grants and assignments of rights and ownership hereunder. Such agreements also shall impose an obligation of confidentiality on such employees with respect to Company's confidential information. It shall be sufficient compliance with this provision of the Agreement if each such employee reads this Agreement and indicates his or her consent to abide by its terms by signing and dating this Agreement or by initialing and dating this paragraph of this Agreement. Nothing contained herein shall limit Developer's ability or right to use independent contractors provided that such independent contractors agree to be bound by the terms of this Agreement.

9. REPRESENTATIONS AND WARRANTIES

Developer makes the following representations and warranties for the benefit of Company:

A. No Conflict. Developer represents and warrants that it is under no obligation or restriction that would in any way interfere or conflict with the work to be performed by Developer under this Agreement. Company understands that Developer is currently working on one or more similar projects for other clients. Provided that those projects do not interfere or conflict with Developer's obligations under this Agreement, those projects shall not constitute a violation of this provision of the Agreement.

B. Ownership Rights. Developer represents and warrants that (1) it is and will be the sole author of all works employed by Developer in preparing any and all Deliverables other than Preexisting Works; (2) it has and will have full and sufficient right to assign or grant the rights or licenses granted in the Deliverables pursuant to this Agreement; (3) all Deliverables other than Preexisting Works have not been and will not be published under circumstances that would cause a loss of copyright therein; and (4) all Deliverables, including all Preexisting Works, do not and will not infringe any patents, copyrights, trademarks or other intellectual property rights (including trade secrets), privacy, or similar rights of any person or entity, nor has any claim (whether or not embodied in an action, past or present) of such infringement been threatened or asserted, nor is such a claim pending against Developer or, insofar as Developer is aware, against any entity from which Developer has obtained such rights.

C. Conformity, Performance, and Compliance. Developer represents and warrants that (1) all Deliverables shall be prepared in a workmanlike manner and with professional diligence and skill; (2) all Deliverables will function under standard HTML conventions; (3) all Deliverables will conform to the specifications and functions set forth in this Agreement; and (4) Developer will perform all work called for by this Agreement in compliance with applicable laws. Developer will repair any Deliverable that does not meet this warranty within a reasonable period of time if the defect does not affect the usability of Company's Website, and otherwise will repair the defect within 24 hours, said repairs to be free of charge to Company. This warranty shall extend for the life of this Agreement. This warranty does not cover links that change over time, pages that become obsolete over time, content that becomes outdated over time, or other changes that do not result from any error on the part of Developer.

D. Accessibility. Designer represents and warrants that all Deliverables will be in conformity with all applicable regulatory requirements, including but not limited to conformance with applicable provisions of the World Wide Web Consortium (W3C) Web Content Accessibility Guidelines ("WCAG") 2.0 Level AA.

10. FORCE MAJEURE

Neither party will be liable for, or will be considered to be in breach of or default under this Agreement on account of, any delay or failure to perform as required by this Agreement as a result of any causes or conditions that are beyond such Party's reasonable control and that such Party is unable to overcome through the exercise of commercially reasonable diligence. If any force majeure event occurs, the affected Party will give prompt written notice to the other Party and will use commercially reasonable efforts to minimize the impact of the event.

11. RELATIONSHIP OF PARTIES

A. Independent Contractor. Developer, in rendering performance under this Agreement, shall be deemed an independent contractor and nothing contained herein shall constitute this arrangement to be employment, a joint venture, or a partnership. Developer shall be solely responsible for and shall hold Company harmless for any and all claims for taxes, fees, or costs, including but not limited to withholding, income tax, FICA, and worker's compensation.

B. No Agency. Company does not undertake by this Agreement or otherwise to perform any obligation of Developer, whether by regulation or contract. In no way is Developer to be construed as the agent or to be acting as the agent of Company in any respect, any other provisions of this Agreement notwithstanding.

12. NOTICE AND PAYMENT

A. Notice. Any notice or other communication given by either Party in connection with this Agreement shall be in writing to the addresses at the beginning of this Agreement and sent via first class mail (postage prepaid) or overnight courier or fax (with a hardcopy sent via one of the prior two mailing methods).

B. Either party may change the address to which notice or payment is to be sent by written notice to the other under any provision of paragraph 12(A).

13. JURISDICTION/DISPUTES

This Agreement shall be governed in accordance with the laws of the State of [State]. All disputes under this Agreement shall be resolved by litigation in the courts of the State of [State] including the federal courts therein and the Parties all consent to the jurisdiction of such courts, agree to accept service of process by mail, and hereby waive any jurisdictional or venue defenses otherwise available to it.

14. AGREEMENT BINDING ON SUCCESSORS

The provisions of the Agreement shall be binding upon and shall inure to the benefit of the Parties hereto, their heirs, administrators, successors and assigns.

15. ASSIGNABILITY

Neither party may assign this Agreement or the rights and obligations thereunder to any third party without the prior express written approval of the other party which shall not be unreasonably withheld.

16. WAIVER

No waiver by either party of any default shall be deemed as a waiver of prior or subsequent default of the same of other provisions of this Agreement.

17. SEVERABILITY

If any term, clause or provision hereof is held invalid or unenforceable by a court of competent jurisdiction, such invalidity shall not affect the validity or operation of any other term, clause or provision and such invalid term, clause or provision shall be deemed to be severed from the Agreement.

18. ENTIRE AGREEMENT; COUNTERPARTS; FAX

This Agreement constitutes the entire understanding of the Parties, and revokes and supersedes all prior agreements between the Parties and is intended as a final expression of their Agreement. It shall not be modified or amended except in writing signed by the Parties hereto and specifically referring to this Agreement. This Agreement shall take precedence over any other documents which may conflict with this Agreement. This Agreement may be executed in one or more counterparts, each of which shall be deemed an original, but all of which together shall constitute one and the same instrument. The parties acknowledge and agree that faxed, emailed, or electronic signatures shall act as original signatures that bind each faxing, emailing, or electronically signing signatory to the terms and provisions of this Agreement.

IN WITNESS WHEREOF, the parties hereto, intending to be legally bound hereby, have each caused to be affixed hereto its or his or her hand and seal the day indicated.

[Company]   [Developer]

By: _____   By: _____

Title: _____   Title: _____

Date: _____   Date: _____

EXHIBIT A

[Note: Attach proposal from the Developer here.]

EXHIBIT B: SCHEDULE FOR DEVELOPMENT OF COMPANY WEBSITE

Task	Date
Initial files transmitted to Developer	As soon as possible
URL registration complete	3 days* after execution of Agreement
URL assigned	As soon as possible after URL Registration
Initial meeting with Company staff to discuss initial design of Website	3 days from receipt of design fee and execution of Agreement
Creation of initial design and posting on private area on Developer server and Passwords and User IDs created by Developer	5 days from initial meeting with Company staff
Review and approval of initial design by Company	5 days from posting of initial design**
Posting of Beta Test Site for Website	2 days from approval by Company
Posting of final Website	5 days from approval by Company of Beta Test Site

* All references to "days" shall mean "business days"

** Any changes requested by Company shall be implemented within 5 days or less by Developer

Appendix 8:

HIPAA Business Associate Checklist

Are you a HIPAA business associate? And if so, what are your responsibilities?

Definition of Business Associate

A HIPAA "business associate" of a covered dental practice is generally a person or entity that does something for the covered dental practice that involves access to patient information, but is not a member of the dental practice's workforce.

Covered. A health care provider is "covered" by HIPAA if it has sent a HIPAA standard transaction electronically (such as submitting a claim), or if someone else has done so on behalf of the covered entity. Certain health plans are also covered by HIPAA, as well as health care clearinghouses.

Patient information. HIPAA applies to information about an individual's physical or mental health, treatment, and payment for healthcare that identifies, or that could be used to identify, the individual.

Workforce. Workforce members are not business associates. HIPAA defines a covered entity's "workforce" as employees, volunteers, trainees, and other persons whose conduct, in the performance of work for the covered entity is under the direct control of such covered entity, whether or not they are paid by the covered entity.

Examples of Possible Business Associates

Billing services, document storage companies, shredding and recycling firms, collection agencies, tech support firms, law firms, and accountants are examples of business associates, if they have access to patient information. A business associate's subcontractor that has access to patient information must also comply with the HIPAA obligations of a business associate.

For more information: see the HIPAA definition of "business associate" in 45 CFR § 160.103, available on the website of the U.S. Government Publishing Office at *www.ecfr.gov/cgi-bin/text-id x?SID=88daf1fb7eb7de8eba602945a9d134d7&node=se45.1.160_1103&rgn=div8.*

A HIPAA "business associate" of a covered dental practice is generally a person or entity that does something for the dental practice that involves access to patient information, but is not a member of the dental practice's workforce.

Obligations of a Business Associate

Business Associate Agreement (BAA)

HIPAA requires a covered dental practice to enter into a compliant business associate agreement with each of it's business associates before allowing the business associate to access patient information. These agreements impose a number of requirements and prohibitions on the business associate.

For example, under the business associate agreement, the business associate must:

- Not use the patient information other than as permitted or required by the contract or required by law

- Report impermissible uses and disclosures, security incidents and breaches to the dental practice

- Ensure that all subcontractors that have access to patient information agree to comply with the requirements in the business associate agreement

- Maintain and make available patient information in accordance with the HIPAA Privacy requirements for patient access, amendments, and accountings of disclosure

- Upon termination, return or destroy all patient information (if not feasible, the business associate must extend the protections of the agreement to the patient information and limit further uses and disclosures to the purposes that make return or destruction infeasible)

For more information: Sample business associate agreement provisions are available on the OCR website at *www.hhs.gov/ocr/privacy/hipaa/understanding/coveredentities/contractprov.html*.

HIPAA Compliance

Business associates are also required by law to comply with applicable provisions of the HIPAA Privacy, Security, Breach Notification and Enforcement Rules. Here are some examples of a business associate's obligations under each of these rules:

Privacy Rule Examples:

- A business associate may use or disclose patient information only as permitted or required by its business associate contract or as required by law.

- A business associate is required to disclose patient information when required by HHS to investigate or determine the business associate's compliance with HIPAA.

- A business associate must not sell patient information except as permitted under the Privacy Rule

- When using or disclosing patient information, or when requesting patient information from a covered entity or another business associate, a business associate must make reasonable efforts to limit the information to the minimum necessary to accomplish the intended purpose of the use, disclosure, or request.

- Business Associate must enter into compliant written agreements with any subcontractor who will have access to patient information

- If the business associate knows of a pattern of activity or practice of a subcontractor that constituted a material breach or violation of the subcontractor's obligation under the contract or other arrangement, the business associate must take reasonable steps to cure the breach or end the violation, as applicable, and, if such steps were unsuccessful, terminate the contract or arrangement, if feasible.

Security Rule Examples

- Identify a Security Official who is responsible for developing and implementing the business associate's HIPAA Security policies and procedures

- Comply with the requirements for administrative, physical and technical safeguards

- Conduct a written risk analysis of potential risks and vulnerabilities to the confidentiality, integrity and availability of electronic patient information held by the business associate

- Implement security measures sufficient to reduce identified risks and vulnerabilities to a reasonable and appropriate level

- Implement a security awareness and training program for all members of the business associate's workforce (including management)

- Apply appropriate sanctions against workforce members who fail to comply with the business associate's HIPAA Security policies and procedures

Breach Notification Rule Examples

- If the business associate discovers a breach of unsecured patient information, the business associate must notify the dental practice without unreasonable delay and in no case later than 60 calendar days after discovery.

- Include in any breach notification to the dental practice:

  o To the extent possible, the identification of each individual whose unsecured patient information has been, or is reasonably believed by the business associate to have been, accessed, acquired, used, or disclosed during the breach

  o Any other available information that the covered entity is required to include in notification to the affected individual(s) (if this information is not available within the timeframe stated above, it must be provided promptly thereafter as information becomes available)

Enforcement Rule Examples

- Provide records and compliance reports as requested by HHS

- Cooperate with HHS complaint investigations and compliance reviews

- Permit access by HHS during normal business hours to its facilities, books, records, accounts and other sources of information , including patient information, that are pertinent to ascertaining compliance with HIPAA

State Law Compliance

HIPAA does not preempt state law that is not contrary to HIPAA, or that is contrary to but more stringent than HIPAA. For example, if a state breach notification law requires notification in a shorter timeframe than HIPAA requires, then in the case of a data breach that requires notification under both HIPAA and the state law, the shorter state law timeframe would apply because the state law is more stringent than HIPAA in this respect.

Potential Consequences of Noncompliance

- Liability for breach of contract under the business associate agreement

- Civil money penalties in the hundreds, thousands or even millions of dollars for violations of HIPAA requirements can be imposed by the federal government

- Settlement agreements and corrective action plans

- Enforcement authorities under HIPAA by state attorneys general

- Criminal penalties apply for certain HIPAA violations

- HHS will develop a methodology under which an individual who is harmed may receive a percentage of any civil monetary penalty or settlement

- HIPAA violations can result in reputational harm and loss of business

---

For More Information

Information about HIPAA is available in the *ADA Practical Guide to HIPAA Compliance: Privacy and Security Manual* available at *adacatalog.org*.

Information about HIPAA is also available on the OCR website at *www.hhs.gov/ocr/privacy*.

See also OCR, Business Associates, at *www.hhs.gov/ocr/privacy/hipaa/understanding/coveredentities/businessassociates.html*.

Appendix 9:

Selecting an EHR Program for Your Dental Practice

Selecting an Electronic Health Records (EHR) program for your dental practice is an important and likely expensive decision. This checklist provides some points to consider when selecting the best program for your practice.

Some initial considerations:

- What are your needs? What are your goals (what do you wish to achieve with use of an EHR program)? In other words, what *must* you have, and what would you *like* to have?

- Will your EHR system need to integrate with an existing practice management system? A patient portal (website)? An e-prescribing system? Any other key systems you use regularly?

- What is your current bandwidth? Would you need to expand it?

- What is your budget? How does this fit with your *needs* and your *wants*?

- Do you participate in any government funded programs (e.g., Medicaid)?

Costs

Purchase Price

Prices can vary substantially depending on the type of EHR model and the program's licensing scheme.

There are two primary models of EHR programs: client-server and Web-based.[19]

Client-server models usually involve significantly more upfront costs. You pay a one-time fee for software and a separate annual maintenance fees.

Web-based is often referred to as "Software as a Service" (SaaS) or "hosted" and may be paid for on a monthly subscription basis.

Licensing Scheme

Some EHR programs are licensed on a per-practice basis, while others are licensed for each individual user or seat. If the program falls under the latter, ascertain if there are different prices for different types of users.

If you believe your practice may grow, consider (x) the cost of licensing additional users at the outset, (y) negotiating a fixed price at which you can later add them, and (z) accepting the risk of an uncertain cost of adding them at a later time.

---

[19] *The client-server model typically involves housing the EHR hardware and software within your practice. Conversely, Web-based models involve you accessing the EHR program through the Internet.*

Additional Costs

Annual Support and Maintenance. Consider the cost of support and maintenance. How much do updates/upgrades cost? Are they both included in the annual support and maintenance fees?

Training. If not included in the purchase price, how much does training cost? Consider also the "cost" of the time lost while your staff completes the necessary training.

Hardware. Will you have to purchase any hardware before implementing the software?

Note: Some of these costs may be offset if you qualify for the Medicare or Medicaid EHR Incentive program.[20] Qualification for the Medicaid incentive program varies from state to state.

Contract. Make sure all costs are documented in the contract.

Remember, cost is only one factor. Vendor reputation and reliability (or lack thereof) may render a lower initial price more costly (in both dollars and disruption) in the long run.

Functionality

- Would you like to be able to prescribe medication through your EHR?
- Would you like to be able to access EHR remotely?
- Would you like your EHR to include educational materials for patients?
- Would you like your EHR to be compatible with mobile devices or tablet computers?
- Can you test the software before purchasing?

Support and Training

What type of customer support is offered? By phone, in person, or Web-based? What's their availability (e.g., 24/7)? Vendor response commitments (also referred to as "service level agreements") may have remedies for failure to respond in a timely manner.

What training (for you and for your staff) is needed? Is it on-site? If not, where is the closest training center? How often is training offered? Is training offered for every new substantial upgrade?

Privacy

If your practice is a covered entity under the Health Insurance Portability and Accountability Act of 1996 (HIPAA), how will the EHR affect your HIPAA compliance program? Vendors providing EHR systems as a service or who provide storage or transmission of PHI may qualify as HIPAA business associates; covered entities are required to sign compliant business associate agreements with their each business associate before permitting the business associate to access patient data.

Does the vendor offer resources to help you update your HIPAA security policies and procedures concerning the new technology?

What would happen if the vendor had a data breach?

---

[20] *For information about the EHR incentive program, visit https://www.cms.gov/Regulations-and-Guidance/Legislation/ EHRIncentivePrograms/index.html?redirect=/EHRIncentivePrograms/*

Supplier Reputation/Reliability/Due Diligence

- How long has the vendor been in business?

- How long have they been selling EHRs?

- How many health care providers currently use their EHR program? Are these respected leaders in the field? Are their circumstances/needs similar to yours?

- Has the vendor evidenced a clear intent to stay in the EHR business?

- Are there any available (online or otherwise) reviews from respected sources for the vendor or its EHR program? What about from peers whose opinions you respect?

- Have you seen a product demonstration (preferably one not controlled by the vendor)? Before the demonstration, it may be worthwhile to prepare a list of (i) things/functions/ features that you wish to see, or that you wish to test yourself, in the demonstration, and (ii) questions you wish to have answered.

Implementation

How long will implementation take? How much will it disrupt your practice? How can you minimize any disruption? What do you need to do (actions you need to take) in preparation for the implementation? Who in your office will coordinate this?

Who will conduct the implementation? Will the EHR vendor hire a third party? If so, does the third party have the same responsibilities and liabilities as the vendor?

Reviewing an EHR Agreement

Warranties. What warranties are excluded? Which are expressly included? For example, do they warranty interoperability with your hardware? Consider not just computer hardware, but also medical devices such as x-ray units and intraoral cameras.

Indemnities. Indemnities are clauses in the agreement where one party agrees to be liable for a specified harm.

Early Termination. Can you terminate the contract for any reason? What are the limitations or costs associated with termination? What is the cost of early termination for SaaS or maintenance services? Can you transfer your patients' EHRs from their program to another? Does the vendor provide transition services?

Confidentiality and Ownership of Data. Where does your data reside? Onsite? At an off-site hosting center? In the "cloud"? It is vital that you know, and that you make appropriate changes to your security plan.

Attorney Review. Having an attorney review an important agreement like this is advisable. Ideally, this will be an attorney experienced in both health care issues and in negotiating software agreements. For some tips on selecting the right attorney, see Question 3: What Does a Dentist Need to Know to Select the Right Attorney?

Appendix 10:

Service Animals in the Dental Office

What Are My Obligations When a Patient Brings an Animal, Such as a "Seeing Eye Dog," to My Dental Office?

When someone brings an animal to the dental office, the dental team must quickly decide what to do. Federal, state and local disabilities laws may require a dental office to allow certain animals in the dental office if the animal meets the definition of "service animal" for people with disabilities. Disabilities laws may also determine which questions the dental team can ask before making a decision about an animal. In some limited instances, the law may permit the dental team to refuse to allow an animal in the dental office. Understanding these laws can help the dental team make appropriate decisions.

Federal, State and Local Laws

This resource and the flowchart that follows are based on a federal law called the "Americans with Disabilities Act" (AwDA), but they do not address any state and local disabilities laws. Some state and local laws give disabled people more rights than the federal AwDA. Dental offices should understand and comply with all federal, state and local laws that apply. The AwDA supersedes any state or local law or regulation that is less protective of individuals with disabilities. For example, the AwDA trumps state or local health codes that prohibit animals on the premises of places that sell food. However, the AwDA does not affect state or local laws that may give a person with a service animal greater protection than the AwDA.

Dogs and Miniature Horses

Only dogs and miniature horses can qualify as "service animals" under the AwDA, although some state disabilities laws may allow additional kinds of animals to be considered service animals. Miniature horses generally range in height from 24 inches to 34 inches measured from the floor to the shoulders and weigh between 70 and 100 lbs. The following factors are set out by the AwDA to help determine whether miniature horses must be accommodated by the facility: (1) whether the miniature horse is housebroken; (2) whether the miniature horse is under the owner's control; (3) whether the dental office can accommodate the miniature horse's type, size, and weight; and (4) whether the miniature horse's presence will not compromise legitimate safety requirements necessary for safe operation of the dental office.

Federal, state and local disabilities laws may require a dental office to allow certain animals in the dental office if the animal meets the definition of "service animal" for people with disabilities.

When is an Animal a "Service Animal"?

Under the AwDA, a dog or miniature horse is service animal only if it has been individually trained to do work or perform tasks for a person with a physical, sensory, psychiatric, intellectual, or mental disability. Examples of "work" or "tasks" performed by a service animal include:

- Guiding people who are blind

- Pulling a wheelchair or retrieving dropped items

- Alerting and protecting a person who is having a seizure

- Alerting individuals who are deaf or hard of hearing to the presence of people, sounds, hazards, etc.

- Calming a person with PTSD during an anxiety attack

- Reminding a person with a mental illness to take prescribed medications

The following, by themselves, are not considered "work" or "tasks" performed by a service animal under the AwDA:

- Providing emotional support, well-being, comfort, or companionship

- Crime deterrence

Questions Which You May NOT Ask a Person With a Service Animal

The AwDA does NOT permit the dental team to ask a person with a service animal:

- To explain or verify the nature of the disability

- To provide any paperwork, certificate, or other document to verify that the animal has been certified, trained, or licensed as a service animal

- To have the animal demonstrate the services it provides

- To require a service animal to wear any special garments.

Questions the Dental Team MAY Ask

If it is not apparent what service the animal provides, then the AwDA does permit the dental team to ask:

- What work or tasks has the animal has been trained to perform (or is in training to perform)?

- Miniature horses only: is the miniature horse housebroken?

Where Can a Service Animal Go?

The AwDA generally requires dental offices to allow disabled people to bring their service animals into all areas of the dental office where patients and the public are normally allowed to go.

Making Reasonable Modifications for a Service Animal

Dental offices must make reasonable modifications in their policies, practices, or procedures to permit people with disabilities to bring in service animals that have been individually trained to do work or perform tasks for the benefit of the person with a disability.

If a Service Animal Poses a Health or Safety Risk

A dental office may refuse to accommodate a service animal that poses a significant risk to the health or safety of other persons in the dental office. The practice that believes it may be necessary exclude a service animal must make an individualized assessment based on reasonable judgment that relies on current medical knowledge or the best available objective evidence to ascertain the nature, duration and potential severity of the risk and the probability that the risk will occur. The practice must also analyze and determine whether the risk can be mitigated by reasonable modifications to the dental practice's policies and procedures. A dental office may NOT refuse to allow a service animal into the dental practice, or for refuse to serve a person with a service animal, for any of the following reasons:

- Allergies of other people in the dental office
- Aggressive breed of dog (although a dental office may exclude an animal based on the individual animal's behavior)
- Fear or dislike of the animal by other people in the dental office

If another person complains about the service animal, inform the person that the animal is a service animal and is legally entitled to be in the facility. You may accommodate the disabled individual and the person with the complaint (e.g., allergies) by assigning them to opposite sides of the room or elsewhere in the facility, but the disabled individual cannot be isolated from, or treated less favorably than, other individuals on the basis of the service animal.

Control of the Service Animal

The service animal must be leashed (or harnessed or tethered), unless such device would interfere with the animals ability to perform its function, or the individual's disability prevents use of such device. In such a case, the individual must maintain control of the animal through voice, signal, or some other means of effective control. If the service animal is unruly and out of control, you may ask the owner to take action to control the animal's behavior. If, after this warning, the owner does not or cannot take effective action to control the animal, your office may exclude the animal. However, you must still give the individual the option to obtain your services without having the unruly animal on the premises.

Damage Caused by a Service Animal

A dental office may not impose charges or other restrictions (such as pet fees, waivers, special cleaning fees, or special entrance or usage fees) on the disabled person. If the service animal causes actual damage, you may seek to handle the damage and charges in the same manner as you would any other damage caused by a patient or member of the public.

Using the Flowchart Tool

If a person with an animal enters your dental office, and it is not immediately clear what service the animal provides, refer to **Step 1** of the flow chart to determine whether the animal meets the AwDA definition of a service animal. If you determine that the animal is a service animal, refer to **Step 2** to determine your dental office's responsibilities under the AwDA to the person and his or her service animal.

Violations of the Americans with Disabilities Act can result in money damages and penalties.

Step 1: Determining whether the animal is a service animal under the AwDA

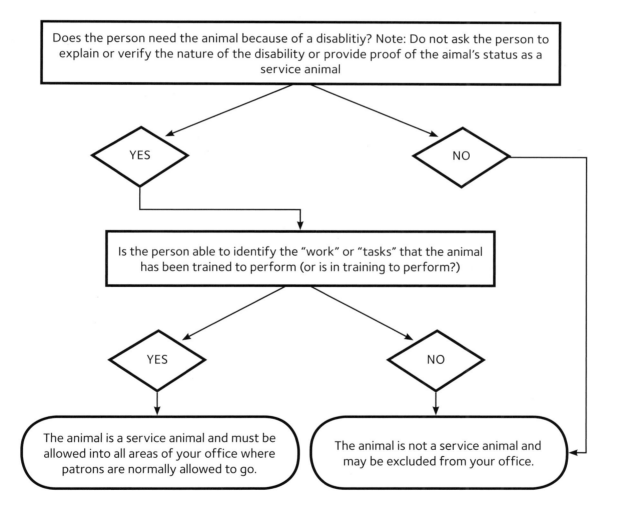

Step 2: Determining your obligations toward a person with a service animal under AwDA

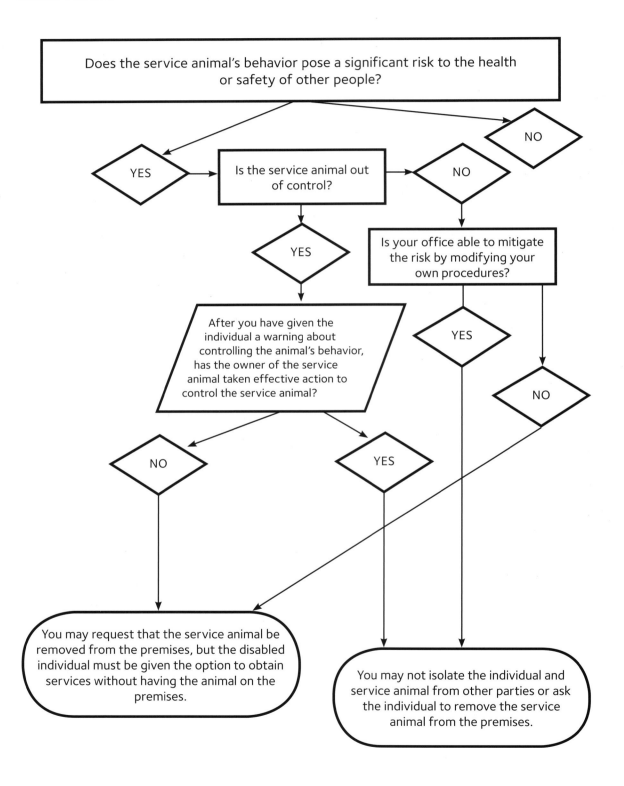

Appendix 11:
Sample HIPAA Business Associate Agreement

(see next page)

Sample HIPAA Business Associate Agreement

This Business Associate Agreement (this "Agreement") is entered into as of _____, 20__, (the "Effective Date") by and between _____ ("Dental Practice") and _____ ("Business Associate").

RECITALS:

WHEREAS, Business Associate performs services for or on behalf of Dental Practice (the "Services") pursuant to that certain _____ Agreement dated _____, 20__ (the "Underlying Agreement"), which Services involve the access, use and/or disclosure of Protected Health Information (as defined below); and

WHEREAS, the parties desire to enter into this Agreement in order to comply with the Health Insurance Portability and Accountability Act of 1996 ("HIPAA") and its implementing regulations, as amended and in effect.

NOW THEREFORE, the parties agree as follows:

1. Definitions. Capitalized terms not otherwise defined in this Agreement shall have the same meaning as those terms in the HIPAA Privacy Rule and Security Rule (as defined below).

   (a)   "Breach," when capitalized, shall have the meaning set forth in 45 CFR § lo164.402 (including all of its subsections).

   (b)   "Electronic Protected Health Information" or "EPHI" shall have the same meaning as the term "electronic protected health information" in 45 CFR § 160.103, limited to information that Business Associate creates, accesses, receives or maintains for or on behalf of Dental Practice.

   (c)   "Protected Health Information" or "PHI" shall have the meaning set forth in in 45 CFR § 160.103, limited to information that Business Associate creates, accesses, receives or maintains for or on behalf of Dental Practice. PHI includes EPHI.

   (d)   "Privacy Rule" means the Standards for Privacy of Individually Identifiable Health Information, codified at 45 CFR parts 160 and 164, Subparts A, D and E, as currently in effect.

   (e)   "Security Rule" means the Standards for Security for the Protection of Electronic Protected Health Information, codified at 45 CFR parts 160 and 164, Subparts A and C, as currently in effect.

   (f)   "Unsecured Protected Health Information" shall have the same meaning as the term "unsecured protected health information" in 45 CFR § 164.402, limited to such information accessed, created, received or maintained by Business Associate.

2. Scope of Use and Disclosure of PHI.

   (a)   **Business Associate Status**. Business Associate acknowledges that it is Dental Practice's "business associate" as defined by HIPAA. Business Associate agrees to comply with the HIPAA regulations as they directly apply to business associates.

(b) **Performance of Service**. Business Associate shall not access, use or further disclose PHI other than as permitted or required by this Agreement, to perform the Services pursuant to the Underlying Agreement or as Required by Law. Business Associate shall not access, use or disclose PHI in any manner that would violate HIPAA if such access, use or disclosure was done by Dental Practice.

  [1. *Uses and Disclosures Permitted By Law*. Business Associate may use or disclose PHI: (A) as is necessary for the proper management and administration of Business Associate's organization, and (B) to carry out the legal responsibilities of Business Associate; provided, however, that any permitted disclosure of PHI to a third party must be either Required By Law or subject to reasonable assurances obtained by Business Associate from the third party that PHI will be held confidentially, and securely, and used or disclosed only as Required By Law or for the purposes for which it was disclosed to such third party, and that any breaches of confidentiality of PHI which become known to such third party will be immediately reported to Business Associate.]

  [2. *Statistical Aggregation*. Business Associate shall not use PHI for any compilation or aggregation of data or for any commercial purpose whatsoever not set forth in this Agreement, unless permitted by Dental Practice in a written document.]

  [3. *De-identification*. Business Associate shall not use PHI to create de-identified PHI for any purpose not set forth in this Agreement, unless permitted by Dental Practice in a written document.]

(c) **Minimum Necessary**. Business Associate shall not access, use or disclose more than the minimum necessary PHI to perform or fulfill the intended permissible purpose, in accordance with this Agreement.

(d) **Privacy Rule**. To the extent Business Associate carries out one or more of Dental Practice's obligations under the HIPAA Privacy Rule, Business Associate shall comply with the requirements of HIPAA that apply to Dental Practice in the performance of such obligation(s).

(e) **Security Rule and Safeguards**. Business Associate shall use safeguards that are appropriate and sufficient to prevent access, use or disclosure of PHI other than as permitted or required by this Agreement. Business Associate shall comply with the Security Rule with respect to EPHI, including implementing Administrative Safeguards, Physical Safeguards, and Technical Safeguards that reasonably and appropriately protect the Confidentiality, Integrity and Availability of EPHI.

(f) **Notification**. Without unreasonable delay, Business Associate shall notify Dental Practice, in writing, of any use or disclosure of PHI not provided for by this Agreement of which Business Associate becomes aware. Without unreasonable delay, Business Associate shall report to Dental Practice in writing of any Security Incident of which it becomes aware in accordance with the Security Rule and Business Associate's obligations under the same. Upon Dental Practice's request, Business Associate shall provide a report of any and all impermissible uses, disclosures and/or Security Incidents.

(g) **Subcontractors**. Business Associate shall ensure that any and all subcontractors that create, receive, maintain or transmit PHI on behalf of Business Associate agree, in writing, to the same restrictions and conditions that apply to Business Associate. Each subcontract agreement must include, without limitation, the provisions of this Agreement. Business Associate shall make such agreements with its subcontractors available to Dental Practice upon request.

(h) **Audit**. Business Associate shall make its internal practices, books, and records relating to the use and disclosure of PHI received from, or created or received by Business Associate on behalf of, Dental Practice available to the Secretary of Health and Human Services and/or Dental Practice, upon request, for purposes of determining and facilitating Dental Practice's compliance with HIPAA.

(i) **Patient Rights**.

1. *Patient Right to Review*. Business Associate shall make PHI maintained in a Designated Record Set available to Dental Practice or, at the direction of Dental Practice, to an Individual, in accordance with §164.524 of the Privacy Rule.

2. *Patient Right to Amend*. Business Associate shall make PHI available for amendment and incorporate any amendments to PHI maintained in a Designated Record Set at the direction of Dental Practice and in accordance with §164.526 of the Privacy Rule. Dental Practice shall be involved in any decision of Business Associate to amend the PHI of an Individual.

3. *Patient Right to Request Accounting*. Business Associate shall document and make available to Dental Practice or, at the direction of Dental Practice, to an Individual, information relating to such Individual as is necessary for Dental Practice to respond to a request for an accounting of disclosures in accordance with §164.528 of the Privacy Rule.

   A. Business Associate agrees to implement an appropriate record-keeping process to ensure compliance with the requirements of this Section.

   B. Business Associate agrees to provide PHI it maintains electronically in a Designated Record Set in an electronic form at the request of Dental Practice or an Individual.

4. *Notice to Dental Practice*. Business Associate shall notify Dental Practice immediately in writing upon receiving a request from an Individual to review, copy or amend his or her medical record information or to receive an accounting of disclosures. Business Associate shall also provide Dental Practice with a prompt written report of the details of its handling of such requests.

(j) **Breach**. Business Associate shall notify Dental Practice of breaches of unsecured PHI in accordance with the requirements of 45 CFR § 164.410. Such notification shall include, to the extent possible, the identification of each Individual whose PHI has been or is reasonably believed to have been accessed, acquired, used or disclosed during the Breach, along with any other information that Dental Practice will be required to include in its notification to an affected Individual, the media and/or the Secretary, as applicable, including, without limitation, a description of the Breach, the date of the Breach and its discovery, the types of Unsecured Protected Health Information involved and a description of Business Associate's investigation, mitigation and prevention efforts.

(k) **Mitigation**. Business Associate agrees to mitigate, to the extent practicable, any harmful effect that is known to Business Associate of a use or disclosure of PHI by Business Associate or a subcontractor or agent of Business Associate in violation of the requirements of this Agreement, the Privacy Rule, the Security Rule or other applicable federal or state law.

3. [Dental Practice Obligations.]

[(a) **Notice of Privacy Practices**. Dental Practice shall notify Business Associate of limitation(s) in its notice of privacy practices to the extent such limitation affects Business Associate's permitted uses or disclosures under this Agreement.]

[(b) **Individual Authorization**. Dental Practice shall notify Business Associate of changes in, or revocation of, authorization by an Individual to use or disclose PHI, to the extent such changes affect Business Associate's permitted uses or disclosures under this Agreement.]

[(c) **Restrictions**. Dental Practice shall notify Business Associate of restriction(s) in the use or disclosure of PHI that Dental Practice has agreed to, to the extent such restriction affects Business Associate's permitted uses or disclosures under this Agreement.]

4. Term and Termination.

(a) **Term**. The Term of this Agreement shall become effective as of the Effective Date, and remain in effect until all PHI is returned or destroyed in accordance with this Section.

(b) **Termination for Cause**. Dental Practice may terminate this Agreement immediately if Dental Practice, in its sole discretion, determines that Business Associate has violated a material term of this Agreement. Dental Practice, at its option and within its sole discretion, may (1) permit Business Associate take steps to cure the breach; and (2) in the event Dental Practice determines such cure is sufficient, elect to keep this Agreement in force.

(c) **Obligations of Business Associate Upon Termination**. Upon termination of this Agreement for any reason, Business Associate shall promptly return to Dental Practice or destroy all PHI received from Dental Practice, or created or received by Business Associate on behalf of Dental Practice, that Business Associate still maintains in any form. Business Associate shall retain no copies of the PHI in any form. Upon request by Dental Practice, Business Associate shall promptly supply a certification executed by an officer (vice president level or above) of the Business Associate confirming that Business Associate has returned or destroyed all PHI and all copies thereof.

(d) **Survival**. The obligations of Business Associate under this Section shall survive the termination of this Agreement.

5. [Limitation of Liability, Indemnification and Insurance.]

[(a) **Limitation of Liability**. To the extent that Business Associate has limited its liability under the terms of the Underlying Agreement, whether with a maximum recovery for direct damages or a disclaimer against any consequential, indirect or punitive damages, or other such limitations, all limitations shall exclude damages to Dental Practice arising out of a breach of this Agreement by Business Associate or any Breach of PHI by Business Associate.]

[(b) **Indemnification**. Business Associate agrees to indemnify, defend, and hold harmless Dental Practice and its directors, officers, affiliates, employees, agents, and permitted successors from and against any and all claims, losses, liabilities, damages, costs, and expenses (including reasonable attorneys' fees) arising out of or related to Business Associate's breach of its obligations under this Agreement, including, but not limited to a Breach of Unsecured Protected Health Information by Business Associate.]

[(c) **Insurance**. Business Associate agrees at the request of Dental Practice, to obtain and maintain insurance coverage against the improper use and disclosure of PHI by Business Associate, naming Dental Practice as a named insured. Promptly following a request by Dental Practice for the maintenance of such insurance coverage, Business Associate will provide a certificate evidencing such insurance coverage.]

6. Miscellaneous Provisions.

(a) **Notices**. Any notice required or permitted under this Agreement will be given in writing and will be sent —

to Dental Practice at: to Business Associate at:

_____   _____

_____   _____

_____   _____

Notices will be deemed to have been received upon actual receipt, one business day after being sent by overnight courier service, or three business days after mailing by first-class mail, whichever occurs first.

(b) **Governing Law**. This Agreement will be governed by, and construed in accordance with the laws of the state of [STATE] without giving effect to choice of law provisions thereof.

(c) **Waiver**. No delay or omission by either party to exercise any right or remedy under this Agreement will be construed to be either acquiescence or the waiver of the ability to exercise any right or remedy in the future. Failure of a party to insist upon strict adherence to any term or condition of this Agreement shall not be considered a waiver by that party of its right thereafter to insist upon strict adherence to that, or any other, term or condition of this Agreement. No waiver of any breach of any provision of this Agreement shall constitute a waiver of any prior, concurrent or subsequent breach of the same or any other provisions hereof, and no waiver shall be effective unless made in writing and signed by an authorized representative of the waiving party.

(d) **Severability.** All provisions of this Agreement are separate and divisible, and if any part or parts of this Agreement are held to be unenforceable, the remainder of this Agreement will continue in full force and effect.

(e) **Amendments**. The parties shall amend this Agreement from time to time by mutual written agreement in order to keep this Agreement consistent with any changes made to the HIPAA laws or regulations in effect as of the Effective Date and with any new regulations promulgated under HIPAA. Dental Practice may terminate this Agreement and, where appropriate, the Underlying Agreement in whole or in part if the parties are unable to agree to such changes by the compliance date for such new or revised HIPAA laws or regulations.

(f) **Interpretation**. In the event of any conflict between the provisions of this Agreement and the Underlying Agreement, the provisions of this Agreement shall control. Any ambiguity in this Agreement shall be resolved in favor of a meaning that permits the parties to comply with HIPAA.

(g) **Automatic Amendment**. This Agreement shall automatically incorporate any change or modification of applicable state or federal law as of the effective date of the change or modification. Business Associate agrees to maintain compliance with all changes or modifications to applicable state or federal law.

(h) **Interpretation**. Any ambiguity in this Agreement shall be interpreted to permit compliance with the HIPAA Rules.

(i) **Independent contractor**. The parties acknowledge and agree that Business Associate is an independent contractor. Nothing in this agreement shall be construed to create any partnership, joint venture, agency, or employment relationship of any kind between the parties. Notwithstanding the foregoing, to the extent that Business Associate is ever determined for any purpose to be an agent of the Dental Practice (under the Federal common law of agency or otherwise), Business Associate shall be acting outside of the scope of agency if Business Associate fails to notify the Dental Practice immediately if Business Associate violates or breaches any provision of this Agreement or violates the HIPAA Rules.

IN WITNESS WHEREOF, the parties have executed this Business Associate Agreement as of the Effective Date.

DENTAL PRACTICE

By: _____

Name: _____

Title: _____

BUSINESS ASSOCIATE

By: _____

Name: _____

Title: _____

Appendix 12:

What Did the US Supreme Court Decide in *North Carolina State Board v. FTC* (2015)?

Q. I've heard about a recent Supreme Court decision concerning the North Carolina State Board of Dental Examiners and teeth whitening. Does the decision have any implications for my practice and what does it mean for the Dental Board in my state?

A. The Supreme Court's decision in *North Carolina State Board v. FTC* (2015) is unlikely to have any direct effect on your practice. It does, however, have important ramifications for dental as well as other licensing and professional boards throughout the United States. The underlying case did revolve around a challenge by the United States Federal Trade Commission to the North Carolina Board's attempt to stop non-dentis ts from performing teeth whitening in the state.

But the case as it reached the Supreme Court involved a much broader issue, namely, whether anti-competitive actions taken by state professional boards comprising mostly members who are market competitors are immune from application of the federal antitrust laws under the "State Action Doctrine." That doctrine is one the Supreme Court announced in a 1943 decision *Parker v. Brown*. In that case, the Court found that even though the Federal antitrust statutes do not make an exception for the states, the states should be free to take anticompetitive actions when it served the public interest. In *Parker*, California had established a commission made up of market competitors in the agricultural field that set pricing and imposed other controls on various agricultural products produced in the state. The Court found that the actions of the commission were exempt from application of the federal antitrust laws.

The ADA believed that the North Carolina case was a clear example of a *Parker*-type situation and spearheaded the submission of a friend-of-the-court brief saying as much. After all, the North Carolina Board was created by a state statute, its members were selected pursuant to a state statute, and it was attempting to enforce a provision of North Carolina's Dental Practices Act, a state statute.

The Supreme Court disagreed, holding that where a state professional board is substantially comprised of market competitors (it did not give a percent threshold), such as practicing dentists, the board must be "actively supervised" by the state. This appears to be a ruling that professional boards, even those established by, and administered in accordance with, state law, are not agencies of the state empowered by themselves to make decisions having potentially anticompetitive effects. Instead, such decisions must be "actively supervised" and approved by an arm of the state that the Supreme Court would recognize as having such power under the State Action Doctrine. It remains to be seen how such "active supervision" will be provided, who can provide it and what subject matter expertise is required to exercise it, and how "active" the supervision must be. In the past, the Supreme Court has imposed the "active supervision" requirement in situations where a state has permitted a private entity (not a state created body) to engage in potentially anticompetitive oversight or regulation.

Some professional boards have expressed their belief that the decision does not apply to them because they choose the market competitor members of their boards differently from the method used to select the North Carolina Board. The fact is, however, that the Supreme Court's decision does not mention the method of selection as constituting a relevant factor in the State Action Doctrine analysis.

Index

Business Associate Agreement, 28, 51, 94, 103-104, 106-108, 110, 114, 118, 133, 167, 192, 194, 215, 222, 230, 240, 252, 254, 256 263-269

Covered Entity, 34, 42, 51, 60, 91, 93, 95, 104, 108, 110, 120, 167, 171, 175-176, 178, 186, 197, 202, 230, 251-253, 256

HIPAA privacy, 12, 25, 28, 42, 44, 59-60, 91, 98, 107, 118-120, 171, 177, 236, 252, 264-265

HITECH, 55, 110, 143

Hygienist, 69, 72, 76, 85, 115, 138

I

I-9 form, 235

Identalloy, 142

Identity theft, 65, 121, 159-160

Immigration and Naturalization (INS), see U.S. Citizenship and Immigration Services

Incorporate, 18-19

Independent contractor, 50, 55, 62, 73, 80, 137, 138-140, 188, 217-218, 220, 223, 230-234

Infection control, 60, 78, 205, 237

Informed consent, 79, 127, 179-183, 191, 193

Informed refusal, 183

Insurance (dental benefit plans), 134-136, 146, 148, 158-160, 162-163, 169-172, 179-180, 185, 209-210

    Contract Analysis Service, 12, 134, 136

    Covered entity, 34, 42, 51, 60, 91, 93, 95, 104, 108, 110, 118, 120, 167, 171, 175-176, 178, 186, 197, 202, 230, 251-253, 256

    Dental claim, 157, 169

    Direct reimbursement, 146

    Discounts, 38, 162

    Explanation of benefits, 169

    Insurance plans, 146, 163

    Multiple visit procedure, 162

    Participating provider, 91, 93, 152, 169-171

    Provider contract, 12, 135, 162, 170

    Usual fee, 162

Insurance, liability, 16, 73, 117, 135, 151-152, 167, 180, 185, 222

Insurance plans, 146, 163

Interpreters, 191-194

Interviewing, 58, 63

Intimate partner violence (IPV), 178

J

K

L

Labs, see Dental lab

Lease, office, 3, 140-141, 186

Leave of absence

    Family and Medical Leave Act (FMLA), 55, 56, 73, 80

    Military Leave (USERRA), 56, 72-73

    Sick leave, 80-81, 239

Liability coverage, 16, 153-154, 185

Libel and slander, 204

License or licensure, 1, 4, 71, 116, 126-127, 147, 176, 215-216, 218

Limited English Proficient (LEP), 193

Limited liability company (LLC), 15, 18-20, 216

Limited partnership, 15, 17-20

M

Malpractice, 1, 3-4, 8, 10-11, 16-17, 28, 43, 79, 102, 113, 127, 145, 151-154, 168, 179, 181-185, 200, 206, 226, 232

Malpractice claim, 10-11, 28, 113, 151-152, 168, 183

Malpractice insurance, 151, 232

Malpractice settlement reporting, 8

Marketing, 8, 31-42, 47-48, 50, 111, 143

Materials, see Dental lab

Medical history, see health history, 65, 180

Medicare or Medicaid, 39-40, 64, 114-115, 125, 150, 164, 187-191, 256

Merchandise, 142-143

Military

    Dues waiver, 73

    Leave, see leave of absence, 72-73

    USERRA, see leave of absence, 72-73

Minimum wage, 74, 138

Minor, 99-100, 182

Multiple visit procedure, 162

Mutual aid agreement, 73

N

National Practitioner Data Bank (NPDB), 11, 168
National Provider Identifier (NPI), 126, 157
Neglect, 9, 99, 111–112, 178
Negative online review, see online review
Negligent referral, 186
New construction, 21, 23, 26, 149
Non-compete, see restrictive covenants
Notices, 51, 74, 219, 221, 226, 229, 234, 268

O

Obesity (re: treating patients), 200
Office design, 20–26, 29, 141
Office manual, 58–59, 67, 73, 236–237, 239
Office safety, 8, 60
Office policies, 58–61, 236–238
Online review, 4, 35, 168
Operating agreement, 20, 216
Original records, 101
OSHA, 7, 56, 60, 74, 76, 85–90, 205, 235–236
OSHA inspection, 87

P

Paperless office, 103
Participating provider, 91, 93, 152, 169–171
Partnership, 15–20, 69, 113, 131, 145, 157, 216, 248, 269
Patient list, 34, 133, 227, 234
Patient protected health information (PHI), 60, 95, 99, 116, 240, 256, 264–268
Patient records, 10, 45, 102–104, 113–114, 137, 165, 171, 176, 209, 220, 222, 226, 232
Payment Card Industry Security Standards, 161
Payments, 114, 117, 125–127, 140, 150, 152–153, 158, 163, 165–167, 170, 190, 245
Payroll taxes, 138, 150, 230
Pet, see service animal
Photo I.D., 202
Posters, workplace, 74
Preemption, 8
Privacy, 59–60, 71, 91–101, 107, 110, 114, 116, 118–122, 123, 127, 153, 171, 175–178, 186, 200, 202, 203–204, 207, 210, 215, 226, 232, 236, 247–248, 252, 256, 264–267

Prescription

Prescription, 68, 70, 141, 143, 188, 202–203, 207
Products, see merchandise
Products liability, 143
Professional limited liability company (PLLC), 20
Prosthesis, 141
Provider contract, 12, 134–135, 162, 170

Q

R

Recordkeeping, 8, 70, 235
Release, see settlement
Records, see patient records
Red Flags Rule (FACTA), 12, 65, 121–122, 161
Referral, 2, 3, 31, 40, 69, 71, 135, 163–164, 168, 186–190, 199, 207, 209, 226–227, 230, 234
Reimbursement, multiple visit procedure, 162
Renovations, 22, 23
Rent, 22, 40, 140–141, 153, 189, 190, 216, 232
Restrictive covenant, 137, 139, 230

S

Sales tax, 143
Scope of practice, 8, 218
Security regulations, 239
Seeing eye dog, see service animal
Self-referral, 186–187, 230
Service animal, 195, 258–262
Settlement, 4, 8, 11, 12, 16, 52, 89, 151–152, 168, 192, 206, 254
Sexual harassment, 57
Sick leave, see leave of absence
Sign language interpreters, 191–193
Slander, see libel and slander
Social Security number, 26, 92, 116, 119, 157, 159–160, 202, 235
Sole proprietorship, 15–17, 20, 85
Specialist, 32, 157, 163
Standard of care, 30, 183, 184–186, 205
Stark law, see self-referral
State dental practice act, 7, 8, 31, 72
Subpoena, 10, 88, 101, 120, 178
Substance abuse, 69–70, 203
Suspension, 67, 154